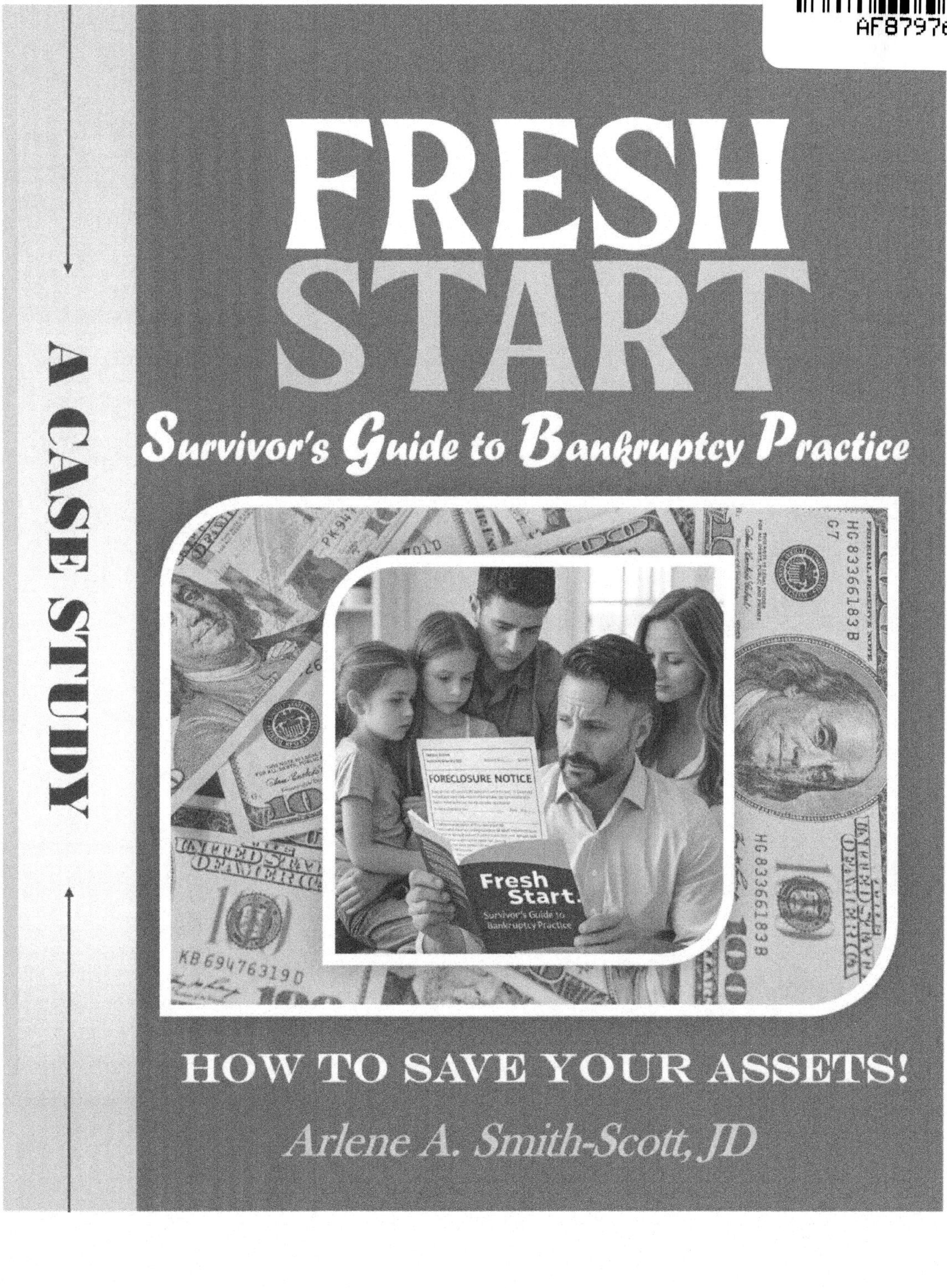
A CASE STUDY
FRESH
START
Survivor's Guide to Bankruptcy Practice
FORECLOSURE NOTICE
Fresh
Start.
Survivor's Guide to
Bankruptcy Practice
HOW TO SAVE YOUR ASSETS!
Arlene A. Smith-Scott, JD

FRESH START

SURVIVOR'S GUIDE TO BANKRUPTCY PRACTICE

Making Informed Bankruptcy Decisions Legal Concepts and Practical Advice

Published by DocWriteReview.com

Library of Congress Preassigned Control Number:
ISBN: 978-1-965060-12-4 - Paperback
ISBN: 978-1-965060-11-7 – eBook

Credit Line:
Cover Design by Arlene A. Smith-Scott

Fresh Start. Survivor's Guide to Bankruptcy Practice

Table of Contents

Fresh Start. Survivor's Guide to Bankruptcy Practice

Fresh Start. Survivor's Guide to Bankruptcy Practice

Fresh Start. Survivor's Guide to Bankruptcy Practice

Fresh Start. Survivor's Guide to Bankruptcy Practice

WELCOME

DocWriteReview understands that your time and money are valuable! We want to offer insightful, encouraging, and informative books, videos, music, and other media, that will make a difference in your life at an affordable price.

WE WANT TO HEAR FROM YOU!

We will enroll you in periodic giveaways, discount programs, event information, and new releases by providing your email. Look for us on Facebook, Twitter, and Instagram.

Thank you for being a member of our family!

WEBSITE: www.DocWriteReview.com

EMAIL: Info@DocWriteReview.com

ALSO BY

Grant Writing, The Unofficial Rulebook
Finding Peace
Why Women Can Teach and Preach the Word of God
Starting Over with God's Grace and Mercy
Devotion, Starting Over with God's Grace and Mercy
Fear Not, Faith to Move Forward
Thank God for Mom

ACKNOWLEDGEMENTS

This book was born out of a desire to illuminate, inform, and empower. Along that journey, I've been fortunate to have the support and encouragement of some incredible individuals.

With special thanks to **John Luke E. Morris** *for being the sounding board that helped make this book possible. Your thoughtful insight, unwavering support, and honest feedback were instrumental in shaping each chapter. I am deeply grateful for your presence throughout this process.*

To all those who continue to challenge the unknown and pursue knowledge, this is for you.

With gratitude and appreciation.

PROLOGUE

SO, YOU'RE THINKING ABOUT filing for bankruptcy to save your home or other property. Maybe you're weighing your options, maybe you're already knee-deep in legalese, or maybe you just woke up in a cold sweat wondering, Wait… what exactly did I sign? Well, you've come to the right place.

The purpose of this book, "Fresh Start: Survivor's Guide to Bankruptcy Practice. Making Informed Bankruptcy Decisions, Legal Concepts and Practical Advice" is to inform, educate, and, most importantly, prepare you for what's ahead. Whether you're hiring an attorney or going solo, you need to understand the key principles and pitfalls of the bankruptcy process. Because at the end of the day, you are your own best advocate. And trust me, you're going to need to be.

Now, let me introduce myself. I'm an African American woman who owned a mortgage company from 1995 to 2008 and I became a bankruptcy attorney. I believed in justice. I believed in fairness. I believed the system worked… until I found out firsthand that it didn't. What I actually experienced? Defamation. Demoralization. Minimalization. And what felt like outright "rape" at the hands of men who schemed, conspired, and straight-up stole my properties.

I'll admit it, I was a little naïve. I expected fair treatment. I didn't get it. I expected good faith. Didn't happen. I expected courts of equity to be, you know, equitable. Nope. Not even close.

After years of mourning (and let's be real, raging), I picked myself up and dug deep into the system that broke me. I learned more than I ever wanted to about how the game is played, because let's be clear, it is a game. And the rules? They weren't made for you or me to win.

But here's the good news: I'm sharing everything I've learned. I'm going to walk you through the bankruptcy process without the confusing legal jargon, just straight talk, real facts, and the concepts you need to know. And we're going to use my story as a case study, the good, the bad, and the "Oh God, why did I do that?" moments, so you'll know exactly what to do (and what to avoid).

And because I like to leave folks with something useful, I'll wrap things up with ten solid pointers that could save you time, money, and maybe even your sanity. So, buckle up, it's going to be a ride. But by the time we're done, you'll be ready to fight back.

Let's get started.

* * PART ONE * *

REORGANIZATION
LIQUIDATION
AUTOMATIC STAY
BANKRUPTCY TRUSTEE
MOTION TO CONVERT
PROOF OF CLAIMS
DISCOVERY
BANKRUPTCY BUY-OUTS
CARVE- OUTS
TAX CONSEQUENCES
PECUNIARY INTEREST
DISCHARGEABILITY
MORTGAGE INSTRUMENTS
DEBTOR'S BUSINESS
AND SO MUCH MORE. . .

Chapter One

CONCEPTS AND CASE STUDY

THIS BOOK HAS TWO main goals.

First, it will help you understand basic bankruptcy concepts that are generally not taught (especially if you own things of value like real estate or a business).

Second, it will demonstrate how the bankruptcy laws might be applied differently depending on who you are, especially if you're a minority, a woman, or someone without a lawyer. Remember that everyone's experience with bankruptcy is different, but the main point here is to help you understand bankruptcy laws so you can protect the things you want to keep.

UNDERSTANDING BANKRUPTCY CONCEPTS

Bankruptcy is basically a legal way for people who are drowning in debt to get some relief. It's also supposed to make sure creditors (people you owe money to) are treated fairly. The following is a list of bankruptcy concepts that will be discussed. Keep in mind, this book isn't meant to show you how to fill out documents, but to show you legal principles and to demonstrate what it can look like if it goes wrong.

1. Automatic Stay - A fundamental protection that takes effect immediately upon filing bankruptcy, temporarily halting most collection actions, foreclosures, repossessions, and lawsuits against the debtor. This provides breathing room to develop a debt resolution plan and prevents creditors from gaining advantages over one another.

2. Proof of Claims Review - The examination of documentation creditors submit to support their claims. Identifying deficiencies in these proofs can lead to disallowance of claims, potentially reducing overall debt.

3. Discovery Powers - The legal right in bankruptcy proceedings to request and obtain relevant documents from creditors. Effective use of discovery can strengthen your position by revealing documentation gaps or procedural errors that might invalidate creditors' claims against you.

4. Expert Witnesses - Professionals hired to testify about specialized topics such as banking practices or document authenticity. Their testimony can strengthen challenges to creditor claims through authoritative knowledge and analysis.

5. Standing - A fundamental legal concept determining whether a party has the legal right to bring a claim against you in bankruptcy court. Challenging a creditor's standing can potentially eliminate certain debts if the creditor cannot legally prove their right to enforce the debt.

6. SEC Regulations and Standing - Securities and Exchange Commission rules govern who can legally enforce mortgage claims. Understanding these

regulations helps identify violations in mortgage handling that could provide defenses against foreclosure or mortgage claims in bankruptcy.

7. Evidence and S-11/A Filings - SEC documents that can be used to challenge creditor ownership claims. These filings may reveal discrepancies between claimed and legal debt ownership, potentially invalidating certain claims against you.

8. Backdated Financial Documents - Documents signed or dated after the fact that creditors might use improperly. Identifying such documents can reveal fraud or misrepresentation, providing grounds to challenge creditor claims.

9. Mortgage Interest Statements (Form 1098) - Tax documents showing who received mortgage interest payments. These can be used to verify or challenge a creditor's standing by potentially contradicting their ownership claims.

10. Personal vs. Corporate Distinction - The legal separation between individual and business entities in bankruptcy proceedings. Understanding this distinction helps protect personal assets from business creditors or vice versa.

11. Pecuniary Interest - The concept of identifying parties with legitimate financial stakes in bankruptcy proceedings. This knowledge helps determine which parties have valid financial interests, potentially excluding certain creditors whose claims don't meet this standard.

12. Settlement Agreement Impacts - How pecuniary interests affect proposed settlements in bankruptcy. This understanding helps evaluate whether settlements fairly reflect true financial interests and prevent agreements that unfairly benefit certain creditors.

13. Buying Out the Bankruptcy Estate - This process allows an interested party (often the debtor, a creditor, or a third party) to purchase all assets in the bankruptcy estate for a negotiated sum. This strategy can benefit the debtor by potentially ending the bankruptcy process more quickly, preserving business continuity, or preventing liquidation of sentimental assets.

14. Carve-Outs - Special arrangements setting aside funds for specific purposes in bankruptcy proceedings. Understanding this helps identify potentially improper arrangements between trustees and creditors that might disadvantage you.

15. Defendant Against a Motion to Convert - This involves defending yourself when creditors or the court attempt to change your bankruptcy from one chapter to another (e.g., from Chapter 11 reorganization to Chapter 7 liquidation). Successfully opposing this motion helps maintain control over your bankruptcy process and potentially preserves your business operations.

16. Contempt of Court - Actions that violate bankruptcy court orders or procedures, potentially resulting in penalties. Knowing what constitutes contempt helps avoid costly mistakes that could negatively impact your case.

17. Ex Parte Communications - Improper communications about your case with the judge when other parties aren't present. Understanding this concept helps maintain case integrity by avoiding inappropriate communications.

18. Dischargeable vs. Non-Dischargeable Debt - The distinction between debts that can be eliminated through bankruptcy and those that cannot. This

knowledge helps develop realistic post-bankruptcy financial expectations and planning strategies.

19. Defamation and Trustee Conduct - Legal recourse may be available if a bankruptcy trustee makes false statements that harm your reputation. Understanding these protections helps preserve your reputation and business goodwill.

20. Emotional and Professional Impacts - The significant personal and professional consequences of bankruptcy beyond financial aspects, including emotional distress, reputation damage, and time lost to legal proceedings. Understanding these impacts helps prepare for the full spectrum of bankruptcy effects.

21. Systemic Issues and Procedural Fairness - Problems within the bankruptcy system that can disadvantage certain debtors, including inadequate trustee oversight, insufficient resources for self-represented litigants, minimal consequences for code violations, and potential discriminatory treatment patterns. Awareness of these issues helps navigate the system more effectively.

Chapter Two

KNOW YOUR VALUE, YOU ARE NOT A FAILURE

IMPORTANT: This information helps the reader maintain emotional resilience during bankruptcy proceedings, preventing them from internalizing financial setbacks as personal failures, which leads to better decision-making and negotiating from a position of strength rather than desperation.

I KNOW THIS IS hard. But hear me, you did not fail. You got up, you tried, and that alone is a victory. Don't let the noise get inside your head, whether it's coming from friends, neighbors, your church family, or even that relentless inner critic. What happened to bring you here today does not define your tomorrow. However, your self-worth and self-determination will move you forward.

OVERCOMING FEELINGS OF FAILURE

Filing for bankruptcy can be an emotional rollercoaster. Many people experience feelings of failure, shame, depression, and anxiety when faced with the reality of financial hardship. However, it is essential to understand that bankruptcy is not a personal failure, it is a legal tool designed to help people regain financial stability. Overcoming the emotional toll of bankruptcy requires a shift in mindset, practical coping strategies, and a focus on the future rather than the past.

One of the first steps to overcoming feelings of failure is to reframe the way you view bankruptcy. Instead of seeing it as a sign of defeat, recognize that it is a responsible and legal way to reset your finances. Many successful individuals and businesses, including well-known figures like Abraham Lincoln and Walt Disney, have gone through bankruptcy and emerged stronger. Bankruptcy does not define a person's worth or intelligence, it is simply a financial restructuring that allows a fresh start. Accepting that life is unpredictable and that financial setbacks can happen to anyone helps remove the stigma and guilt associated with bankruptcy.

It is also important to manage feelings of depression and anxiety by focusing on self-care and mental well-being. Stress and negative emotions can be overwhelming during this time, so taking care of your mental health should be a priority. Seeking support from family, friends, or a therapist can provide reassurance and guidance. Talking about your feelings with a trusted person can help reduce the burden of shame and isolation. Additionally, practicing stress-relieving activities such as exercise, meditation, or journaling can help process emotions and maintain a positive outlook.

Another way to ease the emotional impact of bankruptcy is to focus on practical steps for rebuilding financial health. Instead of dwelling on past mistakes, take proactive measures to create a new financial plan. Learning about budgeting, saving, and responsible credit use can help prevent future financial struggles. Setting small, achievable financial goals, such as saving a portion of each paycheck or building an emergency fund, can provide a sense of progress and control over your financial future.

If feelings of anxiety about the future persist, it can be helpful to educate yourself about what comes next. Understanding that bankruptcy is not the end of financial success but rather a steppingstone to recovery can bring peace of mind. Many people who file for bankruptcy can rebuild their credit, purchase homes, and achieve financial stability within a few years. By focusing on long-term financial goals and making responsible decisions moving forward, bankruptcy can be seen as an opportunity for growth rather than a setback.

Finally, practicing gratitude and self-compassion can significantly impact emotional recovery. It is easy to focus on financial loss, but recognizing the positives, such as supportive relationships, good health, or new opportunities, can help shift perspective. Being kind to yourself and acknowledging that financial hardship does not define you can make a significant difference in overcoming the emotional challenges of bankruptcy.

While filing for bankruptcy can be a difficult and emotional process, it is important to remember that it is not a failure, it is a fresh start. By shifting your mindset, prioritizing mental health, taking practical financial steps, and embracing self-compassion, you can move forward with confidence and create a better financial future.

As we discuss the next steps, I will share my story, too, because we're in this together. I want you to know that you are not alone. Life is unfair. You may not have had the same opportunities as others, but you don't have the luxury of waiting around for some knight on a shining white horse to save you. You must save yourself. You must learn how to become your own advocate.

BIBLICAL PRINCIPALS AND DEBT FORGIVENESS

Sometimes, the hardest thing to do is to forgive ourselves and let go. We need to rely upon something bigger than ourselves. Let's ask the question. What does God think about you? Does God's opinion of you change? Are you a poor steward of his gifts?

Biblical teachings encourage fair lending, responsible borrowing, and mercy in financial dealings. Several passages offer guidance on how debts should be handled and when they should be forgiven, resembling the moral foundation behind bankruptcy laws. The Bible presents a balanced approach to debt. It acknowledges the need for financial mercy through debt forgiveness, much like modern bankruptcy laws providing relief for those who are financially overwhelmed. At the same time, it promotes responsible financial behavior and warns against careless borrowing.

One of the most striking biblical concepts related to bankruptcy is the "Year of Jubilee," found in Leviticus 25:10, which says, "Consecrate the fiftieth year and proclaim liberty throughout the land to all its inhabitants. It shall be a jubilee for you; each of you is to return to your family property and to your own clan." In this year, debts were forgiven, slaves were freed, and land was returned to its original owners. This ensured that financial hardship did not permanently cripple individuals or families. The Jubilee system prevented extreme economic inequality and allowed people to regain financial stability, much like modern bankruptcy laws aim to provide relief and a fresh start for those overwhelmed by debt.

Similarly, Deuteronomy 15:1-2 introduces the "Sabbath Year," which required that debts be canceled every seven years. It says, "At the end of every seven years you must cancel debts. This is how it is to be done: Every creditor shall cancel any loan they have made to a fellow Israelite. They shall not require payment from anyone among their own people, because the Lord's time for canceling debts has been proclaimed." This practice shares similarities with modern bankruptcy in that it acknowledges the need for debt relief after a period of financial burden.

Jesus also taught about debt forgiveness in a more personal and spiritual way. In Matthew 6:12, He instructs His followers to pray, "Forgive us our debts, as we also have forgiven our debtors." While this primarily refers to spiritual forgiveness, the principle of extending mercy in financial matters is present. Likewise, in Matthew 18:23-35, Jesus tells the "Parable of the Unforgiving Servant," where a servant is forgiven a massive debt but refuses to forgive a small debt owed to him by another. The master ultimately punishes the unforgiving servant, illustrating the importance of showing the same grace to others that one has received.

Despite these examples, the Bible also stresses personal responsibility when it comes to debt. Psalm 37:21 states, "The wicked borrow and do not repay, but the righteous give generously." This suggests that debt should not be taken lightly and that those who borrow should strive to fulfill their obligations. Similarly, Proverbs 22:7 warns, "The rich rule over the poor, and the borrower is slave to the lender." These verses encourage caution and wisdom in financial decisions, reinforcing the idea that while debt relief is sometimes necessary, individuals should strive to avoid excessive borrowing when possible.

Ultimately, the Bible presents a balanced view of debt and forgiveness. It encourages lending with kindness, warns against exploiting the poor, and advocates for periodic debt relief to prevent systemic financial oppression. At the same time, it upholds the principle of responsibility, urging individuals to manage their resources wisely. These teachings continue to influence ethical financial practices today, inspiring discussions on fairness, generosity, and economic justice.

Chapter Three

INTRODUCTION TO COURT OF EQUITY AND ITS PREJUDICES

IMPORTANT: This knowledge prepares the reader for the discretionary nature of bankruptcy courts, helping them anticipate potential judicial biases and tailor their presentation, accordingly, potentially resulting in more favorable rulings.

IN THE UNITED STATES, the modern judicial system operates under a unified court structure where both legal and equitable principles can be applied by the same courts. The mission, goals, and mandates of the U.S. judicial system, which encompasses both legal and equitable considerations, can be summarized as follows:

a. Hope of the Court of Equality and Justice

The mission of the U.S. judicial system is to administer justice fairly, impartially, and in accordance with the rule of law. This includes the application of legal and equitable principles to resolve disputes and ensure justice for all individuals.

The goals of the U.S. judicial system include upholding the Constitution, protecting individual rights, and providing access to a fair and impartial forum for the resolution of legal and equitable issues. The system aims to maintain public trust and confidence in the judiciary.

The mandate of the U.S. courts is to interpret and apply the law, including both statutory and common law principles, as well as equitable doctrines. Courts have the authority to grant legal remedies, such as monetary damages, as well as equitable remedies, such as injunctions and specific performance, to address the unique circumstances of each case.

The principles of equity, such as fairness, justice, and conscience, continue to guide the decisions of U.S. courts. The focus is on providing remedies that are just and equitable based on the specific facts and circumstances of each case.

b. Discrimination within the Court System

"I think unconscious bias is one of the hardest things to get at. My favorite example is the symphony orchestra. When I was growing up, there were no women in orchestras. Auditioners thought they could tell the difference between a woman playing and a man. Some intelligent people devised a simple solution: Drop a curtain between the auditioners and the people trying it out. And, lo and behold, women began to get jobs in symphony orchestras." Justice Ruth Bader Ginsburg

WHAT IS RACISM?

Racism has been defined in many ways. Racism refers to the beliefs, attitudes, and actions that perpetuate discrimination or prejudice based on race. It involves treating individuals differently or unfairly because of their racial background.

From the individual beliefs, systemic racism is developed. It is where institutions, policies, and practices within a society perpetuate racial disparities. It goes beyond individual acts to address structural and systemic inequalities that disadvantage certain racial groups. Whether it is racial profiling in law enforcement, discriminatory lending practices, or educational policies that disproportionately affect certain racial groups.

This brings us to the concept of structural racism. It is how societal structures, policies, and power dynamics perpetuate racial inequalities. It considers how historical and systemic factors contribute to ongoing disparities. It is how disproportionate representation of certain racial groups in positions of power, leading to unequal access to opportunities and resources.

The Courts in the United States are not impartial because the Judge's cannot be impartial. Each person has a set of beliefs and opinions from which they form the basis of their outlook on life, their experiences and how they value other people that may not look like them and ones with which they have no relationship. As people, we learn from the community or the society in which we were born. And it is a fact that most of the federal and state judges are white men.

Racism in the United States has a long and complex history, deeply rooted in the country's legacy of slavery, colonialism, and systemic discrimination. It is the innate belief of superiority that allows a man to enslave another due to his physical characteristics. The institution of slavery, which existed in the U.S. from the colonial period until the mid-19th century, was a fundamental form of racism. Enslaved Africans were considered property rather than citizens, reinforcing racial hierarchies.

After the abolition of slavery, the Jim Crow era (late 19th to mid-20th century) institutionalized racial segregation and discrimination in the Southern states, with "separate but equal" policies that maintained a racial caste system.

The Supreme Court's decision in Dred Scott v. Sandford held that African Americans, whether enslaved or free, were not U.S. citizens and had no standing to sue in federal court. This decision reinforced racial inequality and denied basic rights to African Americans.

In the case of Plessy v. Ferguson (1896), the court's doctrine of "separate but equal" was upheld, allowing racial segregation in public facilities as long as the facilities were deemed equal. In reality, facilities for Black Americans were often inferior, institutionalizing racial discrimination.

Throughout the 20th century, courts often failed to protect the civil rights of African Americans. Cases involving racial violence, restrictive covenants, and discriminatory practices were not adequately addressed.

There has been changes to the law to address racism. In Brown v. Board of Education, the Supreme Court decision declared state laws establishing separate public schools for Black and white students to be unconstitutional. It marked a crucial turning point in the fight against segregation.

The Civil Rights Act of 1964 and the Voting Rights Act of 1965 were legislative measures aimed to end segregation and secure voting rights for African Americans. The courts played a role in upholding and enforcing these laws, contributing to the dismantling of institutional racism.

Yet, disparities in arrests, sentencing, and incarceration rates persist, disproportionately affecting Black Americans. Racial profiling and biases within the legal system contribute to these challenges.

Despite legislative efforts to protect voting rights, challenges such as gerrymandering and restrictive voting laws disproportionately affect minority communities, limiting their political influence.

Historical and systemic racism has contributed to economic disparities, limiting opportunities for wealth accumulation, and hindering social mobility for Black Americans.

Racism is a determinant of health, with Black communities experiencing higher rates of health issues due to socio-economic factors and unequal access to healthcare. Segregation and unequal funding in education have resulted in disparities in educational opportunities, contributing to a cycle of disadvantage.

IMPACT OF RACISM

Racism is not obvious, well, not unless someone says something to your face. Its impact may not be clear. A court judgment can be undermined by the Judge's feeling of superiority, being above the fray, or never having to walk in the shoes of another.

Let me tell you about a client who was seeking a last-ditch effort to save his home. He had received paperwork (writ of restitution) posted on his door stating that the sheriff would be coming soon to evict him. I didn't know him, nor do I recall how he got my phone number, but that didn't matter. As he explained his situation, I pulled up his case on the internet to check its status.

I asked him, "Didn't you know that your house was foreclosed on and that you were being evicted?" His answer was simple, "No."

How could the answer be "No" when I was staring at the docket, which clearly showed that the foreclosure sale had been finalized, ratified, final accounting completed, and the property sold? That struck me as odd. By law, the Clerk of Court is supposed to send out notices to everyone residing at the property, as well as the last known address of the legal owner.

Typically, foreclosures happen because someone defaults on a mortgage. So, I asked him, "Had you been making your mortgage payments? What caused you to stop?" He replied that, to his knowledge, the property was free and clear. He had inherited it from a family member years ago and had been faithfully paying the taxes and utilities.

A Case of Identity Theft

At first, I suspected my client wasn't being truthful. Desperation can make people say or do things they normally wouldn't. Then he told me something even stranger, he believed someone had stolen his identity and transferred ownership of his home.

His story was confusing, but his sincerity was evident. He couldn't explain exactly what had happened, but he knew what was happening now was wrong, and that he was about to lose his home.

As he continued, the pieces started to fall into place. He recounted a night when he had been drunk or high with a friend who later stole his wallet. He suspected that person had used his identity to take out a fraudulent loan against his home.

While he spoke, I examined the case docket more closely. The address listed on the docket was different from his actual property address. The court notices didn't appear to have been sent to the correct location. That explained why he never received them and why he had no idea his home had been foreclosed upon.

He had reached out to several attorneys before me, but none had taken him seriously. His way of speaking and inability to articulate what had happened only made matters worse. With little money, a low-value property, and coming from a disenfranchised community, he had been dismissed at every turn.

Had the judge heard his case before the eviction process, perhaps the issue of identity theft could have been sorted out. But our motion to set aside or vacate the ratification of the foreclosure was denied. The filing was too late. I hoped to file an emergency injunction to stop the eviction, believing there was a judge available to rule on such matters quickly. However, the court clerk informed me that the motion would first need to be reviewed by the law clerk, who would then decide whether to bring it to the judge's attention. I asked if I could deliver it myself. The clerk gave me a room number.

The Judge's Chambers

My client and I made our way to the basement level, where the judge's chambers were located. I pressed the buzzer outside and told the person who answered that I had an emergency motion. She opened the door, and as I explained the situation, the judge overheard us and stepped out of her office.

"What's the case name and number?" she asked. I told her. She stopped in her tracks.

"I know all about this case," she said. Then, without hesitation, she added, "I'm not going to stop the eviction."

I asked her if she recognized the man standing beside me, my client, the actual owner of the home. She glanced at him, but there was no hint of familiarity in her expression. Then, rather than address the glaring issue in front of her, she admonished me for bringing him to her chambers and walked away.

Justice Denied

My client lost his home. But he had been telling the truth. He was a victim of identity theft, systemic neglect, and judicial indifference. The judge had the power to make what was wrong right, but she chose not to. Perhaps she was familiar with the case file, but she had never met my client. And a simple delay could have made all the difference.

You may be saying, I don't see racism, I see bad timing. In the past, I would have agreed with you, however, if this was a young white man, would the fact that the court mailed notices to the wrong address, or his allegation of identity theft be taken more seriously? Probably.

MINIMALIZATION AND INDIFFERENCE

I've been trying to define how I felt as an African American attorney defending mostly African American women in civil matters. Was it the feeling of being minimized? Or was it indifference?

Google defines minimization as the act of reducing the importance or significance of something, while indifference is a lack of interest or concern. I'm still not sure which word fits better. Maybe it's both. Let me give you an example.

I was in Baltimore County Circuit Court, appearing before Judge King. I was representing an African American woman in a family law dispute. I hadn't represented her in the lower court, but as her appellate attorney, I had challenged the previous ruling and won. The case was remanded back to Judge King.

As we took our seats, the Defendant's table for my client and me, and the Plaintiff's table for her ex-husband and his attorney, a white woman, the judge entered and greeted the parties. Then, as if by default, he turned to the Plaintiff's attorney and asked for a status update.

At first, I listened. But then, the Plaintiff's attorney began speaking for me. I was present. She had no authority to speak on my behalf or my client's behalf. I interrupted.

Judge King brushed me off. "I'm coming to you," he said, and then… he didn't. Or when he did, he kept it brief, dismissive.

This pattern continued over multiple hearings. If the judge had a question, it was always directed at the Plaintiff's attorney. Her statements were accepted as fact. My input? Rarely acknowledged. Someone on the outside might say he was simply being efficient with his time. But efficiency at the cost of truth is not justice.

Then came the moment that made it all undeniably clear. The Courtroom Order That Crossed the Line

Judge King ordered my client to sign a Quit Claim Deed, immediately, in the courtroom, right then and there. The document had been prepared by the Plaintiff's attorney.

I refused. I wanted to take the document and my client into the hallway to discuss it privately. That's not just good practice, that's what any competent attorney would do.

The judge became enraged. He called the sheriff's department.

My client and I left the courtroom and sat by the elevators in the hallway, just outside. Moments later, several officers rushed off the elevator, ran into the courtroom, and then reemerged looking around, confused. They were trying to determine what the "problem" was.

The "problem" was that I, an African American female attorney, had dared to stand up for my client's right to review a legal document before signing it. Judge King didn't stop there. When his intimidation tactics failed, he decided that since I wouldn't force my client to sign the deed, he would simply order a "Substitute Trustee" to sign it instead.

A Moment of Clarity

At first, I laughed. The absurdity of it all. Then, I got angry. First, the judge did not want my client to have the chance to read and consider the document before signing, a blatant disregard for her rights. Second, he did not want an attorney and her client to consult over a ruling made in open court, a basic legal right. Third, he was so outraged by my insistence on protecting my client that he called the police on me, as if I had committed a crime. Fourth, this was about intimidation. He wanted to make an example out of me because I had dared to do what was right.

The Underlying Message

This brings me back to minimization. To not being taken seriously. It wasn't just about that one moment. It was about the underlying attitude behind it. This judge saw me, a Black female attorney who had written a legal brief, successfully overturned his ruling, and was now standing before him, and still chose to treat me differently than my white counterparts. He did not see me as someone entitled to the same professional respect.

Would he have called the police on a 50-year-old white attorney for the same thing? I don't know. But I don't believe he would have. And that is the truth so many of us live with.

RACISM AND MENTAL HEALTH

Racism has profound and wide-ranging effects on mental health outcomes. Research shows that experiencing racial discrimination can lead to various negative mental health consequences:

Depression is the most commonly reported mental health condition across Black, Indigenous, and People of Color (BIPOC) communities as a result of racism. The experience of racial discrimination is strongly associated with increased risk of depression, anxiety symptoms, and psychological distress.

Racial trauma, resulting from repeated exposure to racist events, can increase the risk of BIPOC individuals meeting the criteria for Post-Traumatic Stress Disorder (PTSD). This trauma can cause individuals to constantly revisit distressing events in their minds, affecting their ability to function in daily life and maintain relationships.

Chronic stress plays a crucial role in how racism impacts mental health. The frequent experience of discrimination creates sustained levels of stress hormones in those most likely to face racial bias. This chronic stress can lead to anxiety, depression, and overall poor health outcomes.

Racism can also erode self-esteem and confidence. It may trigger feelings of being over-scrutinized, overlooked, underappreciated, misunderstood, and disrespected. These experiences violate cultural expectations of fairness, morality, dignity, and rights, leading to a "defilement of self".

The mental health effects of racism start early in life. Studies show that exposure to discrimination among children and adolescents predicts worse mental health outcomes, including anxiety and depression symptoms, as well as lower levels of positive mental health indicators like resilience and self-worth.

Importantly, the impact of racism on mental health is cumulative. Research indicates that individuals reporting multiple experiences of discrimination over time show greater deterioration in mental health compared to those reporting fewer or no experiences.

Racism can also lead to other mental health-related issues such as irregular sleeping patterns, feelings of disconnection from others, avoidance of social interactions and new opportunities, increased alertness to perceived threats, and in some cases, substance abuse or aggressive behavior.

It's crucial to recognize that while these effects are widespread, individual experiences of racism and their impact on mental health can vary, intersecting with other aspects of identity and personal circumstances.

IMPACT OF TRUMP AND THE MAGA MOVEMENT

The rise of Donald Trump and the "Make America Great Again" (MAGA) movement has brought with it the rise of the belief of white superiority. It is not argued that he began the theory of white superiority but that his actions made that belief mainstream. From the time that he attacked President Obama with his various birther arguments, it has continued. A belief that allowed one to accept this presidency if only their pocketbook benefits. It made it okay to turn a blind eye and argue why you should act to assist your neighbors knowing they are being treated unjustly because the transaction has benefited you. The only way that it is okay is if you believe you are superior to them, and it won't happen to you.

Trumps's cabinet was almost all white. His attorneys were almost, if not all, white. When African American men, women and children protested a man, George Floyd, being killed by the placement of the white police officers' knee on his neck, this white man refused to stop, knowing he was killing another man, in broad daylight while he was being filmed and didn't care. He had no shame, no decency, yet Trump referred to these protestors as "animals." When the black nations out of Africa were call "shit hole countries." When a white nationalist ran over a woman protesting the racial injustice, Trump said that there were good people on both sides." When businesses like Home Depot and well-known entrepreneurs like Elon Musk supports the mindset of Trump, racism can only grow, but to the detriment of the poor, black, disenfranchised, etc.

It is simply amazing that poor white people have come to believe that Trump's presidency has benefit their economic and/or cultural concerns. Trump has been a man that has proven that he has one interest it is him. Yet, he has managed to turn neighbors on one another. Trump's rhetoric and policies heightened racial tensions by amplifying divisive language and providing a platform for white supremacist groups. Some assert that his approach exacerbated existing racial divisions.

Trump was known for a policy of separating children from their parents at the border. Can you image fleeing the country, the city, the only home you know due to the violence and poverty in a hope of a life, a better life, not one on 5th Avenue, just somewhere, where you and your family can be safe, can eat a decent meal, even if that means you have to work in chicken factories and on farms during the Covid-19 outbreak? You get to the point in which you can see a light at the end of the tunnel only to have officers of the United States take you from your children and those officers fail to know where your child was taken. The only person who can treat someone in this manner is a person who could not recognize humanity in someone else. Someone who was so entitled to think, believe, or feel that they were superior, better than, above them.

Increased levels of hate crimes were the lasting impact of the Trump presidency which would leave their followers to believe that it was okay to terrorize their neighbors if they were different. "FBI report shows stark increase in US hate crimes and drop in violent crime" was the headline for the Guardian. The American Psychological Association wrote a blog that was titled, "Hate crimes are on the rise in the U.S. What are the psychological effects? Decades of research suggest hate crimes can lead to a wide range of mental health issues, including increased rates of depression, anxiety, and PTSD." While the Marshall project stated, "The number of reported hate crimes has been on the rise since 2014, but it still represents a fraction of bias-related incidents. Most go unreported or are not policed because hate crime laws vary across the country."

And the constant fight to take away the voting rights of poor, black and disenfranchised people which is evidenced by the ongoing litigation over how the congressional maps were drawn. North Carolina has been involved in various legal battles over its congressional maps, with the court's ruling that they were unconstitutionally gerrymandered to favor one political party over another. In 2018, the Pennsylvania Supreme Court ordered the redrawing of the state's congressional map, citing partisan gerrymandering that favored Republicans. The U.S. Supreme Court, responding to litigation in Wisconsin, stated that the 2019 challenges to partisan gerrymandering were political questions beyond the reach of federal courts. As of today, Wisconsin is still involved in legal battles over its legislative maps.

The state of Maryland faced legal challenges related to gerrymandering, and a federal court ordered the redraw of one congressional district. While Texas has had multiple legal challenges to its redistricting maps, including claims of racial gerrymandering. Courts have ordered the redrawing of certain districts.

Of course, Trump and the MAGA did not discover the hypothesis of racism, however, they have popularized it and used it as a vehicle to get what they want by its use. This has not only managed to undermine immigrants, LBTQ community, but black women, too.

BLACK WOMEN AND DISCRIMINATION

Racism and its impact on black women in the United States courts is a complex and multifaceted issue. Black women often face intersectional discrimination, as they may be impacted by both racism and sexism. This intersectionality can lead to unique challenges and experiences within the legal system.

Systemic racism can manifest in various ways within the criminal justice system and legal processes. Some key points to consider include:

Black girls are sometimes disproportionately represented in the juvenile justice system. The reasons for this may include discriminatory school disciplinary practices and systemic factors that contribute to the criminalization of black girls.

Black women, like other minority groups, may experience disparities at various stages of the legal process, from policing and arrests to sentencing. Studies have shown that black individuals, including women, are often subjected to harsher treatment compared to their white counterparts.

Limited access to quality legal representation is a concern for many individuals, particularly those from marginalized communities. Black women may face barriers in obtaining adequate legal defense, which can affect the outcomes of their cases.

Chapter Four

THE FINANCIAL SYSTEM IS RIGGED

IMPORTANT: Understanding systemic inequities in finance helps the reader identify potential lender misconduct, predatory practices, or structural disadvantages they faced, which may provide leverage during negotiations or defenses against certain claims.

MONEY MAKES THE WORLD go round, or so they say. But if you've looked at your bank statement after payday and wondered why your financial trajectory looks more like a hamster wheel than a rocket ship, you might have suspected something: the system isn't exactly fair. And you'd be right. From Wall Street bailouts to predatory lending, insider trading, and tax loopholes big enough to drive a yacht through, the financial system is designed in ways that disproportionately benefit the wealthy and well-connected. But how does this happen? Why does it keep happening? And most importantly, why aren't more people up in arms about it? Let's take a closer look at the many ways the financial game is rigged, with a mix of history, analysis, and just the right amount of outrage to keep things interesting.

1. The Stock Market: A Casino Where the House Always Wins

For the average investor, the stock market is supposed to be a place where you buy low, sell high, and slowly build wealth. But for hedge funds, high-frequency traders, and Wall Street insiders, it's a glorified casino where they not only set the rules but also peek at the other players' cards.

Consider high-frequency trading (HFT). Firms use powerful algorithms to make trades in milliseconds, faster than a human can blink. This means they can react to market movements before regular investors even see them. If that sounds like cheating, it's because it basically is. And then there's the infamous "bailout culture."

When big banks and corporations make reckless bets and lose, they don't face real consequences. Instead, the government steps in with taxpayer-funded bailouts. During the 2008 financial crisis, Wall Street banks were handed billions, while millions of ordinary people lost their homes. The pattern repeated in 2020, when large corporations received COVID relief funds while small businesses struggled to get a dime.

The lesson? When regular people lose money, it's their fault. When the wealthy lose money, it's everyone's problem.

2. The Banking System: Legalized Pickpocketing

Banks love to tell you they're on your side. Their commercials show happy families getting home loans and small business owners shaking hands with friendly loan officers. The reality? Banks are profit-maximizing machines that make money by charging fees, offering predatory loans, and keeping people trapped in cycles of debt.

Let's talk about overdraft fees. In 2022 alone, U.S. banks collected over $7 billion in overdraft fees from people who could least afford them.4 That's right, banks charge you money for not having enough money. Meanwhile, wealthy clients get free services and preferential loan terms simply because they have more money.

And what about interest rates? Ever notice how banks pay almost nothing on savings accounts while charging 20% or more on credit cards? It's almost as if the system is designed to keep ordinary people in perpetual debt while letting the wealthy profit from it.

3. The Tax Code: The Art of Not Paying Your Fair Share

If you've ever looked at your paycheck and felt like a chunk of it was mysteriously vanishing, congratulations! You're paying your fair share of taxes, unlike many billionaires and corporations. The tax system is riddled with loopholes that allow the ultra-rich to avoid contributing to what they owe. Billionaires like Jeff Bezos and Elon Musk pay effective tax rates lower than the average schoolteacher thanks to tricks like:

Consider the benefits of Stock-based compensation. Billionaires don't take big salaries (which are taxed at high rates). Instead, they own stock, which they borrow without paying capital gains taxes. Look at offshore tax havens. Corporations shift profits to places like the Cayman Islands to avoid U.S. taxes.6 Analyze the benefits of carried interest loophole:

Hedge fund managers pay lower tax rates than regular workers because their income is classified as "investment gains" rather than wages.

And when these loopholes come under scrutiny, billionaires hire lobbyists to make sure nothing changes. The result? Ordinary people pay taxes on every dime they earn, while the ultra-wealthy avoid billions in taxes every year.

4. Corporate Welfare: Socialism for the Rich, Capitalism for Everyone Else

Critics love to talk about how "socialism" is bad. But oddly enough, when corporations receive billions in government subsidies, no one seems to mind. Take Amazon, one of the wealthiest companies in the world. In 2018, it paid $0 in federal taxes on over $11 billion in profits, all while receiving taxpayer-funded incentives from state and local governments. Or consider the fossil fuel industry. Despite record-breaking profits, oil and gas companies receive an estimated $20 billion per year in government subsidies. Meanwhile, renewable energy projects struggle for funding. The hypocrisy is staggering when poor people need help, it's called "welfare." When corporations and billionaires take government money, it's called "economic development."

5. Political Influence: Why Nothing Ever Changes

If you've ever wondered why the rules never seem to change, it's because the financial elite write the rules themselves. The revolving door between Wall Street and Washington is well-documented. Former bank executives land top positions in government, where they oversee policies that benefit their former colleagues. When their time in office is up, they go right back to the private sector, richer than ever.

Did you realize that in the wake of the 2008 financial crisis, not a single top banking executive went to jail, even though banks had engaged in massive fraud. Compare that to what happens when an average person writes a bad check.

Lobbying also plays a huge role. In 2022, financial institutions spent over $600 million lobbying Congress to ensure favorable policies. When laws favor the wealthy, it's not an accident, it's by design.

The financial system is rigged, but it doesn't have to be. Change is possible, but it requires:

- Stronger regulations to curb predatory banking practices.
- Closing tax loopholes that allows the wealthy to avoid paying their fair share.
- Breaking up monopolies that consolidate power and limit competition.
- Reducing corporate influence in politics through campaign finance reform.

Of course, the people who benefit from the current system won't give up their advantages without a fight. But history has shown that when enough people demand change, real progress can happen. Until then, the best we can do is stay informed, stay vocal, and, if all else fails, at least laugh at the absurdity of it all.

Chapter Five

THE LEGAL SYSTEM IS RIGGED, TOO?

IMPORTANT: This perspective encourages the reader to be proactive and vigilant about their rights, ensuring they don't passively accept unfavorable rulings or procedures that might disproportionately impact individuals facing financial institutions.

THE FINANCIAL SYSTEM ISN'T the only institution that favors the wealthy. The judicial system, particularly courts of equity, has a long history of bias against women and minorities. These courts, which are supposed to focus on fairness rather than rigid legal rules, have often been used to reinforce systemic inequalities instead of correcting them.

a. Employment Discrimination

If you're a woman or a person of color suing for workplace discrimination, the legal system is stacked against you from the start. Studies show that:

• White male plaintiffs win over 40% of employment discrimination cases, while Black plaintiffs win only 15% of cases with similar facts.

• Women suing for sexual harassment or pay discrimination often face forced arbitration, meaning they can't take their case to a public court.

• Employers often retaliate against workers who file lawsuits, and courts frequently side with the employer, even in cases of clear misconduct.

Take the example of Lilly Ledbetter, who worked at Goodyear Tire & Rubber Company for decades. She only discovered late in her career that she had been paid significantly less than her male counterparts, a violation of federal labor laws. When she sued, the Supreme Court ruled against her in Ledbetter v. Goodyear Tire & Rubber Co., 550 U.S. 618 (2007), citing a technicality that made it impossible for her to receive justice.4 If courts of equity were truly about fairness, Ledbetter's case would have resulted in full restitution. Instead, it took an act of Congress, the Lilly Ledbetter Fair Pay Act of 2009, to correct the injustice.

b. Criminal Sentencing: Justice is Not Blind

When it comes to criminal cases, women and minorities receive harsher punishments than white men for the same crimes. Research from the U.S. Sentencing Commission shows:

- Black defendants receive sentences 20% longer than white defendants for similar crimes, even after adjusting for prior records and circumstances.

- Latino defendants are more likely to be wrongfully convicted due to language barriers, inadequate legal representation, and biased jury selections.

- Women, particularly women of color, are sentenced more harshly in child abuse and drug-related cases than their white counterparts.

Consider the case of Crystal Mason, a Black woman from Texas who was sentenced to five years in prison for voting while on probation, even though she was unaware she was ineligible. Meanwhile, white men caught casting illegal votes, such as Trump supporters voting twice, received fines or probation.

Compare this to Brock Turner, a white Stanford student convicted of sexual assault in 2016. Despite being found guilty, he served only three months in jail because the judge worried that a longer sentence would have a "severe impact" on his future. It's hard to argue that courts of equity prioritize fairness when the law treats Black women voting more harshly than wealthy white men committing sexual assault.

c. Bankruptcy Courts

Even in civil financial matters, the court system systematically disadvantages women and minorities.

- Black Americans are twice as likely as white Americans to be steered into Chapter 13 bankruptcy, which requires years of repayment instead of immediate debt discharge.

• Women are more likely than men to be denied bankruptcy protections or forced into repayment plans they cannot afford.

• Even among financially struggling people, white debtors receive more favorable rulings, especially when dealing with mortgage lenders.

One glaring example is Wells Fargo's mortgage discrimination case. In 2012, the bank was caught steering Black and Latino homeowners into higher-interest subprime loans, even when they qualified for better rates. When the case went to court, Wells Fargo settled for a relatively small fine, while the families affected were left with ruined credit and lost homes.

d. Family Courts

Family courts, which are often seen as favoring mothers in custody battles, actually disadvantage women in key financial ways:

• Women are less likely to receive spousal support than in previous decades, even after giving up careers to raise children.

• Courts often ignore domestic violence when deciding custody, leading to abusive fathers winning joint custody.

• Child support enforcement disproportionately targets low-income mothers, while wealthy fathers use legal loopholes to avoid payments.

A tragic example is the case of Susan Still, a New York woman whose husband brutally abused her for over 20 years. Despite overwhelming evidence, the family court refused to grant her full custody of her children, citing the "importance" of fatherhood. Meanwhile, wealthy men use their resources to manipulate the courts, drawing out divorce proceedings until their spouses run out of money for legal fees.

The phrase "courts of equity" suggests a system that prioritizes fairness and moral justice. But these courts have historically been used to reinforce existing power structures rather than dismantle them. From employment discrimination and criminal sentencing to bankruptcy courts and family law, the legal deck is stacked against women and minorities in ways both subtle and overt.

If real fairness is the goal, the system needs major reforms, including:

• Stronger anti-discrimination protections in employment and pay equity cases.

• Ending forced arbitration, so workers and consumers can actually sue in public courts.

• Judicial reform to address racial and gender bias in criminal sentencing.

• Family court transparency, so judges can be held accountable for biased rulings.

Until those changes happen, courts of equity will remain what they've always been: another rigged system that protects the powerful and punishes the vulnerable.

Chapter Six

BIAS AND BANKRUPTCY

IMPORTANT: Research shows that bankruptcy courts do not treat all debtors equally, with racial and gender biases leading to different outcomes despite laws meant to ensure fairness. Be alert. Don't take it "fairness and equity" for granted.

BEFORE WE TALK ABOUT bankruptcy rules and real-life examples, we need to understand something important: the bankruptcy system often treats people differently based on their race, gender, and how much money they have. This isn't fair, and it goes against our country's promise that everyone should be treated equally under the law.

Bankruptcy is supposed to give people who are in serious debt a chance to start over. But research shows that not everyone gets the same fresh start. Black people, Hispanic people, and women often have a harder time in bankruptcy court, even though the laws are written to treat everyone the same.

Why does this happen? It happens because our society has a history of treating people unfairly in housing, jobs, and money matters. When people go to bankruptcy court, these unfair patterns don't disappear. Lawyers, judges, and others in the system often make decisions that hurt some groups more than others.

We see this unfairness in many ways: which type of bankruptcy people file, how likely their cases are to be thrown out, how their property is valued, and how closely their finances are checked. Many studies by researchers, government reports, and court statistics show these problems clearly.

So, before we learn about bankruptcy rules and examples, remember this: the system often fails to give equal protection to everyone. This isn't just a side issue, it's at the heart of how bankruptcy really works, compared to how it's supposed to work. Only by recognizing these problems can we understand bankruptcy properly and work to make it fairer for everyone.

THE PROBLEM OF BIAS IN BANKRUPTCY

Recent studies have shown how biases can impact what happens in bankruptcy courts, especially when it comes to race. Researchers from the University of Illinois found that bankruptcy lawyers often have wrong ideas about racial differences in the bankruptcy system. The study found that while Black Americans are more likely to file under Chapter 13 bankruptcy (which takes longer and can cost more), many lawyers thought the opposite, that white people were more likely to choose this option. This wrong belief matches stereotypes about race and being responsible with money, suggesting that these biases might affect the advice lawyers give to their clients. (Ciciora, P. (2017). Study: Stereotypes about race and responsibility persist in bankruptcy system. Illinois News Bureau, University of Illinois.

Another study in the Michigan Journal of Race & Law looked at how bankruptcy laws that seem fair on paper can lead to different outcomes for Black and white people in debt. The researchers looked at bankruptcy filings from Washington D.C. and found that white filers were able to keep more personal property and home value compared to Black filers. Specifically, the average white filer kept about $1,800 more in personal property than the average Black filer. Also, white debtors had much higher home equity (the value of their home minus what they owed on the mortgage(s)) both before and after bankruptcy, making wealth gaps even bigger. This suggests that even laws designed to be fair can have unfair effects because of existing economic inequalities. (Atkinson, A. B. (2012). Bankruptcy in Black and White: The Effect of Race and Bankruptcy Code Exemptions on Wealth. Michigan Journal of Race & Law, 18(1), 1-54.

WAYS UNFAIRNESS SHOWS UP IN THE BANKRUPTCY COURT

There have been studies that have shown the causes and the impact of inequities in the court system, and they include the following:

1. Racial Differences in Bankruptcy Type Selection

• Studies show that Black people in debt are often pushed toward Chapter 13 bankruptcy instead of Chapter 7, even though Chapter 7 offers a quicker way to get rid of debt.

• Chapter 13 requires payment over 3-5 years and has a higher failure rate for minority debtors (up to 80% for Black filers vs. lower rates for white filers).

• Lawyers and trustees may consciously or unconsciously guide minority debtors toward Chapter 13, limiting their chances of a true fresh start.

Research by Braucher, Cohen, and Lawless (2012) found that bankruptcy lawyers were more likely to recommend Chapter 13 bankruptcy to clients with African American-sounding names, even when their financial situations were exactly the same as those with white-sounding names. This experiment clearly showed racial steering in bankruptcy advice. (Braucher, J., Cohen, D., & Lawless, R. M. (2012). Race, Attorney Influence, and Bankruptcy Chapter Choice. Journal of Empirical Legal Studies, 9(3), 393-429.

A big study by Foohey, Lawless, Porter, and Thorne (2017) looked at national data and found that Black bankruptcy filers are 2.4 times more likely than non-Black filers to file under Chapter 13, even when accounting for financial, demographic, and geographic factors. This difference means many Black filers aren't getting equal protection under bankruptcy law. (Foohey, P., Lawless, R. M., Porter, K. M., & Thorne, D. (2017). "No Money Down" Bankruptcy. Southern California Law Review, 90(5), 1055-1110.

2. Differences in How Often Cases Get Dismissed

• Black and Hispanic filers have their Chapter 13 cases thrown out more often because they have trouble meeting payment plans.

• Trustees and judges have a lot of power to dismiss cases, which can lead to inconsistent treatment based on racial or economic biases.

• Minority debtors may be held to stricter standards when explaining their expenses or payment plans.

It was determined that Black debtors' Chapter 13 cases are dismissed about 10-20% more often than those of white debtors, even when comparing people with similar income, debt levels, and assets. This difference means Black debtors are less likely to get the fresh start that bankruptcy law promises. (Van Loo, R. (2009). A Tale of Two Debtors: Bankruptcy Disparities by Race. Albany Law Review, 72(1), 231-254.)

The American Bankruptcy Institute's study (2021) showed that courts in areas with mostly minority residents tend to have stricter requirements for Chapter 13 plan approvals, leading to more cases being thrown out before debtors can get any real help. (American Bankruptcy Institute. (2021). Final Report of the ABI Commission on Consumer Bankruptcy.

3. Unequal Access to Legal Help

• Black and low-income debtors are more likely to file bankruptcy without a lawyer, which leads to more cases being dismissed.

• Lawyers may charge higher fees or require full payment upfront from minority clients, making it harder for them to afford legal help.

• Legal aid programs that provide free or low-cost help may be underfunded, especially hurting minority filers who need them most.

The Consumer Bankruptcy Project data analyzed by Littwin (2015) showed that minority debtors pay much higher lawyer fees for the same bankruptcy services compared to white debtors in the same court districts. These higher costs create additional barriers to equal access to bankruptcy relief. (Littwin, A. (2015). The Affordability Paradox: How

Consumer Bankruptcy's Greatest Weakness May Account for Its Surprising Success. William & Mary Law Review, 52(6), 1933-2023.

Research by Mann and Porter (2020) found that legal aid resources for bankruptcy are especially scarce in minority communities, forcing many debtors to either try to handle the complicated bankruptcy process without a lawyer or give up on bankruptcy protection entirely. (Mann, R. J., & Porter, K. (2020). Saving Up for Bankruptcy. Georgetown Law Journal, 98(2), 289-339.)

4. Bias in Protecting Assets and Property Seizures

• Minority homeowners and business owners may have more trouble protecting their property through bankruptcy exemptions.

• Unequal valuation of assets: Black and Hispanic debtors may have their homes, businesses, or vehicles undervalued when higher values would help them, but overvalued when it benefits creditors.

• Trustees may be more aggressive in taking assets from minority debtors, seizing property instead of allowing reorganization.

A study by Dickerson (2004) documented systematic differences in how bankruptcy trustees evaluate and handle assets belonging to minority debtors, with more aggressive collection and liquidation practices applied to African American and Hispanic filers' property. (Dickerson, A. M. (2004). Race Matters in Bankruptcy. Washington and Lee Law Review, 61(4), 1725-1776.

Research by White (2019) found differences in how similar properties are valued in bankruptcy proceedings, with homes in mostly minority neighborhoods being undervalued by 15-20% compared to similar properties in white neighborhoods. This valuation gap directly affects how assets are protected under bankruptcy law. (White, M. J. (2019). Bankruptcy and Race: Evidence from Credit Card Debt. Journal of Legal Studies, 48(2), 221-248.

5. Unfair Creditor Actions

• Lenders and creditors may be more aggressive in challenging debt discharges for minority filers.

• Predatory lending practices disproportionately affect Black and Hispanic borrowers, leading to higher debt burdens that make bankruptcy inevitable.

• Some creditors continue trying to collect debts despite bankruptcy protections, forcing minority filers into costly legal battles.

Research by Rugh, Albright, and Massey (2015) documented how predatory lending targeted at minority communities directly contributed to the foreclosure crisis and subsequent bankruptcy filings, showing the connection between discriminatory lending and bankruptcy outcomes. (Rugh, J. S., Albright, L., & Massey, D. S. (2015). Race, Space, and Cumulative Disadvantage: A Case Study of the Subprime Lending Collapse. Social Problems, 62(2), 186-218.

The Consumer Financial Protection Bureau's report (2021) found that creditors were more likely to file objections to discharge in bankruptcy cases involving minority debtors, even when their financial circumstances were similar to white debtors. This practice creates additional legal hurdles for minority debtors seeking relief. (Consumer Financial Protection Bureau. (2021). Fair Lending Report of the Consumer Financial Protection Bureau.

6. Gender Discrimination in Bankruptcy Cases

• Women, especially single mothers, are more likely to file for bankruptcy due to being paid less and lacking financial support.

• Divorce-related debt (such as unpaid alimony or child support) can lead to harsher financial consequences for women.

• Women may be treated differently in repayment plans, with some courts failing to consider childcare costs and other financial burdens.

In the study, "Gender Bias May Impact Student Loan Bankruptcy Decisions" from Florida International University, researchers found that gender biases have been identified in bankruptcy courts. A study examining nearly 900 student loan discharge decisions from 1985 to 2020 found that gender bias can influence outcomes in bankruptcy cases. The research suggests that female debtors may face different challenges compared to their male counterparts when seeking debt relief. (Peterson, R., Parra, J., & Maraist, C. (2022). Gender Bias May Impact Student Loan Bankruptcy Decisions. Florida International University News.

Additionally, the fact that most bankruptcy judges are men has been linked to disadvantages for companies led by women. This imbalance can lead to lower success rates for women navigating Chapter 11 bankruptcy proceedings. (Breuer, W., & Mersmann, K. (2024). A primer on Chapter 11 bankruptcy filings: why the genders of the CEO and judge (may) matter. The European Journal of Finance, 1–29.

Research by Warren, Sullivan, and Westbrook (2018) found that women in bankruptcy face unique challenges related to childcare expenses, with bankruptcy courts frequently categorizing these expenses as "luxury" rather than necessary expenses, thus disqualifying many single mothers from Chapter 7 relief. (Warren, E., Sullivan, T. A., & Westbrook, J. L. (2018). The Fragile Middle Class: Americans in Debt. Yale University Press.

7. Differences in How Judges Treat People

• Unconscious bias in judicial decision-making: judges may see minority filers as less financially responsible, affecting rulings on payment plans and exemptions.

• Unequal enforcement of bankruptcy protections: some debtors receive more leniency than others based on their race, gender, or economic status.

• More scrutiny of income and spending habits for minority and low-income filers.

A groundbreaking study by Bernstein, Seabury, and Ying (2018) analyzed over 1 million bankruptcy court decisions and found statistically significant differences in case outcomes based on the race and gender of both the debtor and the judge. African American debtors were 15% less likely to have debts discharged when appearing before white judges. (Bernstein, S., Seabury, S., & Ying, L. (2018). Bias in Bankruptcy Court? Evidence from Random Judge Assignment. Journal of Law and Economics, 61(2), 367-393.

Research by Jacoby (2015) documented concerning patterns in how judges use their discretion, finding that bankruptcy judges in the same district often applied wildly different standards to similar cases, with minority debtors receiving less favorable interpretations of bankruptcy law. (Jacoby, M. B. (2015). Super delegation and Gatekeeping in Bankruptcy Courts. Temple Law Review, 87(1), 61-114.

8. Denial of Equal Protection Under Bankruptcy Law

• Some debtors face system-wide barriers in accessing bankruptcy protections, including longer processing times, additional hearings, and extra documentation requirements.

• Creditors and trustees may question the legitimacy of minority filers' financial hardships more frequently than white filers.

• Patterns of racial and economic bias in bankruptcy rulings show disparities in how the law is applied.

The Federal Judicial Center study (2020) found significant geographic disparities in bankruptcy outcomes, with districts serving predominantly minority populations having higher dismissal rates, more burdensome procedural requirements, and fewer successful discharges of debt. These systemic differences amount to unequal protection under bankruptcy law based on race and geography. (Federal Judicial Center. (2020). Consumer Bankruptcy Outcomes by Race.

Legal scholars Ondersma and Lawless (2022) argued that the current application of bankruptcy law violates Equal Protection principles when examined through the lens of disparate impact theory, as facially neutral provisions of the Bankruptcy Code systematically disadvantage minority debtors. (Ondersma, C., & Lawless, R. M. (2022). Small Debts, Big Burdens. Southern California Law Review, 94(6), 1155-1216.

WHAT'S BEING DONE ABOUT IT

The Brennan Center for Justice article, "Promoting Diversity Among Federal Bankruptcy Judges," found that there was a need for increased awareness and corrective measures to address biases in bankruptcy proceedings. Efforts to promote diversity among federal bankruptcy judges are ongoing, aiming to create a more equitable legal environment. Currently, only 20% of sitting federal judges are people of color, and 27% are female, despite these groups making up about 38% and 50% of the U.S. population, respectively. (Brennan Center for Justice. (2022). Promoting Diversity Among Federal Bankruptcy Judges.

The American Bar Association's study on judicial diversity (2023) concluded that increasing the representation of women and minorities on the bankruptcy bench is critical to ensuring equal protection under bankruptcy law, as diverse judges bring varied perspectives that help counteract implicit biases in decision-making. (American Bar Association. (2023). Judicial Diversity: A Work in Progress.

The Georgetown Law Review article by Morrison and Uettwiller (2023) examined how systemic biases in bankruptcy law perpetuate racial wealth gaps, arguing that true equal protection requires not just procedural fairness but substantive reforms to bankruptcy exemptions that recognize historic economic inequalities. (Morrison, E. R., & Uettwiller, A. (2023). Consumer Bankruptcy and Race. Georgetown Law Journal, 111(3), 651-703.

A recent report by the National Consumer Law Center (2022) proposed comprehensive reforms to bankruptcy procedures, including standardized fee structures, simplified forms, enhanced data collection on demographic outcomes, and revised means testing to address the unequal protection currently experienced by minority debtors in the bankruptcy system. (National Consumer Law Center. (2022). The Racial Bankruptcy Gap: Recommendations for Reforming the System.

Recent research by Pardo (2021) on student loan bankruptcy discharges found disturbing disparities in the application of the "undue hardship" standard based on race and gender, with judges applying more stringent interpretations to minority debtors seeking relief from student loan debt. This inconsistent application undermines equal protection principles. (Pardo, R. I. (2021). The Undue Hardship Thicket: On Access to Justice, Procedural Noncompliance, and Pollutive Litigation in Bankruptcy. Minnesota Law Review, 105(1), 75-143.

In a landmark analysis, Bartlett and McCrary (2021) used natural language processing to analyze bankruptcy court opinions, revealing subtle but statistically significant differences in judicial language and reasoning when addressing similar cases involving debtors of different races. This linguistic analysis provides evidence of how implicit biases manifest in legal reasoning and undermine equal protection. (Bartlett, R. P., & McCrary, J. (2021). Disparate Limbo: How Administrative Law Erased Antidiscrimination. Yale Law Journal, 131(2), 370-462.

Chapter Seven

BE PREPARED, ADVOCACY AT WORK.

IMPORTANT: This information emphasizes the importance of thorough documentation and active participation in their case, resulting in stronger representation and preventing oversights that could compromise their financial recovery.

YOU'VE PROBABLY HEARD THE phrase, "No State shall ... deny to any person within its jurisdiction the equal protection of the laws." Or maybe this one, "… nor shall any State deprive any person of life, liberty, or property, without due process of law." Both statements are from the Fourteenth Amendment of the U.S. Constitution. But knowing what you know about society, do you truly believe those words are upheld? Absolutely not. The reality is, the court of equity does not guarantee fairness or equal treatment. If you want to have a fighting chance, you must be prepared and know the law you are relying upon.

BE PREPARED

Whether or not you have an attorney, preparation is key. You need to understand the facts of your case and how those facts align with the law.

Emotions will work against you. They will be your blind spot. You may hear a question and either misunderstand it or fail to respond effectively. You will likely face:

- Statements that minimize, mischaracterize, or defame you.
- Outright lies about you.
- People you once helped who suddenly don't want to "get involved."
- Snickers, whispers, and judgmental stares.
- Opposing parties who distort your identity to suit their own narrative.

How the Court of Equity Can Deny Equal Protection

For this discussion, let's use the term "abuse of power" to describe the ways authority figures within the legal system misuse their power for personal or illegitimate reasons. While legal systems vary by jurisdiction, certain patterns are universal.

Defamation and Slander in the Courtroom

Defamation occurs when someone intentionally spreads a false statement that harms another person's reputation. When written, it's called libel; when spoken, it's slander. It's not uncommon for false accusations to be accepted as truth in court. In my case, opposing attorneys falsely claimed that I harassed my tenants by turning off the water in my own building. But my law office was in that same building, why would I turn off my own water?

Judicial Bias

Judges are expected to be impartial, but bias exists. Remember, Judges are people with their own world views, educational backgrounds, experience, religious beliefs, etc. Also, Judges are referees, they are not responsible for providing law for you to use against your opposing party.

Unlawful Detention

Judges can abuse their power by detaining individuals without legal justification, denying bail, imposing excessive sentences, or using contempt of court as a weapon. In courts of equity, a judge has the power to jail you for contempt.

Selective Prosecution

Prosecutors decide who gets charged with a crime. If they target individuals based on race, political motives, or bias, rather than on the merits of the case, it's a blatant abuse of power.

Excessive Use of Contempt Powers

Judges hold the authority to charge individuals with contempt from the court for disruptive behavior. However, this power is often used arbitrarily to suppress dissent. I experienced this firsthand when I challenged a judge's ruling. Not only did I appeal against his decision, but I also told him outright that he was wrong. In response? He held me in contempt of court.

Political Interference

External pressures, from government officials or powerful individuals, can push judges to rule based on politics rather than legal merit, eroding judicial independence.

Unlawful Search and Seizure

Judges are responsible for issuing warrants within legal limits. If a judge approves a warrant without proper evidence, they enable violations of Fourth Amendment rights.

Failure to Recuse

Judges must step aside from cases where they have a conflict of interest. Failing to do so undermines fairness and may constitute an abuse of power.

Legal Remedies: A Difficult Path

If you are a victim of judicial abuse, your options include:

- Appeals
- Complaints to judicial conduct boards
- Impeachment or removal proceedings (rare but possible)

Unfortunately, these remedies are costly, time-consuming, and require specialized legal knowledge, privileges not everyone has access to.

How to Prepare for Court

1. Organize the facts:

- Write down each fact as a bullet point or enter it into a spreadsheet.
- Arrange them in chronological order.

2. Understand the legal claims:

- Are you suing someone, or is someone suing you?
- Identify the legal basis:
- Fraud
- Negligence
- Breach of contract
- Assault
- And so on.

3. Research the legal elements:

- Google the elements of each legal claim.
- If it's a breach of contract case, consider:
- What contract are you relying on?
- Was there a valid offer and acceptance?
- Was consideration (something of value) given?
- Does the contract need to be in writing?
- Did you perform your obligations under the contract?
- Did the opposing party fail to perform?
- How were you damaged?

Additionally, the Fourteenth Amendment promises equal protection under the law, but reality tells a different story. The court of equity is not about fairness; it's about power, preparation, and strategy. If you find yourself in court, do not expect justice to be handed to you. Be prepared. Know the law. Control the facts. And never let emotions blind you.

Chapter Eight

NOT ALL ATTORNEYS ARE THE SAME

IMPORTANT: This knowledge guides the reader in selecting representation with appropriate bankruptcy expertise and experience with similar cases, potentially saving thousands of dollars and preserving more assets through skilled advocacy.

WHEN YOU HEAR THE word "attorney," what comes to mind? Maybe you envision a slick, fast-talking character from a legal drama, impeccably dressed and always a step ahead. Or perhaps you picture a stressed-out, coffee-fueled professional drowning in paperwork. Either way, the reality is this: not all attorneys are the same. Just as not all doctors have the same bedside manner, not all lawyers possess the same skills, strategy, and, let's be honest, basic human decency.

A good attorney is more than just a walking, talking legal encyclopedia. Knowledge of the law is essential, of course, but the practice of law requires far more than simply reciting statutes and case law. A great attorney must be a master communicator, a brilliant strategist, a tough negotiator, and, when the situation calls for it, an unwavering warrior in the courtroom.

KNOWLEDGE: BEYOND THE BASICS

Let's start with the obvious; a lawyer must know the law. But knowing the law doesn't just mean being able to quote legal precedent or cite statutes from memory. It means understanding how laws are applied in real-world scenarios, anticipating legal trends, and staying ahead of the ever-changing landscape of legislation and court decisions. A good attorney doesn't just memorize; they interpret, analyze, and apply the law in ways that best serve their clients.

Imagine going to a doctor who only remembers what they learned in medical school 20 years ago and hasn't read a single new study since. Would you trust them with your health? The same applies to lawyers. The legal field is constantly evolving, and attorneys must stay sharp, informed, and adaptable. The best attorneys don't just pass the bar; they raise it.

COMMUNICATION: MORE THAN LEGAL JARGON

Ever had a conversation with someone who was technically speaking the same language as you, but you had no idea what they were saying? Legalese is notorious for making simple things sound like an ancient incantation. A great attorney understands that effective communication isn't about impressing clients with big words, it's about making sure they actually understand what's happening in their case.

The best attorneys break things down in a way that makes sense. They listen to their clients, address concerns, and translate complex legal concepts into plain English (or Spanish, French, or whatever language their client speaks). A lawyer who can't communicate clearly is like a GPS that only gives directions in Morse code, technically accurate, but practically useless.

STRATEGY: THE LEGAL CHESSBOARD

Law isn't just about what you know; it's about how you use that knowledge. The best attorneys are master strategists, always thinking three moves ahead. Every case, whether it's a high-stakes corporate lawsuit, a divorce battle, or a criminal defense, requires careful planning, calculated risks, and an ability to anticipate the opponent's next move.

An attorney without strategy is like a general marching into battle without a plan. You wouldn't want to go to war with a leader who just "wings it," and you certainly don't want a lawyer who does the same. A strong legal strategy can mean the difference between winning a case and watching it crumble like a poorly baked soufflé.

NEGOTIATION: THE ART OF THE DEAL

Most legal disputes don't go to trial. Instead, they are resolved through negotiation, making an attorney's ability to strike a favorable deal one of their most valuable skills. The best lawyers know when to push, when to compromise, and when to walk away. Negotiation isn't about getting everything you want—it's about getting the best possible outcome for your client while avoiding unnecessary risks.

Think of an attorney as a professional poker player. They have to read the room, understand their opponent, and know when to play their cards. Some attorneys negotiate with finesse, getting favorable settlements without ever stepping foot in a courtroom. Others bulldoze through negotiations like a wrecking ball, making things worse for everyone. The difference between the two? Skill, experience, and knowing when to hold 'em and when to fold 'em.

ADVOCACY: A CLIENT'S STRONGEST SHIELD

At the core of every great attorney is a fierce advocate. Whether it's in a courtroom, a boardroom, or a mediation session, a lawyer must be willing to fight for their client's best interests. Advocacy isn't just about arguing, it's about standing up for what is right, making compelling arguments, and ensuring that justice is served.

A strong advocate isn't just aggressive; they are persuasive. They know how to present a case in a way that resonates with judges, juries, and opposing counsel. They don't just yell louder, they argue smarter.

ETHICS AND INTEGRITY: BECAUSE CHARACTER MATTERS

Not all attorneys are ethical, and let's face it, lawyers have a bit of a reputation. The phrase "shady lawyer" exists for a reason. But the best attorneys operate with integrity, putting their client's best interests ahead of personal gain. Ethics in law aren't just about following rules; they're about ensuring justice is served fairly and honestly.

A great lawyer understands that their reputation is their most valuable asset. No matter how skilled or experienced they are, if they lose the trust of their clients, their career is as good as over. A lawyer's word should mean something, and the best attorney honors that.

THE TAKEAWAY: CHOOSING THE RIGHT ATTORNEY

So, what does all of this mean for someone looking for legal representation? It means that hiring an attorney isn't just about finding someone with a law degree. It's about finding someone who is knowledgeable, communicative, strategic, skilled at negotiation, a strong advocate, and above all, ethical.

Remember, I told you that I thought I knew Brett Weiss. I worked with him on the Maryland Bankruptcy Bar, he wrote a book on Chapter 11 Bankruptcy, etc. But I didn't ask other attorneys about him, nor did I get a referral from someone who actually worked with him. You don't know a person until you sleep with them, night after night.

Not all attorneys are the same, and when it comes to legal matters, who you choose can make all the difference. The best attorneys are not just experts in the law, they are problem solvers, protectors, and, when needed, warriors for justice. So, choose wisely. After all, your future may depend on it.

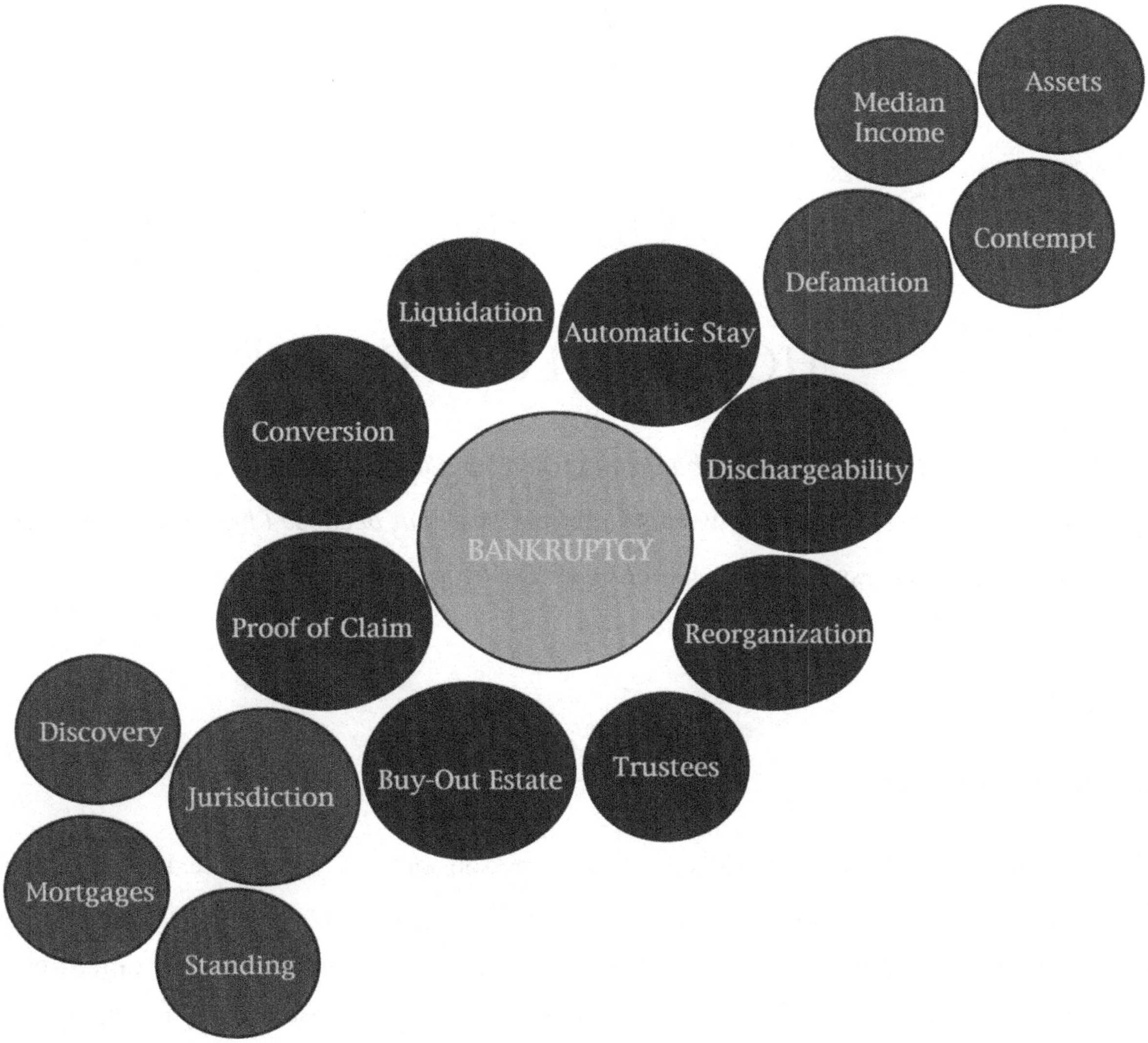
Assets
Median Income
Contempt
Defamation
Liquidation
Automatic Stay
Conversion
Dischargeability
BANKRUPTCY
Proof of Claim
Reorganization
Discovery
Jurisdiction
Buy-Out Estate
Trustees
Mortgages
Standing

Chapter Nine

HOW DID I GET HERE?

I WILL BE ADDRESSING both bankruptcy concepts and practice to help you succeed. I want you to know that I know what I am talking about because I have experienced the bankruptcy process as both a Debtor and a Bankruptcy Attorney. I have been there and done that.

MY PERSONAL STORY

Has anyone ever tried to crush you? Was that person someone you expected to help? Were you denied fair access to the laws of the land? Well, that is my story. It has taken me six years to speak, my truth. I was depressed and had anxiety for the longest time. I even considered suicide. I questioned my life. I questioned my purpose. But my testimony only comes from the testing of my faith and my belief that there is a bigger plan for my life. A plan that I am not controlling. It is my belief that the best way that I can be an intercessor for someone else is to stand for truth and justice. To prevent what occurred to me from happening to someone else.

I am going to tell my story. However, I will use it as a case study to assist you. I will break down some core principles to help you to understand how to save your home or your real properties, even though mines were taken from me.

BACKGROUND

After I graduated law school, I worked for two mortgage companies in the early nineties. By 1995, I started my own mortgage company, Strategic Alliance Funding, Inc. I obtained a warehouse line which allowed me to finance my own loans and sell them on the secondary mortgage market. By the early 2000s, I invested in commercial properties that I converted into mixed-use and a historic mansion with multi-unit dwelling.

Do you remember when the housing market collapsed in 2008? George W. Bush was the president. You probably remember when then Senator Barack Obama and Senator John McCain came to the white house to discuss our countries' financial future. One of the largest banks and financial institutions, Lehman Brothers, went out of business. The availability of capital came to a halt. People were laid off. Real property depreciated across the country.

At that time, I was caught in the middle of the mess. I owned a mortgage company that could not provide a mortgage. I had real properties that were not breaking even. I used all my cash to renovate a historic multi-unit mansion after purchasing it while the market was high. I was behind on everything. My home and the mixed used properties, too. I had no other income besides the rentals. Several of my tenants were hit hard and did not pay their rent.

In 2009, I filed a Chapter 11 Bankruptcy in the U. S. Bankruptcy Court for Maryland in Baltimore. I hired an attorney. It is my belief that his total cost was approximately forty-five thousand dollars. He prepared my schedules, my various pleadings, and attended motion and confirmation hearings. For those of you who do not know, a Chapter 11 allows you keep your property by working out an agreement with your creditors to pay them over a specific period. Sometimes, if the creditor disagrees with the proposed plan or settlement, the court can decide.

With all that was going against me, my creditors as well as the court approved my bankruptcy case, which is called a plan confirmation. I was able to modify the terms on my properties in Laurel, Maryland. The term was for four years, with one additional year, since the bankruptcy was running for five years. The creditor who held the note on the historic mansion appeared at the hearing under one name and later sold the debt.

What was significant was that I had a law degree since 1993, however; I had never taken the Maryland bar examination, nor had I desired to practice law. I took two bar prep courses and later passed the bar exam in 2012.

Calls and Contradictions

After my bankruptcy plan confirmation in 2011, I received telephone calls from various individuals that were unknown to me concerning the historic mansion. Eventually, John Davenport contacted me and said that his company purchased my mortgage note from the liquidation sale of assets held by Greenpoint Mortgage Company, a division of Lehman Brothers Assets. I contacted the Bankruptcy attorney to inquire about the validity of the statements. After all, Capital One Bank appeared in my court proceeding stating that they were the owners of the debt. Capital One Bank held out the fact that they had the legal rights to make all decisions regarding this debt.

John Davenport offered me a short payoff, or an amount less than what would have been owed. It was an attractive offer; however, I was still in bankruptcy. I spent months trying to seek a refinance on a large commercial dwelling, it was not happening. I finally decided to dismiss the bankruptcy and try to refinance the property, afterwards. I moved to dismiss the bankruptcy case. The case was heard. The Judge stated I had done a good job in the bankruptcy and stated that it was his opinion that I should completed it, however, he granted my request.

The day after the court granted my motion for dismissal, the purported mortgage lender on the historic mansion sent letters to all the tenants of the building demanding that they pay the lender directly, which eventually prevented any possible refinance of the property. This set up a legal battle. It also forced me back into bankruptcy.

Don't Hire Brett Weiss!

I completed my bankruptcy schedules and my first day pleadings for a second Chapter 11 bankruptcy. I later hired an attorney who I had known in the industry, Brett Weiss. In fact, he even wrote a book about Chapter 11 bankruptcies. I believe he amended my schedules and attended one meeting, really a two-fer. The Meeting of the Creditors and the meeting with the U. S. Trustee both occurred on the same day, in the same room, one after the other.

Shortly thereafter, I received a couple of emails. He did not return my telephone calls, nor did he respond to pleadings filed by my creditors. I spoke to the attorney who helped me in my first case. He said to protect yourself, so I filed responses to the creditors' pleadings. I used the previous Disclosure Statement and Plan as a template and filed both of those documents, too.

A hearing was scheduled for the various pleadings. Brett Weiss contacted me the Friday before the hearing was scheduled and pressured me to withdraw. He stated that I was responding to the pleadings and therefore waived my right to his counsel. I didn't receive an email or call for more than six weeks and suddenly, here he is. My thought at the time was don't make someone represent you that will not work for you.

The following Monday, the day of the hearing, Brett Weiss is the first person I saw when I walked into the courtroom. Judge Scheider told me that he received a motion to withdraw as counsel from Brett Weiss and what did I have to say about it. I should have said that he disappeared and wouldn't return my telephone calls or email me, but I told him to allow him to withdraw. I didn't throw him under the bus.

I did not understand the significance of what I was facing. The Creditor, Patapsco Bank aka as Howard Bank, from the Laurel Properties filed a Motion to Convert from Chapter 11 to a Chapter 7 with the alleged note holder on the historic mansion joining with them. The Judge gave me a one-month extension to hire someone else. Brett Weiss had asked for a downpayment of Twenty-Thousand Dollars, \$20,000.00. After his behavior, frankly, I did not want another attorney. I did not know who to trust. Yet, I was in the business of doing small Chapter 13 and Chapter 7 Bankruptcies.

Chapter Ten

WHAT IS A BANKRUPTCY?

IMPORTANT: This foundational information ensures the reader comprehends the legal process they're entering, the different Bankruptcy chapters available, and the implications of each, helping to make an informed decision about whether bankruptcy is the right solution.

BANKRUPTCY IS LIKE HITTING the financial reset button. Imagine your bills are like dirty laundry piling up. At some point, you've got too much, and no matter how hard you try, you just can't wash it all. Bankruptcy is basically asking a judge to help clean up the mess when you don't have enough money to pay your debts.

Like with everything in life, there's a catch. Bankruptcy doesn't make your money problems magically disappear; it just gives you a structured way to deal with them. Some debts might get erased, some might get reduced, and some might stick around like that one annoying relative who won't take a hint.

THE DIFFERENT FLAVORS OF BANKRUPTCY

Think of bankruptcy like ice cream, it comes in different flavors, but instead of tasting sweet, they all just taste like a little bit of regret and relief both mixed together. The most common types for regular folks and businesses are Chapter 7, Chapter 13, and Chapter 11.

Chapter 7 - The "Fresh Start" Bankruptcy

This is the most common type, and it is considered liquidation. It's like a garage sale for your debts. You give up some of your stuff (not all, don't panic), and in exchange, most of your debts are wiped away. It's usually over in a few months, so it's fast and effective. But not everyone qualifies, you must show that you really don't have the money to pay back your debts.

**Best for people with a lot of debt and not much income.

**The biggest downside is that you might have to give up some of your belongings, but there are laws that protect essentials like your house, car, and favorite couch (probably).

Chapter 13 - The "Let's Make a Deal" Bankruptcy

Instead of wiping out your debts, this one lets you set up a payment plan to pay back what you can over 3 to 5 years. It is a reorganization, really, it's like making a deal with your creditors: "I'll pay what I can, but let's be reasonable." This is great for people who have a steady income but just need a little breathing room.

**Best for people who make decent money but have fallen behind on things like mortgage payments or car loans.

**Biggest downside is that you still have to pay a good chunk of your debt, just overtime.

Chapter 11 - The "Big Business Shuffle" Bankruptcy

This one is mostly for businesses. It, too, is a reorganization. It lets a company restructure its debt while staying open. Think of it as a company saying, "Hey, we messed up, but if you give us time, we'll fix it." Some big names like Toys "R" Us, Hertz, and even Marvel Comics have used Chapter 11 to get back on their feet.

**Best for businesses and high net worth individuals that are struggling but still have potential.

**Biggest downside is that it may be expensive and complicated, like trying to assemble IKEA furniture without the instructions.

The Bottom Line

Bankruptcy isn't the end of the world! It's just a way to get back on your feet when debt gets out of control. The key is to know which type is right for your situation. Chapter 7? Quick and clean, but you might lose some assets. Chapter 13? A payment plan to catch up. Chapter 11? Mostly for businesses trying to stay afloat.

If you're drowning in debt, bankruptcy might be an option, but it's always good to talk to a professional before making any big moves. Because let's be real, financial problems are stressful enough without trying to figure out legal jargon on top of it!

DO YOU NEED TO BE BROKE TO FILE FOR BANKRUPTCY?

Nope, you don't have to be flat-out broke to file for bankruptcy. Bankruptcy is a legal tool designed to help folks and businesses manage overwhelming debt, regardless of their current wealth or income. It's not about having zero dollars; it's about having more debt than you can handle. For instance, even if you're earning a good salary or own valuable assets like a home or car, you might still qualify for bankruptcy. The key factor is whether your debts are unmanageable based on your income and assets.

So, it's not about being penniless; it's about finding a feasible way to tackle your debts.

Why Did Donald Trump File Multiple Bankruptcies?

Donald Trump, the businessman (not the individual), has filed for bankruptcy several times. But here's the twist: these bankruptcies were strategic moves for his companies, not personal bankruptcies. Trump used bankruptcy laws to restructure debt and keep his businesses afloat during tough times.

Between 1991 and 2009, Trump's businesses, including casinos and hotels, filed for Chapter 11 bankruptcy protection six times. Chapter 11 allows companies to reorganize their debts while continuing operations. This approach can be a savvy business move to renegotiate debt terms and emerge stronger.

So, while Trump's companies faced financial hurdles, he used bankruptcy laws as a tool to manage debt and attempted to turn things around. Remember, bankruptcy isn't a sign of failure; it's a legal option to help manage debt and work towards a more stable financial future.

DEBT LIMITS IN BANKRUPTCY

A decision-making factor is the debt limits, if any, that must be considered. Debt Limits are the amounts for a type of debt that as allowed. As of 2024, Chapter 7 bankruptcy has no specific debt limits, but individuals must pass the means test to qualify based on income and expenses. Chapter 11 bankruptcy, commonly used by businesses but also available to individuals, has no debt limits, making it an option for those who exceed Chapter 13's thresholds. Chapter 13 bankruptcy, designed for individuals with regular income, imposes debt limits that are periodically adjusted.

As of June 21, 2022, the Bankruptcy Threshold Adjustment and Technical Corrections Act set a combined debt limit of $2,750,000 for both secured and unsecured debts, removing the previous separate limits. Before this change, Chapter 13 filers were subject to a secured debt limit of $1,257,850 and an unsecured debt limit of $419,275. Additionally, Chapter 7 has asset exemptions that vary by state, allowing filers to protect certain assets from liquidation, while Chapter 13 allows individuals to retain assets by structuring a repayment plan.

THE KEY PLAYERS IN BANKRUPTCY

Before you file a bankruptcy, you must understand the key players in the bankruptcy process. Think of a bankruptcy case like a courtroom drama, except with more spreadsheets and fewer surprise witnesses. Here are the main characters:

1. The Debtor – That's you (or the business) filing for bankruptcy. You're the one drowning in debt and looking for relief.

2. The Creditors – These are the people or companies you owe money to, like credit card companies, banks, landlords, or even Uncle Joe if you borrowed cash from him.

3. The Bankruptcy Trustee – This is a court-appointed person who oversees your case, makes sure everything is done fairly, and distributes money to creditors (if there's any to give).

4. The Bankruptcy Judge – This is the big boss who makes final decisions in your case, like approving payment plans or deciding whether debts can be wiped out.

5. The U.S. Trustee (in some cases) – This is a government official who makes sure the bankruptcy process isn't being abused (think of them as the IRS's distant cousin).

6. Your Bankruptcy Attorney (optional but recommended) – A lawyer who helps you navigate the process, file the paperwork correctly, and make sure you don't accidentally mess up your case.

HOW THE PLAYERS DIFFER IN EACH TYPE OF BANKRUPTCY

Each bankruptcy chapter has a different "game plan," so the roles of these players change slightly depending on which one you file.

Chapter 7 - The "Sell and Wipe" Bankruptcy

• Debtor's Role: Fill out paperwork, attend a short court hearing, and give up non-essential assets in exchange for getting most debts erased.

• Creditors' Role: They can object to certain debts being wiped out, but most just wait to see if they get any money.

• Trustee's Role: This person sells off any non-exempt assets (like extra cars or vacation homes) and gives the money to creditors. If you don't have assets to sell, the trustee just oversees the case.

• Judge's Role: Mostly signs off on the case unless there's a dispute.

REMEMBER: The trustee plays a big role in liquidating assets, while creditors don't have much say unless they challenge a discharge.

Chapter 13 - The "Make a Deal" Bankruptcy

• Debtor's Role: Propose a repayment plan to pay some or all the debt over 3-5 years. Must stick to the plan or risk the case being dismissed.

• Creditors' Role: They can object to the payment plan, but if it's approved, they must accept what they're given.

• Trustee's Role: Acts like a referee, making sure the debtor sticks to the payment plan and distributing the money to creditors.

• Judge's Role: Decides whether the repayment plan is fair and approves or denies it.

REMEMBER: The trustee acts more like a financial manager instead of a liquidator, and creditors have a bigger say in shaping the payment plan.

Chapter 11 – The "Big Business Shuffle" Bankruptcy

• Debtor's Role: Usually a business (though individuals can file too). The company keeps running while working out a repayment plan with creditors.

• Creditors' Role: They play a BIG role. They can vote on the repayment plan, negotiate terms, and even propose their own restructuring ideas.

• Trustee's Role: Not always appointed. If one is involved, they monitor the case rather than take control of the business.

• Judge's Role: Heavily involved, approving the plan and making sure creditors and debtors negotiate in good faith.

REMEMBER: The debtor (business) often stays in control, and creditors have a lot more power in shaping the outcome.

FINAL TAKEAWAY

Before filing a bankruptcy, make sure you understand the role of the Trustee as well as the type of assets you may have in order to determine the best solution for you.

- In Chapter 7, the trustee is in charge of selling things off, and the debtor is mostly hands-off.

- In Chapter 13, the debtor makes a payment plan, and the trustee ensures they follow through.

- In Chapter 11, the debtor stays in control, and creditors have a bigger voice in the process.

Each type of bankruptcy has different rules, but the key players remain the same, they just wear different hats depending on the chapter.

TRUSTEE'S FIDUCIARY DUTY

The bankruptcy trustee is like a financial referee in the bankruptcy process. They are appointed by the court to make sure everything is handled fairly and according to the law. Think of them as the middleman between the person filing for bankruptcy (the debtor) and the people they owe money to (the creditors).

A fiduciary duty is a fancy way of saying, "I have to put someone else's best interests ahead of my own." Trustees have this legal responsibility, which means they must act honestly, fairly, and without any personal gain. If they mess up or play favorites, they can get into serious trouble.

Who does the trustee owe this duty to?

1. To the Creditors (Mostly!)

- The trustee's main job is to get as much money as possible to pay off debts.
- In Chapter 7, this means selling off non-exempt assets and distributing the cash to creditors.
- In Chapter 13 and Chapter 11, this means making sure the debtor sticks to the payment plan.
- The trustee can challenge unfair transactions (like if the debtor gave away assets to friends before filing).

2. To the Bankruptcy Court and System

- The trustee must follow bankruptcy laws and make sure no one is abusing the system.

- If they catch fraud (like hiding assets), they can report it to the judge.

3. To the Debtor (Sort of…)

- The trustee must be fair, but they aren't really on the debtor's side.

- However, they must follow the law and make sure the debtor isn't treated unfairly by creditors.

Again, the Trustee's Role in Different Bankruptcy Differs.

• Chapter 7 Trustee – Focuses on selling assets and giving money to creditors. Think of them as a liquidator.

• Chapter 13 Trustee – Acts like a financial manager, making sure the debtor makes payments and distributes the money fairly.

• Chapter 11 Trustee – Usually, there isn't one unless the court appoints one for fraud or mismanagement. If there is a trustee, they oversee the business restructuring.

The trustee is not your lawyer or your enemy, they are there to make sure the bankruptcy process is fair and that creditors get as much repayment as possible. Their fiduciary duty is mainly to the creditors, but they also must follow the law and make sure no one is cheating on the system.

WHEN CHAPTER 7 BANKRUPTCY SHOULD NOT BE USED

While Chapter 7 bankruptcy can provide significant debt relief for individuals and businesses struggling with overwhelming financial burdens, it is not always the best solution. In certain situations, filing for Chapter 7 may not provide the relief expected, and in some cases, it could even create more financial problems. Understanding when Chapter 7 is not the right option is essential before making a decision.

One of the main reasons Chapter 7 may not be suitable is that it does not erase all types of debt. Some financial obligations, such as child support, alimony, most tax debts, and student loans, are generally non-dischargeable. If a significant portion of a person's debt falls into these categories, filing for Chapter 7 may not provide much relief. Additionally, debts that arise from fraudulent activity or intentional wrongdoing cannot be discharged, meaning that individuals with these types of obligations will remain responsible for repayment even after bankruptcy. If the goal of filing for Chapter 7 is to eliminate most debts, it is crucial to assess whether the majority of financial liabilities qualify for discharge under bankruptcy law.

Another major drawback of Chapter 7 is the potential loss of valuable assets. Unlike Chapter 13 bankruptcy, which allows individuals to create a repayment plan while keeping their property, Chapter 7 involves the liquidation of non-exempt assets to pay creditors. This means that if a debtor owns significant assets, such as a second home, an extra vehicle, expensive jewelry, or a business, those assets may be sold off by the bankruptcy trustee. For individuals who want to retain their property, filing for Chapter 7 may not be the best choice. Instead, exploring Chapter 13 or other debt relief alternatives might be a better strategy to protect assets.

Eligibility for Chapter 7 bankruptcy is also determined by income level. The bankruptcy system includes a "means test" to ensure that Chapter 7 is reserved for those who genuinely cannot afford to pay their debts. If a debtor's income is too high and they have disposable income left after necessary expenses, they may be required to file for Chapter 13 instead, where they would be responsible for repaying a portion of their debts over a structured period. This restriction makes Chapter 7 unsuitable for individuals who earn a steady income but are simply looking for a quick way to erase debt without attempting repayment.

The long-term impact on credit is another factor that makes Chapter 7 bankruptcy an unfavorable option for some. A Chapter 7 bankruptcy filing remains on a person's credit report for up to ten years, making it difficult to obtain loans, credit cards, or even secure housing. In some cases, employers check credit history as part of their hiring process, which means that filing for bankruptcy could negatively affect employment opportunities. For those who anticipate needing credit in the near future for major purchases, such as buying a home or financing a vehicle, the damage to credit may outweigh the immediate benefits of filing for Chapter 7.

Another important consideration is how filing for Chapter 7 affects co-signers. If a debtor has a co-signer on a loan, such as a family member or friend who agreed to be responsible for the debt if the debtor fails to pay, the bankruptcy discharge will not protect the co-signer. Once the primary borrower's obligation is erased, the creditor can pursue the co-signer for full repayment. This can create financial strain for the co-signer, who may have only agreed to help based on the assumption that the debtor would continue making payments. If protecting a co-signer's financial well-being is a priority, filing for Chapter 7 may not be the best decision.

Some individuals also choose to avoid Chapter 7 bankruptcy due to personal or ethical concerns. Some people believe in repaying their debts no matter how difficult the situation may be. They may feel that filing for bankruptcy is a moral failure or a way of avoiding responsibility. In these cases, individuals may prefer to explore alternatives such as debt settlement, credit counseling, or negotiating directly with creditors. While these options may take longer to resolve financial difficulties, they align better with the values of those who are uncomfortable with the idea of declaring bankruptcy.

Ultimately, deciding whether to file for Chapter 7 bankruptcy requires careful consideration of an individual's financial situation, goals, and priorities. While it can provide a fresh start for those who have little income and overwhelming unsecured debt, it is not a one-size-fits-all solution. If debts cannot be discharged, valuable assets may be lost, or future financial opportunities could be compromised, it may be worth considering alternative approaches. Consulting with a qualified bankruptcy attorney or financial expert can help individuals assess their options and determine the best course of action for their unique circumstances.

UNDERSTANDING THE VARIOUS TYPES OF DEBT

Debt is a common part of modern life, allowing individuals and businesses to finance large purchases, cover unexpected expenses, and manage financial obligations over time. However, not all debt is the same. Different types of debt have unique characteristics, repayment structures, and legal implications. Understanding the various categories of debt is essential for making informed financial decisions and knowing how different obligations are treated under the law, including in bankruptcy proceedings.

1. Secured Debt

Secured debt is backed by collateral, meaning that the borrower pledges an asset to guarantee repayment. If the borrower fails to repay the debt, the lender has the legal right to take the collateral to recover the outstanding balance. Because these loans are secured by valuable property, they often come with lower interest rates than unsecured loans. The most common types of secured debt include:

• Mortgage Loans: A home loan is secured by the property itself. If the borrower fails to make payments, the lender can foreclose on the home and sell it to recover the debt.

• Auto Loans: Car loans are secured by the vehicle. If the borrower defaults, the lender can repossess the car.

• Secured Credit Cards: Some credit cards require a cash deposit as collateral, which acts as security for the lender in case the borrower defaults.

• Pawn Shop Loans: A borrower provides a valuable item as collateral in exchange for a short-term loan. If the loan is not repaid, the pawn shop keeps and sells the item.

Secured debt is considered a lower risk for lenders, but borrowers must be aware that failure to make payments can result in the loss of the pledged asset.

2. Unsecured Debt

Unsecured debt is not backed by collateral, meaning lenders provide credit based solely on the borrower's creditworthiness and promise to repay. Because there is no asset securing the loan, unsecured debt typically carries higher interest rates than secured debt. Common types of unsecured debt include:

• Credit Card Debt: One of the most common forms of unsecured debt, credit card balances accrue interest if not paid in full each month.

• Medical Debt: Bills for healthcare services, including hospital visits, surgeries, and medical treatments, fall under unsecured debt.

• Personal Loans: Loans issued by banks, credit unions, or online lenders that do not require collateral. These can be used for various purposes, such as consolidating debt or covering unexpected expenses.

• Student Loans (in some cases): While federal student loans are unsecured in the sense that they do not require collateral, they have special protections for lenders and are not easily discharged in bankruptcy.

• Utility Bills: Past-due payments for electricity, water, internet, and other utilities are unsecured debts.

Because unsecured debt lacks collateral, lenders rely on legal actions such as debt collection, lawsuits, or wage garnishment to recover unpaid balances if a borrower defaults.

3. Revolving Debt

Revolving debt allows borrowers to use and repay credit on an ongoing basis. Instead of receiving a fixed loan amount upfront, borrowers have access to a credit limit that they can borrow against repeatedly, as long as they make minimum payments and do not exceed the limit. Examples of revolving debt include:

• Credit Cards: The most common form of revolving debt, credit cards allow users to make purchases up to a set limit. Interest is charged on unpaid balances carried over from month to month.

• Home Equity Lines of Credit (HELOCs): A HELOC allows homeowners to borrow against their home's equity and use the funds as needed. It functions similarly to a credit card but is secured by the home.

• Retail Store Credit Accounts: Department stores and other retailers often offer revolving credit accounts for purchases.

Revolving debt differs from installment debt because there is no set repayment period, and borrowers can choose how much to pay each month as long as they meet the minimum requirement.

4. Installment Debt

Installment debt involves borrowing a fixed amount of money and repaying it in regular, scheduled payments (installments) over a set period. The monthly payments include both principal (the amount borrowed) and interest. Common types of installment debt include:

• Mortgages: A home loan that is typically repaid over 15 to 30 years in fixed monthly payments.

• Auto Loans: A car loan that is paid in equal installments over a few years.

• Personal Loans: Borrowers receive a lump sum and repay it in fixed payments over a set term.

• Student Loans: Loans used to finance education expenses, repaid in monthly installments after the borrower leaves school.

Installment debt provides predictability because borrowers know exactly how much they owe each month and when the debt will be fully paid.

5. Priority Debt

Priority debt is a special category of debt that receives higher legal priority than other types of debt, especially in bankruptcy cases. These debts must be paid before most other debts when a borrower files for bankruptcy. Examples of priority debt include:

• Child Support and Alimony: Court-ordered payments for the support of a child or former spouse. These obligations cannot be discharged in bankruptcy.

• Certain Tax Debts: Some federal, state, and local tax debts are considered priority debts and must be paid in full.

• Criminal Fines and Restitution: Money owed due to legal penalties or court-ordered restitution.

Because priority debts take precedence over other obligations, they are generally not dischargeable in bankruptcy and must be repaid in full.

6. Non-Dischargeable Debt

Some debts cannot be eliminated in bankruptcy, regardless of financial hardship. These debts include:

• Student Loans (except in cases of extreme hardship): Most student loans remain due even after bankruptcy.

• Child Support and Alimony: These obligations cannot be discharged under any circumstances.

• Most Tax Debts: Some older tax debts may be discharged, but many remain collectible.

• Debts Arising from Fraud: If a borrower incurred debt through fraudulent means, the court may rule that the debt must still be paid.

Non-dischargeable debts are crucial to consider when filing for bankruptcy because they will remain a financial responsibility even after the case is finalized.

7. Business Debt

Business debt refers to financial obligations incurred by companies. It can be secured or unsecured and is treated differently depending on whether the business is a sole proprietorship, partnership, or corporation.

• Small Business Loans: Loans issued to business owners to fund operations often require personal guarantees.

• Vendor Debt: Unpaid balances for goods or services received on credit.

• Business Credit Cards: Similar to personal credit cards but used for business expenses.

When a business files for bankruptcy, business debts may be discharged or restructured depending on the type of bankruptcy chosen.

REMEMBER: Understanding the different types of debt is crucial for managing finances effectively and making informed decisions about borrowing and repayment. Secured debt is backed by collateral, while unsecured debt relies solely on the borrower's promise to repay. Revolving debt allows continuous borrowing, whereas installment debt follows a fixed repayment schedule. Some debts, such as priority and non-dischargeable debts, have special legal protections that make them difficult to eliminate. Whether handling personal or business debt, knowing these distinctions can help individuals and companies navigate financial challenges, avoid unnecessary risks, and explore the best options for repayment or relief.

Chapter Eleven

BANKRUPTCY, CONTRACTS AND THE UNIFORM COMMERCIAL CODE

IMPORTANT: Knowing who can legally enforce a mortgage, how contractual obligations are handled in bankruptcy, and what protections exist under the UCC can help homeowners avoid wrongful foreclosure, challenge improper creditor claims, and make informed financial decisions.

WHEN FINANCIAL DIFFICULTIES ARISE, homeowners and property owners may consider bankruptcy to protect their assets, including their home. However, bankruptcy does not exist in a vacuum, it is deeply intertwined with Contract Law and the Uniform Commercial Code (UCC). Understanding these three legal areas is essential for any homeowner facing financial distress because they collectively determine who has the legal right to enforce debts, what obligations exist under a mortgage contract, and how bankruptcy may impact these legal relationships.

THE FOUNDATIONS OF BANKRUPTCY LAW

Bankruptcy Law provides individuals and businesses with relief from overwhelming debt through a legal process that may discharge certain debts or restructuring payments. Governed primarily by the U.S. Bankruptcy Code, it establishes the rules for debtors seeking relief, creditors attempting to recover what they are owed, and the courts that oversee the process. However, bankruptcy law does not exist in isolation. The enforcement of contracts, including mortgage agreements and promissory notes, as well as secured transactions governed by the UCC, directly impact bankruptcy proceedings.

THE ROLE OF CONTRACT LAW

At its core, Contract Law governs agreements between parties, ensuring that obligations are enforceable by law. When a homeowner takes out a mortgage, they enter a contract with the lender. This contract outlines rights, duties, payment terms, and potential consequences for default. In the context of bankruptcy, understanding contract law is critical because:

1. Mortgage contracts are legally binding agreements. Homeowners must understand their rights and obligations before signing.

2. Bankruptcy does not eliminate contractual obligations unless explicitly discharged. Even in Chapter 7 bankruptcy, secured debts like mortgages remain unless the debtor surrenders the property.

3. Modifications and reaffirmations require legal consideration. In Chapter 13, debtors can renegotiate terms, but this must be done within contract law principles.

4. The enforcement of contracts determines creditor rights. Lenders can only enforce their claims if they follow proper contractual and legal procedures.

THE UNIFORM COMMERCIAL CODE AND ITS IMPACT ON BANKRUPTCY

The Uniform Commercial Code (UCC) standardizes laws governing commercial transactions, including secured transactions, which are highly relevant to mortgages. Article 3 of the UCC covers negotiable instruments like promissory notes, while Article 9 deals with secured transactions and liens. Understanding the UCC is crucial in bankruptcy cases because:

i. The UCC determines who is entitled to enforce a debt. In mortgage-backed securities, loans are often sold, and homeowners must know who holds their note.

ii. Lost or improperly assigned notes can impact on foreclosure rights. If a lender cannot prove ownership under UCC standards, their claim may be challenged.

iii. The UCC ensures compliance with secured transactions. Creditors must perfect their security interests properly, or their claims may be deemed unsecured in bankruptcy court.

The "holder in due course" doctrine protects certain creditors. This affects whether debtors can assert defenses against lenders.

THE IMPACT OF THE UCC ON DEEDS, ASSIGNMENT OF DEEDS, AND MORTGAGE MODIFICATIONS

The UCC significantly impacts deeds, the assignment of deeds, and mortgage modifications:

1. Deeds and Title Transfers: While the UCC primarily governs secured transactions, mortgage lenders must ensure proper chain of title when transferring ownership of a note. If an entity does not have the right to enforce under UCC standards, its claim to the property may be invalid.

2. Assignment of Deeds: Many mortgages are assigned multiple times between financial institutions. The UCC requires proper negotiation and endorsement of the promissory note. If an assignment is not done correctly, the entity attempting to foreclose may lack standing.

3. Mortgage Modifications: When a loan is modified, it constitutes a new contract under contract law. Additionally, UCC Article 9 requires any changes in security interest to be properly recorded to maintain priority.

Who Is Entitled to Enforce a Debt?

A key concept in both UCC and bankruptcy proceedings is determining who has the right to enforce a debt. In mortgage transactions, the entity that can legally enforce the promissory note must meet certain criteria under the UCC:

- Holder of the Note: The entity in physical possession of the note, with proper endorsements.

- Non-Holder in Possession with Rights of a Holder: A party that has been assigned the note but lacks direct endorsement.
- Person Not in Possession but with the Right to Enforce: A party that has lost the note but can prove rightful ownership.

If a lender cannot establish one of these statuses, they may lack standing to foreclose or collect payments in bankruptcy proceedings. This issue has been central to legal battles following the 2008 financial crisis, where securitization led to confusion over note ownership.

WHY HOMEOWNERS MUST UNDERSTAND ALL THREE LEGAL AREAS

For homeowners, the intersection of Bankruptcy Law, Contract Law, and the UCC is more than just legal theory, it determines their ability to protect their home and financial future. Here's why understanding all three is essential:

1. Protecting Against Wrongful Foreclosure: If a lender cannot prove ownership of the mortgage note under UCC standards, foreclosure attempts may be challenged.
2. Navigating Bankruptcy Effectively: Homeowners can make informed decisions about restructuring debts, protecting assets, and challenging improper creditor claims.
3. Ensuring Legal Compliance in Mortgage Agreements: Understanding contract law prevents homeowners from signing predatory loan agreements.

4. Defending Against Fraudulent Assignments: Some lenders attempt to enforce debts without proper legal standing, and a well-informed homeowner can fight back.

5. Making Informed Decisions on Loan Modifications and Reaffirmations: Bankruptcy may allow renegotiation of terms, but only if the homeowner understands their contractual rights.

The legal landscape surrounding homeownership, debt, and bankruptcy is complex, requiring an understanding of Bankruptcy Law, Contract Law, and the Uniform Commercial Code. These three areas work together to determine a homeowner's rights, obligations, and options when financial hardships arise. Knowing who is entitled to enforce a mortgage, how contractual obligations are treated in bankruptcy, and what protections the UCC provides can mean the difference between saving a home and losing it to foreclosure. Homeowners who take the time to educate themselves on these laws will be in the strongest position to protect their assets and make informed financial decisions in times of crisis.

Chapter Twelve

REAFFIRMATION AGREEMENTS

LET ME EXPLAIN WHAT A reaffirmation agreement is in bankruptcy in a way that's easy to understand.

Imagine you owe money on a bunch of things, like credit cards, medical bills, and maybe a car loan. When you file for bankruptcy, most of these debts can be wiped away so you can have a fresh start. That's the main point of bankruptcy!

But what if you really want to keep your car? This is where a reaffirmation agreement comes in.

A reaffirmation agreement is basically a promise you make during bankruptcy that says, "Even though I'm filing for bankruptcy, I want to keep paying for this specific thing (like my car), and I agree that this particular debt won't be wiped away like my other debts."

Here's how it works:

• You tell the bankruptcy court you want to keep paying for your car

• You sign a special paper (the reaffirmation agreement) with the company that gave you the car loan

• This paper says you'll keep making payments just like before your bankruptcy

• The bankruptcy court has to approve this agreement

The important thing to know is that if you sign a reaffirmation agreement and later can't make the payments, the company can take back your car AND you'll still owe them money for it, even after your bankruptcy is over!

That's why it's super important to think carefully before signing one of these agreements. You should only do it if you're absolutely sure you can keep making the payments.

Know the Exception

So, let's talk about something called the "undue hardship" exception for reaffirmation agreements in bankruptcy.

Imagine this: Your friend Maria filed for bankruptcy because she had too many bills she couldn't pay. She has a car loan with Monthly Motors for her old Honda that she needs to get to school and her part-time job. The car payment is $300 per month.

Monthly Motors tells Maria, "If you want to keep your car, you need to sign a reaffirmation agreement promising you'll keep paying us, even though you're in bankruptcy."

Maria really needs her car, but after paying for rent, food, and other basic stuff, she would only have about $200 left each month, not enough for the $300 car payment! This would create an "undue hardship" for her.

Here's what Maria could do:

1. She could go to the bankruptcy judge and explain her situation.

2. The judge might say, "I can see this reaffirmation agreement would create an undue hardship for Maria because the payments are too high compared to her income."

3. The judge might not approve the reaffirmation agreement because it's not in Maria's best interest.

The cool thing is, Maria might still be able to keep her car! This is called "ride-through" or "pay and drive" in some places. As long as Maria keeps making payments on time, Monthly Motors might let her keep the car even without a reaffirmation agreement.

The big difference? If Maria can't make payments later and Monthly Motors will take back the car, they can't come after Maria for any extra money they didn't get from selling the car. That's because without the reaffirmation agreement, Maria's personal responsibility for the loan was wiped away in bankruptcy!

So, the undue hardship exception is like a safety net that helps protect people in bankruptcy from promising to pay debts they really can't afford.

Chapter Thirteen

MORTGAGE TRUST AND OTHER FINANCIAL INSTRUMENTS

IMPORTANT: This knowledge helps the reader identify potential weaknesses in mortgage securitization that could be challenged during bankruptcy, potentially reducing mortgage debt or preventing foreclosure.

WHEN DEALING WITH MORTGAGES and mortgage notes for sale, different types of trusts can be used to manage, protect, and transfer assets efficiently. Trusts offer legal and financial advantages, such as asset protection and tax benefits, but they can also create complexities and challenges. In some cases, trust can obscure ownership, making it difficult for outsiders to determine who controls a property or financial asset. This essay will examine the various types of trusts, their strengths and weaknesses, the role of an indenture trustee, and the ways trusts can be used to shield ownership from public view.

TYPES OF TRUSTS IN MORTGAGE HOLDING

Trusts come in various forms, each designed for different purposes. Some trusts allow the owner to retain control, while others remove the assets from their estate entirely. The choice of trust depends on the specific goals of the person or entity holding the mortgage or mortgage note.

One common type is a revocable trust, which allows the trust creator, or grantor, to make changes or even dissolve the trust entirely. This flexibility makes revocable trusts appealing, particularly for estate planning, as they enable a smooth transfer of assets to heirs without going through probate. Additionally, revocable trusts provide some degree of privacy because they are not part of public probate records. However, they offer little protection from creditors or lawsuits, as the grantor still maintains control over the assets.

In contrast, an irrevocable trust is far more restrictive. Once established, the grantor cannot modify or reclaim the assets placed within it. This lack of control is the main disadvantage, but it also provides significant benefits, particularly in asset protection. Since the trust owns the assets rather than the individual, they are generally protected from lawsuits and creditors. Additionally, irrevocable trusts can reduce estate tax burdens, making them a useful tool for wealth preservation.

A land trust is a specialized type of trust used to hold real estate, including mortgages. Unlike traditional ownership, where the property owner's name is publicly recorded, land trusts allow property to be held under the trust's name. The trustee technically owns the property, while the beneficiaries retain full control over its use and decisions. This structure creates an additional layer of privacy by keeping ownership information out of public records. However, land trusts do not offer strong legal protection against creditors or lawsuits. If someone sues the beneficiary, a court may still force the sale of the trust's property.

For those interested in investing in real estate but not directly holding property, a Real Estate Investment Trust (REIT) may be a better option. A REIT is a company that owns and manages income-generating properties or mortgage-backed securities. Investors buy shares in the REIT, similar to stocks, and earn dividends from the company's profits. The main advantage of REITs is that they provide an opportunity to invest in real estate without the responsibility of direct ownership. They are also highly liquid, as shares can be bought and sold like stocks. However, because REITs must distribute most of their earnings to investors, they have limited ability to reinvest profits for growth.

An asset protection trust is designed specifically to shield assets from legal claims. Often set up in offshore jurisdictions with favorable laws, these trusts make it difficult for creditors or litigants to access the assets. This type of trust is particularly useful for individuals in high-risk professions, such as doctors or business executives, who may face lawsuits. However, asset protection trusts can be expensive to establish and maintain, and some legal systems impose restrictions on their use.

The Role of an Indenture Trustee

In mortgage-backed securities and other financial agreements, an indenture trustee plays a crucial role in overseeing transactions and ensuring compliance with contractual obligations. Unlike a typical trustee who manages assets for beneficiaries, an indenture trustee represents bondholders or investors in a mortgage-backed security. Their primary responsibility is to ensure that payments from mortgage borrowers are correctly distributed to investors. If a borrower defaults on a loan, the indenture trustee may also be responsible for taking legal action on behalf of the investors. While a trustee directly manages a trust's assets, the indenture trustee acts more like a referee, ensuring that agreements are upheld and that all parties comply with their obligations.

HOW TRUSTS CAN HIDE OWNERSHIP FROM PUBLIC VIEW

One of the key reasons individuals and corporations use trusts is to obscure ownership. By structuring real estate or financial holdings under a trust, the true owner can remain hidden from public records. This is especially common in land trusts, where the property is legally owned by the trust rather than by an individual or business. If someone searches public property records, they will only see the trust's name, not the actual person or entity behind it.

In addition to land trusts, business entities such as Limited Liability Companies (LLCs) and corporations can be combined with trusts to further mask ownership. For example, an individual might set up an LLC to hold a property, then place that LLC into a trust. This layering of ownership structures makes it incredibly difficult to trace the real owner. In some cases, these methods are used for legitimate privacy concerns, such as preventing unwanted solicitations or protecting individuals from targeted lawsuits. However, the same strategies can also be misused to hide assets from creditors, evade taxes, or conceal illegal activities.

Another common tactic is the use of offshore trusts, which are established in foreign jurisdictions with strict privacy laws. These countries, often referred to as tax havens, do not require disclosure of trust beneficiaries. Even if a legal dispute arises in another country, it can be nearly impossible for authorities to access the trust's details. While offshore trusts can provide robust asset protection, they are often scrutinized by tax authorities and regulatory agencies, as they have been linked to tax evasion and money laundering.

Even within the United States, some states offer stronger trust privacy laws than others. States such as Delaware, Nevada, and South Dakota have become popular for setting up trusts due to their favorable asset protection laws and minimal disclosure requirements. In these states, trusts are not required to publicly list beneficiaries or trustees, making them attractive for those seeking financial anonymity.

Challenges and Ethical Considerations

While trusts provide numerous financial benefits, they also raise ethical and legal concerns. The ability to obscure ownership can lead to abuses, such as hiding assets from divorce settlements, evading debts, or even laundering money. Governments have introduced regulations to prevent misuse, but enforcement remains difficult due to the complexity of trust structures. Financial institutions and legal professionals must navigate the fine line between legitimate asset protection and unethical concealment.

Trusts play a significant role in mortgage holding and financial transactions, offering advantages such as privacy, tax benefits, and asset protection. Different types of trusts serve various purposes, from estate planning to real estate investment and legal shielding. The role of an indenture trustee is crucial in ensuring compliance with financial agreements, particularly in mortgage-backed securities. However, trusts can also be used to obscure ownership, making it challenging to trace property and financial interests. While these structures are legal, they come with ethical and regulatory concerns, particularly when used to evade financial obligations. Understanding the complexities of trusts is essential for investors, legal professionals, and policymakers seeking to balance privacy with financial transparency.

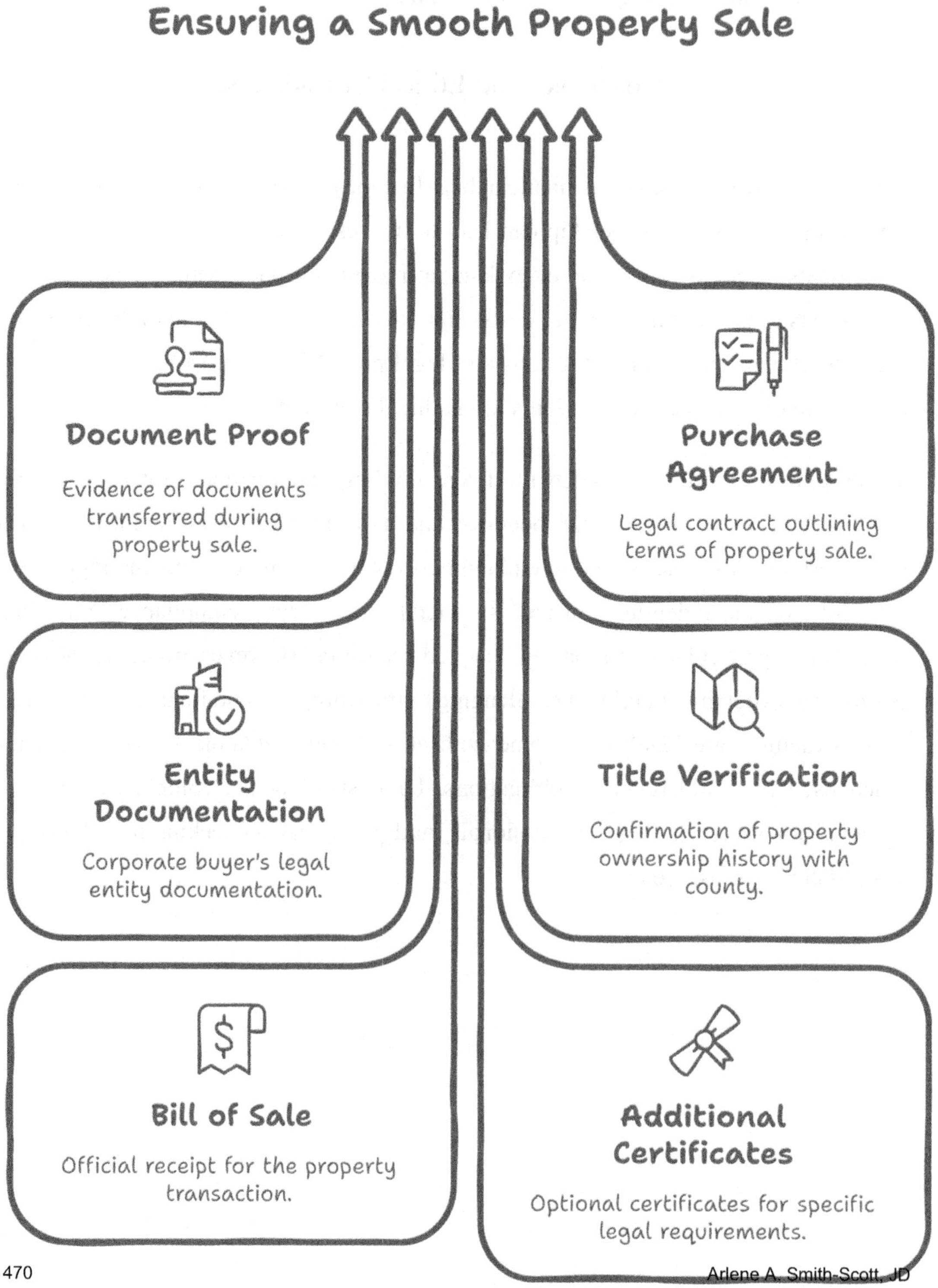
Ensuring a Smooth Property Sale
Document Proof
Evidence of documents transferred during property sale.
Purchase Agreement
Legal contract outlining terms of property sale.
Entity Documentation
Corporate buyer's legal entity documentation.
Title Verification
Confirmation of property ownership history with county.
Bill of Sale
Official receipt for the property transaction.
Additional Certificates
Optional certificates for specific legal requirements.

Chapter Fourteen

BANKRUPTCY TRUSTEES GET PAID!

IMPORTANT: How the Trustee gets paid may affect how much of your money goes to fees instead of paying off your debts. It also helps you pick the right type of bankruptcy for your situation and spot any unfair deals that could take more from your estate than necessary.

BANKRUPTCY TRUSTEES ACT AS FIDUCIARIES responsible for managing bankruptcy estates. The compensation a trustee receives will differ depending on whether the bankruptcy is Chapter 7, Chapter 11, and Chapter 13. Also, the Trustee may engage their own law firms or affiliated real estate agencies which can create potential conflicts of interest.

CHAPTER 7 TRUSTEE COMPENSATION

Chapter 7 trustees are primarily compensated through statutory commissions based on monies disbursed to parties in interest, as established in 11 U.S.C. § 326(a):

• 25% on the first $5,000

• 10% on amounts between $5,001 and $50,000

• 5% on amounts between $50,001 and $1,000,000

• 3% on amounts exceeding $1,000,000

In *In re Rowe,* 750 F.3d 392 (4th Cir. 2014), the court clarified that the statutory commission represents a cap rather than an entitlement. The Fourth Circuit upheld a reduction in the trustee's commission where the court found the trustee had not demonstrated sufficient benefit to the estate relative to the commission sought.

Real-Life Scenario

Consider a Chapter 7 trustee who administers an estate with $2,000,000 in assets. The trustee hires their own law firm at $425 per hour for 100 hours of legal work and employs their affiliated real estate firm to sell property which shares one-half of the 6% commission. The potential compensation breaks down as follows:

1. Statutory Commission:

- 25% of first $5,000 = $1,250

- 10% of next $45,000 = $4,500

- 5% of next $950,000 = $47,500

- 3% of remaining $1,000,000 = $30,000

- Total commission: $83,250

2. Attorney Fees:

- 100 hours at $425/hour = $42,500

3. Real Estate Commission:

- 3% of $2,000,000 = $60,000

Bankruptcy Rule 2014 requires disclosure of all connections with the debtor, creditors, and other parties in interest. And the trustee would have to overcome the presumption against self-dealing established in *In re Interwest Business Equipment, Inc.*, 23 F.3d 311 (10th Cir. 1994), where the court held that a trustee hiring their own firm creates an inherent conflict requiring particularly careful scrutiny.

CHAPTER 11 TRUSTEE COMPENSATION

In Chapter 11 cases, trustees are less common since debtors typically remain in possession. However, when appointed, Chapter 11 trustees are subject to the same statutory commission structure as Chapter 7 trustees under 11 U.S.C. § 326(a). Additionally, in complex reorganizations, trustee compensation may be enhanced through:

1. Success Fees: *In In re Intelogic Trace, Inc.*, 200 B.R. 538 (Bankr. S.D.N.Y. 1996), the court approved a success fee for achieving a particularly beneficial reorganization.

2. Hourly Rates: Per *In re Busy Beaver Building Centers, Inc.,* 19 F.3d 833 (3rd Cir. 1994), reasonable hourly rates may be approved for trustees performing specialized services.

A Chapter 11 trustee overseeing the reorganization of a medium-sized business with substantial real estate holdings worth $2,000,000 might:

1. Receive Statutory Commission:

- Maximum of $83,250 (calculated as in the Chapter 7 example)

2. Bill Legal Services:

- 200 hours of specialized legal work at $425/hour = $85,000

3. Obtain Real Estate Commissions:

- 3% commission on property sales = $60,000

The bankruptcy court would likely apply the standards established in *In re Marvel Entertainment Group, Inc.*, 234 B.R. 21 (D. Del. 1999), which held that the court must ensure that the trustee is not double-dipping by receiving both commission and legal fees for essentially the same work. However, under *In re Drexel Burnham Lambert Group, Inc.*, 133 B.R. 13 (Bankr. S.D.N.Y. 1991), the court would examine whether the legal services performed were distinct from trustee duties and whether they were necessary for the estate's administration.

CHAPTER 13 TRUSTEE COMPENSATION

Chapter 13 standing trustees receive compensation differently than their Chapter 7 and 11 counterparts. Their payment is governed by 28 U.S.C. § 586(e), which establishes:

1. A percentage fee not to exceed 10% of all payments received under plans

2. An annual salary set by the Attorney General, not to exceed $235,756 (as of 2024, adjusted annually)

In *Nardello v. Balboa (In re Nardello),* 514 B.R. 105 (D.N.J. 2014), the court clarified that Chapter 13 standing trustees are entitled to their percentage fee on all payments received, regardless of whether those payments are ultimately distributed to creditors.

Real-Life Scenario

A Chapter 13 Trustee who manages 1,000 active cases with average monthly payments of $500 might:

1. Receive Percentage Fee:

- 10% of $500,000 monthly payments = $50,000/month

- But limited by the statutory salary cap

2. Legal Services:

- Unlike Chapter 7 or 11 trustees, Chapter 13 standing trustees rarely provide legal services to the estates they administer, as this would create significant conflicts with their administrative duties.

3. Real Estate Services:

- If property valued at $2,000,000 needed to be sold in Chapter 13 cases, using the trustee's affiliated real estate agency (3% commission = $60,000) would likely be prohibited under *In re Franklin,* 802 F.2d 324 (9th Cir. 1986), which established strict limits on conflicts of interest for standing trustees.

Conflict of Interest Concerns

The scenario where a trustee hires their own law firm and uses their affiliated real estate agency creates significant conflict of interest issues across all chapters. The seminal case of *Woods v. City National Bank & Trust Co.,* 312 U.S. 262 (1941), established that bankruptcy courts must exercise special vigilance to prevent conflicts of interest and ensure that estate professionals do not engage in self-dealing.

More recently, in *In re AFI Holding, Inc.,* 530 F.3d 832 (9th Cir. 2008), the Ninth Circuit emphasized that trustees must avoid even the appearance of impropriety and must place the interests of the estate above their own financial interests.

Court Review and Approval Process

Under 11 U.S.C. § 330, all trustee compensation and professional fees are subject to court review for reasonableness. The landmark case of *In re Manoa Finance Co.,* 853 F.2d 687 (9th Cir. 1988), established that courts must examine the following factors:

1. The time spent on services

2. The rates charged for such services

3. The necessity of the services

4. The benefit to the estate

5. The complexity and novelty of the issues

6. The preclusion of other employment due to acceptance of the case

When a trustee hires their own law firm or affiliated real estate agency, the court will typically require:

a. Full disclosure under Bankruptcy Rule 2014

b. Evidence that the arrangement benefits the estate more than hiring independent professionals

c. Competitive market rates for all services provided

d. Proof that services do not duplicate trustee duties

Bankruptcy law allows trustees to earn compensation through various channels, but strict ethical and legal constraints limit self-dealing. When trustees engage their own firms or affiliates, courts apply heightened scrutiny and may require independent examiners to review fees. To maximize lawful compensation, trustees should prioritize efficient estate administration, maintain clear boundaries between fiduciary and professional roles, and fully disclose any relationships that could impact their duties.

Chapter Fifteen

JURISDICTION OF THE BANKRUPTCY COURT

IMPORTANT: Jurisdiction will determine which court has power over your financial situation, your property (even across state lines), and your creditors, while establishing clear boundaries for what legal issues the court can and cannot address. This knowledge helps you anticipate the protection you'll receive from the automatic stay, recognize which legal problems bankruptcy can solve, and make informed decisions about whether filing bankruptcy is the right solution for your specific financial circumstances.

HAVE YOU EVER WONDERED how bankruptcy courts get the power to make decisions about people's money and property? This is called "jurisdiction," and it's like the court's territory or playground where it has special powers. Let's break down how jurisdiction works in bankruptcy in a way that's easy to understand.

WHAT DOES "JURISDICTION" MEAN?

Jurisdiction is the legal power of a court to make decisions about certain people and certain things. Think of it like this. Each court has a specific "zone of control," and if you or your property falls within that zone, the court can make decisions about you or your property. In bankruptcy, there are three types of jurisdictions:

First, "subject matter jurisdiction" means bankruptcy courts can handle bankruptcy cases, but not other types of cases like criminal trials or divorce proceedings.

Second, "personal jurisdiction" means the court has power over specific people or companies.

Third, "in rem jurisdiction" means the court has power over specific property.

When Does a Bankruptcy Court Have Jurisdiction Over You?

The bankruptcy court gets jurisdiction over you (personal jurisdiction) when:

(a) You file for bankruptcy voluntarily. This is the most common situation. When you sign those bankruptcy papers and file them with the court, you're basically saying, "Hey court, I'm giving you the power to handle my financial situation."

(b) Someone forces you into bankruptcy (involuntary bankruptcy). This happens when your creditors (people you owe money to) file bankruptcy against you. This is rare for regular people but can happen to businesses.

Real Life Example: John lives in Texas and files for Chapter 7 bankruptcy in the Texas bankruptcy court. The court now has personal jurisdiction over John, and he must follow all the court's orders about his finances.

When Does a Bankruptcy Court Have Jurisdiction Over Your Property?

Bankruptcy courts have jurisdiction over all your property that's part of the "bankruptcy estate." The bankruptcy estate includes all property you own when you file bankruptcy; some property you acquire within 180 days after filing (like inheritance or life insurance proceeds); and income you earn from property of the estate

Real Life Example: Sarah files for bankruptcy in California. She owns a house in California, a vacation cabin in Colorado, a car, bank accounts, and jewelry. The California bankruptcy court has jurisdiction over ALL of these items, even the cabin in Colorado, because they all become part of Sarah's bankruptcy estate.

Jurisdiction Over Other People and Companies

Here's where things get interesting. The bankruptcy court's power doesn't just cover you (the debtor). It can also extend to:

- Creditors: People or companies you owe money to,
- Your spouse (in certain situations),
- Companies that have your property, and
- People who owe you money.

Real Life Example: Maria files for bankruptcy. The bankruptcy court now has the power to stop Bank ABC from foreclosing on her house, prevent Credit Card Company XYZ from calling her about debts, and stop her landlord from evicting her (at least temporarily). All these entities are subject to the bankruptcy court's jurisdiction for matters related to Maria's bankruptcy.

When the Bankruptcy Court DOESN'T Have Jurisdiction

The bankruptcy court doesn't have jurisdiction over:

(i) People who aren't involved in your bankruptcy case,

(ii) Property that isn't part of your bankruptcy estate,

(iii) Certain government actions (like criminal prosecutions or tax collection activities)

(iv) Certain domestic relations matters (like divorce or child custody)

Real Life Example: Tom files for bankruptcy. The bankruptcy court has no power to stop his traffic ticket case in municipal court. It also can't stop his divorce proceedings, although it can affect how property is divided into the divorce.

The Automatic Stay: Jurisdiction in Action

The best example of bankruptcy jurisdiction in action is something called the "automatic stay." When you file bankruptcy, an invisible legal shield (the automatic stay) immediately protects you. This shield stops most collection actions against you, including:

• Foreclosure of your home

• Repossession of your car

• Wage garnishments

• Lawsuits for money you owe

• Utility shutoffs

• Evictions (in some cases)

• Harassing collection calls

This automatic stay is possible because the bankruptcy court has jurisdiction over you AND your creditors for matters related to your debts.

Real Life Example: Dave files for Chapter 13 bankruptcy. The day before, ABC Bank was planning to foreclose his house, DEF Auto was planning to repossess his car, and his employer had received a wage garnishment order. Once Dave files bankruptcy, the court's jurisdiction stops all these actions immediately.

How Far Does Bankruptcy Court Jurisdiction Reach?

Bankruptcy court jurisdiction is surprisingly broad and can reach across state lines. A bankruptcy filed in Florida has jurisdiction over the filer's property in California A US bankruptcy court can have jurisdiction over a debtor's property in foreign countries (though enforcing this can be complicated) The court has jurisdiction over creditors from anywhere in the country

Real Life Example: Rachel files bankruptcy in New York. She has creditors in all 50 states, a timeshare in Mexico, and a small bank account in Canada. The New York bankruptcy court's jurisdiction extends to all these items and entities, though dealing with the foreign property might require extra legal steps.

Important Limits to Bankruptcy Court Jurisdiction

Bankruptcy courts are "courts of limited jurisdiction." This means they can't handle every type of legal issue. Some matters must be decided by regular federal courts (called "district courts"). These include:

- Personal injury
- Lawsuits
- Certain tax disputes
- Some constitutional questions
- Complex legal issues outside of bankruptcy law

Real Life Example: Mark files for bankruptcy. During his bankruptcy, he was injured in a car accident and wants to sue the other driver. While the bankruptcy court has jurisdiction over any money Mark might win from the lawsuit (since that's potential property of his bankruptcy estate), the actual personal injury lawsuit must be filed and decided in a regular civil court, not the bankruptcy court.

The Bottom Line on Bankruptcy Jurisdiction

Bankruptcy court jurisdiction is powerful but has specific boundaries. When you file bankruptcy, the court gains jurisdiction over you and your property, no matter where it's located. The court also gains limited jurisdiction over your creditors regarding your debts.

However, the court doesn't have jurisdiction over unrelated legal matters or people not involved in your bankruptcy.

Chapter Sixteen

JURISDICTION AND THE DEBTOR'S BUSINESS

IMPORTANT: A business entity, such as LLC, Corp, etc., is legally distinct from personal assets, meaning its assets and liabilities are generally not included in a personal bankruptcy estate. This distinction is crucial because it helps protect the business from being directly impacted by an owner's personal financial troubles, as long as business and personal finances remain separate and corporate formalities are followed.

WHEN AN INDIVIDUAL (LET'S call her Jane) owns a separate business entity, be it a Limited Liability Company (LLC), a close corporation, or an S-Corp, that business is legally distinct from her personal assets. This separation means that the business's assets and liabilities are generally not automatically included in Jane's personal bankruptcy estate.

Let's delve into the concept of "separate" business entity further. When a person owns a business, the legal structure of that business plays a huge role in how it is treated during bankruptcy. A business that is legally separate from its owner, like an LLC, S-Corp, or close corporation, has its own rights, responsibilities, and assets. This means that if the owner files for personal bankruptcy, the business itself doesn't automatically become part of the bankruptcy estate. Instead, only the debtor's ownership interest in the business is considered.

For example, imagine Jane, a lawyer, owns a law firm structured as an LLC. If she files for personal bankruptcy, the trustee overseeing her case can only claim Jane's ownership interest in the firm but cannot seize the firm's bank accounts or office furniture, as those belong to the business. The firm can continue operating unless the trustee takes further action to sell Jane's ownership share. However, if Jane's law practice were a sole proprietorship instead of an LLC, the situation would be very different.

A sole proprietorship is not a separate legal entity, which means all of its assets, including client payments, office supplies, and any business property, become part of Jane's personal bankruptcy estate. The trustee could liquidate these assets to pay creditors.

The trustee has several options when handling a debtor's business in bankruptcy. If the business has significant value and the debtor owns it outright, the trustee might attempt to sell it. In rare cases, the trustee might even try to take over the business and run it until it can be sold. However, if the business is deeply tied to the debtor's personal services, like a solo law practice, the trustee may find it difficult to sell and may instead abandon it, allowing the debtor to keep operating.

One issue that can complicate matters is how the debtor interacts with the business. If the debtor fails to keep business and personal finances separate, such as using business funds to pay personal expenses, the trustee may argue that the business is not truly independent. In such cases, the trustee might attempt to "pierce the corporate veil," meaning they could go after the business's assets as if they were the debtor's personal property. Courts are cautious about allowing this, but it can happen if the debtor has treated the business like an extension of their personal finances rather than as a legally separate entity.

For business owners in bankruptcy, maintaining clear separation between personal and business finances is critical. Keeping business bank accounts separate, paying oneself a formal salary instead of taking business profits directly, and ensuring that all corporate formalities are followed can help protect the business from being pulled into the bankruptcy estate. Additionally, if the business has multiple owners, a buy-sell agreement can prevent a trustee from selling the debtor's share to an outsider.

Ultimately, a separate business entity provides protection, but only if it is properly maintained. If the business is truly independent, the trustee can typically only sell the debtor's ownership stake rather than seizing the company's assets. However, if the debtor treats the business as a personal bank account, the trustee may have grounds to go after it. Understanding the legal distinctions between personal and business assets can make the difference between losing a business in bankruptcy and keeping it intact.

Scenario: Jane's Law Practice Renting Property She Owns Personally

Let's say Jane owns a building personally and rents a unit to her law practice, which operates as an LLC. Here's how bankruptcy considerations might play out. If Jane owns a law practice and rents office space from herself, the law practice has rights as a tenant, just like any other business renting a space. If there is a formal lease agreement between Jane and her law firm, the law firm is allowed to stay in the office as long as it follows the terms of that lease. Even if Jane files for personal bankruptcy, the lease doesn't just disappear. The trustee in charge of her bankruptcy will review all of her assets, including the building she owns, but the law practice still has the right to stay in the rented space because the lease remains valid.

However, there are situations where the law practice could be evicted from the premises. If it stops paying rent or breaks the lease agreement, the trustee could take steps to remove it. Since Jane's building has become part of the bankruptcy estate, the trustee now controls it and may decide that the best option is to terminate the lease and rent the space to someone else who might pay more. But the trustee can't just do this on a whim. They have to get permission from the court before making any big changes to existing lease agreements.

One question that often comes up in bankruptcy is whether the trustee can take money from the law firm's bank account. Normally, the answer is no, because Jane's law practice is an LLC, which means it is a separate business entity from Jane as a person. That separation protects the law firm's money from being taken just because Jane is in personal financial trouble. But there is an exception. If the trustee can prove that Jane has been treating the law practice like her personal bank account, moving money around improperly or paying personal expenses with business funds, the trustee can argue that the law firm is not actually separate from Jane. If the court agrees, the trustee could be allowed to take money from the law firm's bank account to help pay off Jane's debts. This is called "piercing the corporate veil," and courts don't approve it unless there is strong proof that the business was not actually being run as a separate entity.

In summary, as long as Jane's law firm follows the lease agreement, it has the right to stay in its office space. The trustee may try to end the lease if it benefits Jane's bankruptcy estate, but they need court approval to do so. The law firm's bank account is generally protected, but if Jane has mixed her personal and business finances too much, the trustee might try to argue that the law firm isn't truly separate and could try to seize its funds.

DISTINCTION BETWEEN PERSONAL AND BUSINESS ASSETS

Understanding distinctions ensures that both personal and business assets are appropriately managed and protected in bankruptcy situations. Therefore, when an individual files for personal bankruptcy but owns a separate corporation, the general rule is that the corporation itself is not automatically included in the bankruptcy estate. This is because corporations, LLCs, and other separate legal entities have their own assets, liabilities, and legal identity, distinct from their owners.

However, the individual's ownership interest in the corporation, whether it's stock in an S-Corp or membership interest in an LLC, can be part of the bankruptcy estate and subject to the trustee's control. Courts have consistently held that while a bankruptcy trustee can step into the debtor's shoes regarding ownership rights, they do not automatically gain access to the corporation's assets unless specific conditions apply.

One case that illustrates this distinction is *In re Albright,* 291 B.R. 538 (Bankr. D. Colo. 2003). In that case, the debtor was the sole member of an LLC, and the bankruptcy court ruled that because there were no other members in the LLC, the bankruptcy trustee could take full control of the company and its assets. This happened because a single-member LLC does not have the same protections as an LLC with multiple members. However, if the business had multiple owners, the trustee would generally only be able to access the debtor's ownership interest and not the business's property or accounts.

To put this in real-life terms, imagine Jane, a solo attorney, owns Jane's Legal Services, LLC, which operates as a successful law practice. Jane personally files for Chapter 7 bankruptcy because she has overwhelming credit card debt and medical bills. Since her law firm is an LLC, its assets, such as client trust accounts, office computers, and legal contracts, do not automatically become part of her personal bankruptcy case. However, her membership interest in the LLC does become part of the bankruptcy estate, meaning the trustee could try to sell it if there is value. But selling a law firm's membership interest is complicated because lawyers cannot transfer ownership of a legal practice to non-lawyers, which makes the interest less valuable.

A case that supports this principle is *In re First Protection, Inc.,* 440 B.R. 821 (9th Cir. B.A.P. 2010), where the court recognized that a business's separate legal identity must be respected unless there is strong evidence that the debtor was using the corporation as a personal piggy bank. This means that as long as Jane's law firm follows proper corporate formalities, the trustee cannot touch its bank accounts, legal contracts, or client funds just because Jane is personally in financial trouble.

However, there are exceptions. If Jane commingles funds, meaning she uses the law firm's bank account to pay personal expenses or deposits personal money into the firm's accounts, the trustee may argue that the company is not really separate. This is known as piercing the corporate veil, and courts will only allow it when the owner has failed to respect the corporation's independence. A case that highlights this issue is *In re Turner,* 335 B.R. 140 (Bankr. N.D. Cal. 2005), where the court allowed the trustee to go after corporate assets because the debtor was using the corporation's accounts as if they were personal checking accounts.

If Jane also owns the office building where her law practice is located and rents it to her firm, the law practice has tenant rights under the lease agreement. Even if Jane's bankruptcy trustee takes control of the building, the law firm cannot simply be evicted without cause. Under 11 U.S.C. § 365, the trustee must either assume or reject the lease, and eviction can only happen if the lease is violated. A real-life example of this is *In re Tudor Motor Lodge Associates,* 102 B.R. 936 (Bankr. D.N.J. 1989), where the court upheld the rights of a corporate tenant in a bankruptcy case, stating that the corporation's leasehold interest remained intact despite the owner's personal bankruptcy.

If the trustee wants to access the law practice's bank accounts, they must prove that the business is not truly separate or that fraud was involved. Courts are very hesitant to allow this unless there is clear evidence of wrongdoing. The case of *In re Munford, Inc.,* 97 F.3d 449 (11th Cir. 1996) reinforces this, as the court ruled that a trustee cannot simply seize business assets without proper legal justification.

So, when an individual like Jane files for bankruptcy, her business remains separate as long as corporate formalities are followed. The trustee may control her ownership interest in the company but cannot take the company's assets unless they prove misuse or fraud. The law firm retains its tenant rights and cannot be evicted without cause. Courts generally respect the corporate veil, but when a business owner fails to separate personal and business finances, they risk losing that protection. Understanding these legal principles can make the difference between keeping a business intact and losing it in bankruptcy.

BOTTOM LINE

- A business entity, like Jane's Law Practice, LLC, is legally separate from its owner. In personal bankruptcy, the trustee doesn't automatically gain control over the business's assets.
- The law practice's rights as a tenant are protected under the lease agreement, and eviction would depend on lease violations or strategic decisions by the trustee to benefit the bankruptcy estate.
- Trustees can only access the law practice's bank accounts if they can demonstrate that the business is not truly separate from the owner's personal affairs, a challenging legal standard to meet.

Understanding these distinctions ensures that both personal and business assets are appropriately managed and protected in bankruptcy situations.

WHEN TRUSTEE VIOLATES THE LAW

If a bankruptcy trustee garnishes a law firm's bank account and evicts the law firm without legal justification, several legal violations could occur. Since a law firm operating as an LLC or corporation is a separate legal entity from the individual debtor, the trustee does not automatically have the right to seize the law firm's assets or evict it from its office unless specific legal conditions are met. If the trustee wrongfully takes these actions, the law firm and the debtor may have legal grounds to challenge them.

What Should Happen if the Trustee Garnishes the Law Firm's Bank Account?

A trustee cannot simply freeze or garnish a business's bank account just because the owner of the business filed for personal bankruptcy. The law firm's assets belong to the business, not the individual debtor, and they are not part of the bankruptcy estate unless the trustee proves otherwise. Under 11 U.S.C. § 541, only the debtor's personal property becomes part of the bankruptcy estate, and corporate assets are excluded unless the trustee successfully "pierces the corporate veil."

If the trustee wrongfully garnishes the law firm's bank account, the law firm should immediately file a motion to compel the trustee to release the funds, arguing that the funds belong to the business, not the debtor. A case that supports this principle is *In re First Protection, Inc.,* 440 B.R. 821 (9th Cir. B.A.P. 2010), where the court ruled that corporate assets should not be included in an individual owner's bankruptcy estate unless there is strong evidence that the corporate structure is being abused.

Additionally, the law firm could sue the trustee for conversion, which is the wrongful taking of someone else's property. Courts have recognized that a trustee who improperly seizes assets that are not part of the bankruptcy estate may be liable for damages. *In In re Graves,* 609 F.3d 1153 (10th Cir. 2010), the court held that trustees must act within their legal authority and could be held accountable if they wrongfully take property belonging to third parties.

What Should Happen if the Trustee Evicts the Law Firm?

If the law firm is renting space from the debtor (for example, if the debtor owns the office building personally and rents it to their law practice), then the law firm has rights as a tenant under the lease agreement. Even though the debtor's property becomes part of the bankruptcy estate, the lease does not automatically terminate just because of the bankruptcy filing. Under 11 U.S.C. § 365, a trustee must either assume or reject an existing lease, and they cannot evict a tenant without cause.

If the law firm has been paying rent and following the lease terms, the trustee has no legal right to evict it without court approval. A case that supports this is *In re Tudor Motor Lodge Associates,* 102 B.R. 936 (Bankr. D.N.J. 1989), where the court ruled that a valid lease remains in effect even if the property's owner files for bankruptcy. If the trustee tries to evict the law firm without legal grounds, the firm can file an emergency motion to stay eviction, requesting the court to stop the wrongful eviction.

If the eviction has already taken place, the law firm may be able to file a lawsuit for wrongful eviction and damages. In *In re LJC Corp.*, 983 F.2d 1060 (6th Cir. 1993), the court held that a trustee who evicts a tenant without following proper legal procedures could be liable for damages, including lost business income and relocation costs.

How Can the Law Firm Fight Back?

If a trustee wrongfully garnishes the law firm's bank account or evicts the law firm, the law firm should take the following steps:

- File a motion with the bankruptcy court demanding the return of garnished funds and an order preventing further interference.
- Challenge the eviction by filing an emergency motion arguing that the lease remains valid and the eviction is unlawful.
- Sue the trustee for damages if the actions resulted in financial harm, such as lost revenue or disruption of business operations.

Trustees must follow strict legal procedures when handling a bankruptcy estate. If they overstep their authority and improperly seize corporate assets or evict a law firm without cause, the law firm has strong legal grounds to challenge their actions and seek damages.

CASE STUDY

In my case, a lease agreement that existed between myself as the debtor and my business, a Limited Liability Corporation in good standing, should not have been impacted by the bankruptcy proceedings. This lease agreement specifically reflected that rental payments were to be used to cover the expense of improvements to the property. However, this arrangement was incorrectly characterized and treated as "non-payment of rent" during the bankruptcy proceedings.

On January 8, 2016, the Trustee filed a motion to compel me (the Debtor) and my law firm (a separate legal entity in good standing) to turn over the real property, alleging nonpayment of rent. Subsequently, on March 22, 2017, an order was issued compelling both myself and my law firm to turn over the real property and all possessory interests, whether as tenant or landlord.

This action fundamentally violated established bankruptcy jurisdiction principles and represented disparate treatment under the law for several key reasons:

VIOLATION OF BANKRUPTCY JURISDICTION

The bankruptcy court's jurisdiction extends to the debtor and the debtor's estate, but not automatically to separate legal entities that are not in bankruptcy. By compelling my law firm, a distinct LLC in good standing, to surrender its leasehold rights, the court effectively extended its jurisdiction beyond its proper boundaries. This overreach contradicts the fundamental principle that bankruptcy proceedings should not infringe upon the rights of non-debtor entities absent extraordinary circumstances.

The Bankruptcy Code (11 U.S.C. § 365) specifically addresses treatment of leases in bankruptcy and provides that unless a lease is properly rejected according to statutory procedures, the legal rights of parties to that lease remain intact. The treatment of the lease as simply "non-payment of rent" ignored the documented purpose of the rent allocation (bathroom installation) and the separate legal status of the tenant LLC.

DISPARATE TREATMENT UNDER THE LAW

This treatment represents a significant departure from how other similarly situated parties would be treated under bankruptcy law:

1. Had any other third-party business entity been the tenant, it would have been entitled to the protections of its lease agreement and would have required a separate adversary proceeding to terminate its tenancy rights.

2. The characterization of an improvement-for-rent agreement as "non-payment" ignored the economic reality of the arrangement, which would typically be recognized as valid consideration in other commercial contexts.

3. The order compelling turnover of "all possessory interests" effectively stripped rights from a non-debtor entity without the procedural protections that would normally be afforded to such entities, such as a full adversary proceeding with appropriate discovery and evidentiary standards.

4. Most importantly, the law firm, as a separate legal entity, should have been entitled to its own day in court to defend its leasehold rights independent of the bankruptcy proceedings against me personally.

This case illustrates how bankruptcy proceedings can sometimes improperly disregard the separate legal personhood of business entities, particularly when they are closely associated with the debtor. The proper approach would have been to respect the lease agreement with the LLC and address any issues through proper adversary proceedings that recognized the distinct legal status of the law firm as a separate entity from myself as the individual debtor.

Chapter Seventeen

PROOF OF CLAIMS AND MORTGAGE DEFICIENCES

IMPORTANT: Understanding what is a Proof of Claim (POC) and how it may establish a creditor's right to repayment from the debtor's estate, impacting how and whether creditors will be paid. Knowing when a POC must be filed and the consequences of deficiencies or missing documentation can help identify potentially invalid claims.

A PROOF OF CLAIM (POC) is a legal document filed by a creditor in a bankruptcy case to establish its right to receive payments from the debtor's estate. It serves as the creditor's formal assertion that the debtor owes a specific debt and must include supporting documentation to verify its validity. A properly filed Proof of Claim generally includes:

• The amount of the debt owed as of the bankruptcy filing date.

• The basis for the claim (such as a loan, mortgage, or contract obligation).

• Supporting evidence like promissory notes, loan agreements, assignments, and endorsements.

• A breakdown of any interest, fees, or costs included in the claim.

Whether a POC is filed or not depends on the type of bankruptcy case and specific circumstances.

When a Proof of Claim is Filed:

In Chapter 7 (Liquidation) cases, if there are assets available for distribution to creditors, bankruptcy trustee will notify creditors to file a Proof of Claim. Unsecured, secured, and priority creditors must file a POC to participate in the distribution of assets.

In Chapter 13 (Reorganization) cases, creditors must file a POC to receive payments under the debtor's repayment plan. If a creditor does not file a POC, they may not be entitled to receive payments from the plan.

In Chapter 11 (Business Reorganization) cases, if the debtor objects to a creditor's claim, or if the claim is disputed or not listed in the bankruptcy schedules, the creditor must file a POC. Creditors wishing to vote on the reorganization plan must file a claim.

When the Claim is Not Scheduled or Is Listed as Disputed, Contingent, or Unliquidated

If a creditor is not listed in the debtor's bankruptcy schedules or their claim is listed as disputed, contingent, or unliquidated, they must file a POC to assert their right to repayment.

When a Proof of Claim is NOT Filed:

i. When the Creditor's Claim is Properly Listed in a No-Asset Chapter 7 Case

ii. If the debtor has no assets to distribute, the court may issue a "no-asset" notice, meaning creditors do not need to file a POC because no funds will be available for distribution.

iii. When a Secured Creditor Does Not Seek Payment from the Bankruptcy Estate

iv. If a creditor holds a mortgage or car loan and chooses to foreclose or repossess the collateral rather than seek repayment from bankruptcy, they may not file a POC.

v. When the Creditor Agrees with the Amount and Classification in the Debtor's Bankruptcy Schedules

vi. If the debtor lists a creditor's claim correctly and the creditor does not dispute the information, filing a POC may not be necessary unless required by the trustee or court.

vii. When a Debtor or Another Party Files the Proof of Claim on Behalf of the Creditor

viii. In some cases, the debtor or trustee may file a POC on behalf of a creditor (especially in Chapter 13 cases where the debt is included in the repayment plan).

In summary, filing a Proof of Claim is essential for a creditor to assert their right to repayment in most bankruptcy cases. However, there are situations, such as no-asset Chapter 7 cases or when a secured creditor opts for foreclosure, where filing is unnecessary. Whether or not a POC is required depends on the type of bankruptcy, the creditor's role, and the specifics of the debtor's financial situation.

Mortgage Related Claims

In mortgage-related bankruptcy claims, the creditor must also provide evidence of standing, meaning they must demonstrate that they have the legal right to enforce the debt. This is typically shown through a complete chain of titles, which includes proper assignments, endorsements, and allonges attached to the original promissory note.

CASE STUDY

In my case, U.S. Bank, NA filed a Proof of Claim purporting to establish its right to collect on my mortgage debt. However, this filing was critically deficient in several key ways:

Lack of Endorsements

A valid Proof of Claim in a mortgage case must include an endorsed note that transfers ownership from the original lender to the current claimant. The Proof of Claim did not contain any endorsements from Capital One Bank or Lehman Brothers, making it unclear how U.S. Bank, NA obtained ownership of the debt.

Absence of Assignments

A creditor filing a Proof of Claim should provide properly recorded assignments showing the chain of ownership from lender to lender. In this case, there were no recorded assignments demonstrating how U.S. Bank, NA acquired the loan from Capital One Bank or Lehman Brothers, raising serious concerns about their standing.

Missing Allonges

An allonge is an additional document attached to a promissory note when there is no room for further endorsements. It serves to validate the transfer of the note to a new holder. The Proof of Claim failed to include any allonges supporting the transfer of the debt, leaving a significant gap in the evidence of ownership.

The Legal Impact of These Omissions

Without endorsements, assignments, or allonges, U.S. Bank, NA's claim is legally questionable because:

i. It fails to demonstrate a clear chain of title, meaning there is no verified proof that U.S. Bank, NA actually owns the note.

ii. The bankruptcy court may reject the claim if the creditor cannot prove it has the right to enforce the debt.

iii. It raises the possibility of a fraudulent or erroneous claim, as multiple entities could attempt to collect on the same debt without proper documentation.

Why This Matters?

A Proof of Claim is not just a formality; it is the legal foundation for a creditor's right to collect. When key documents like endorsements, assignments, and allonges are missing, it undermines the legitimacy of the claim and calls into question whether the claimant truly has standing in the bankruptcy court.

In this case, U.S. Bank, NA's failure to provide these essential documents suggests a critical defect in their claim. If they cannot produce the necessary paperwork, their Proof of Claim should have been challenged and potentially disallowed by the bankruptcy court. As with any financial dispute, following the paper trail is crucial, and in this instance, the lack of documentation speaks volumes.

U.S. Bank vs. GreenPoint Mortgage Funding Lawsuit

There was a high-profile lawsuit between U.S. Bank, NA and GreenPoint Mortgage Funding, Inc. (GreenPoint) The lawsuit claimed that GreenPoint's business model was to structure, originate, and sell loans rather than service them. This distinction was highly significant in my bankruptcy case because it provided crucial evidence that GreenPoint was not the true owner of my debt.

A creditor must establish their legal standing by proving they have the right to enforce a debt. A party filing a Proof of Claim in bankruptcy court must demonstrate an unbroken chain of title, showing a clear transfer of ownership from the original lender to the entity attempting to collect the debt. When GreenPoint sold loans without retaining servicing rights, it meant that any subsequent claims of ownership by parties tied to GreenPoint needed to be closely scrutinized. If Lehman Brothers were the actual owner of my debt, then any claims made by GreenPoint or entities purchasing distressed notes from them could be legally flawed.

The Implications for a Distressed Mortgage Note Sale

When an individual asserts that a party purchased a note from a distressed mortgage note sale held by GreenPoint, several legal concerns arise:

Questionable Chain of Title

If GreenPoint's business was merely to originate and sell loans and not to service or retain ownership, then any entity claiming ownership of a mortgage note from GreenPoint must provide clear proof of a legitimate transfer.

If a distressed note was later sold without proper endorsements, assignments, or supporting documentation, it raises serious doubts about whether the new party truly holds the right to enforce the debt.

Standing Issues in Bankruptcy Court

Bankruptcy law requires a creditor to prove that they have standing to collect on a debt. If an entity claiming ownership of the mortgage note cannot show proper assignments and a continuous chain of title, their claim may be legally defective and subject to challenge. This issue becomes particularly relevant when multiple parties claim ownership of the same debt, as improper documentation can lead to wrongful foreclosure attempts or invalid claims in court.

Potential for Fraudulent Transfers

When a distressed mortgage note is sold without transparency and adequate documentation, it raises concerns that the transfer may have been done to manipulate ownership records or fabricate standing. If a party is trying to collect on a debt without proof that it legally acquired the note, this could constitute fraud upon the bankruptcy court, as courts rely on accurate records to make determinations about debt enforcement.

Legal Precedent and the Role of GreenPoint's Business Model

The U.S. Bank vs. GreenPoint lawsuit supports the argument that GreenPoint was not the final owner of the loan, reinforcing the claim that subsequent transfers must be thoroughly examined. Any party purchasing a distressed note from GreenPoint must prove that they obtained proper title from the actual legal owner of the debt, not just from a company that once held it in its pipeline of originations.

Why This Matters in Bankruptcy?

The distinction between a lender that originates and sells loans versus one that owns and services them is crucial in personal bankruptcy cases. A party attempting to enforce a mortgage note must prove its legal right to do so through a properly documented chain of title. In my case, the U.S. Bank vs. GreenPoint Mortgage Funding lawsuit provided essential evidence that GreenPoint was never the true owner of my debt. This meant that any entity claiming ownership through a distressed note sale linked to GreenPoint must be closely examined to determine whether they actually hold a valid interest in the debt.

If a party cannot produce valid assignments, endorsements, and loan sale agreements, they may lack standing to enforce the note, making their claims against the debtor invalid in bankruptcy court. This principle protects debtors from fraudulent or improperly documented claims, ensuring that only legally valid creditors are permitted to participate in the bankruptcy process.

Chapter Eighteen

THE POWER OF DISCOVERY AND THE RECORD

IMPORTANT: This knowledge empowers the reader to request crucial documentation from creditors that may reveal improper practices or documentation gaps, potentially invalidating claims against their estate.

IMAGINE YOU'RE ABOUT TO take a big test, but you aren't allowed to study, ask questions, or even see the material beforehand. That would be unfair, right? Well, in court, something similar would happen if lawyers didn't have a process called discovery.

Discovery is how both sides gather information before trial. It's like detectives gathering clues to solve a mystery. Lawyers use discovery to collect facts, documents, and witness statements to build the record, which is all the evidence that will be used in court. Without discovery, trials would be full of surprises, and no one would have a fair chance of proving their case.

What Is Discovery and Why Is It So Important?

Discovery is the process where both sides exchange important information before trial. It makes sure that no one can hide evidence or spring surprises at the last minute. Here's how lawyers use discovery to strengthen the record:

- Depositions – This is when a witness or party in the case answers questions under oath before trial. A lawyer might ask a doctor, "What injuries did the patient suffer?" or ask a company executive, "Did you know the product was defective?" The answers are recorded and can be used later if someone changes their story.

- Requests for Documents – Lawyers ask for things like emails, contracts, medical records, or police reports. These documents can prove what really happened. For example, in a car accident case, phone records might show that a driver was texting right before the crash.

- Interrogatories – These are written questions that one side sends to the other. The person answering must respond truthfully, helping lawyers gather key facts before trial.

- Requests for Admissions – These are yes-or-no questions that help narrow down the issues. If someone admits, "Yes, I was at the scene of the crime," that fact is settled and doesn't have to be argued in court.

- Expert Reports and Inspections – If a case involves a complex issue, experts may be brought in during discovery. For example, in a medical malpractice case, a doctor might review records and write a report saying whether a mistake was made. Or, in a construction case, engineers might inspect a building to see if it was built correctly.

How Discovery Shapes the Record

The record, the collection of all the evidence used in a case, begins in discovery. If a lawyer doesn't gather the right documents or interview the right witnesses, key evidence may never make it into the record. And if something isn't part of the record, the judge or jury won't consider it when deciding the case.

What Happens If Discovery Fails?

If Discovery isn't done properly, the case can fall apart. Imagine suing a company for selling a dangerous product, but your lawyer never asks for safety reports during discovery. If those reports later show the company knew the product was unsafe, but they weren't added to the record, it might be too late to use them in court.

Courts can also limit or block discovery, which can be dangerous for justice. If a judge unfairly refuses to let a lawyer see important documents or stops an expert from testifying, it weakens the record and can lead to a wrong decision. In some cases, higher courts can review and overturn unfair rulings, but only if the record shows that mistakes were made.

Discovery and the Record Work Together

Discovery is the foundation of a case, and the record is the final product. If discovery is weak, the record is weak. And if the record is weak, the case might be lost, even if the truth is on your side. In court, you don't just tell the truth, you prove it. And discovery is where that proof begins.

THE POWER OF THE RECORD IN COURT

Imagine you are telling a story, but instead of just words, you have proof, photos, letters, expert opinions, even diagrams to help explain your point. That's exactly what happens in court when lawyers build a "record." A record is all the evidence, testimony (what people say in court), documents, expert opinions, graphs, and anything else that helps prove a case. This record is not just important; it is the foundation of winning or losing in court. Without a strong record, even the best lawyer can struggle to prove their case.

Building a Strong Record: The Backbone of a Case

A case is only as strong as the proof behind it. That's why lawyers work hard to gather all the right evidence. Think about a murder mystery. If the detective only has one clue but the suspect has ten alibis, the case falls apart. The same thing happens in court. Here's how a strong record is built:

(a) Testimony from Witnesses – This is when people come to court and answer questions under oath. A witness might say, "I saw the defendant run away from the crime scene," or "I was with the defendant at the time of the crime, so they couldn't have done it." Witnesses help tell the story, but their words alone aren't always enough.

(b) Documents and Physical Evidence – This includes contracts, emails, medical records, or even something physical like a broken car part in an accident case. Documents can prove what happened when people's memories fade.

(c) Expert Witnesses – Sometimes, regular people don't have the knowledge to explain something complex. That's where experts come in. If a doctor testifies about how an injury happened or an engineer explains why a bridge collapsed, their testimony helps make sense of the evidence.

(d) Graphs, Diagrams, and Visual Aids – Courts rely on more than words. Diagrams and graphs help explain things visually, especially when cases involve complicated facts. For example, a graph showing how a company's pollution increased over time might be more powerful than just saying, "The pollution got worse."

What Happens If a Record Can't Be Built?

If there's little or no record, it's like trying to prove a case with no evidence. Even if a lawyer knows the truth, without proof, they can't convince a judge or jury. A case without a strong record is like a puzzle missing half the pieces—it won't make sense, and the court won't rule in favor of that side.

A weak record also makes appeals (asking a higher court to review a case) nearly impossible. When a case goes to appeal, the higher court doesn't redo the trial. Instead, it reviews the record from the lower court. If key evidence isn't there, the appeal is likely to fail, even if a mistake was made.

When a Court Denies Evidence or an Expert Witness

Sometimes, a judge may say, "No, this witness or piece of evidence can't be used in court." This can be devastating. If a judge wrongly excludes a key expert or important documents, the record becomes incomplete, and the case may become much harder to prove.

For example, imagine someone suing a drug company, claiming their medicine caused serious harm. If the judge refuses to allow a scientist to testify about the dangerous effects of the drug, the case may be unfairly weakened. When courts wrongly deny evidence, it can lead to unjust outcomes, meaning the wrong side might win, not because they were right, but because crucial proof was kept out.

The Record Is Everything

In law, having the truth on your side isn't enough, you have to prove it. A strong record made up of testimony, documents, expert opinions, and visual aids is what makes or breaks a case. If a lawyer doesn't build a good record, their case may fall apart. And if a judge unfairly stops evidence from being included, it can lead to unfair results.

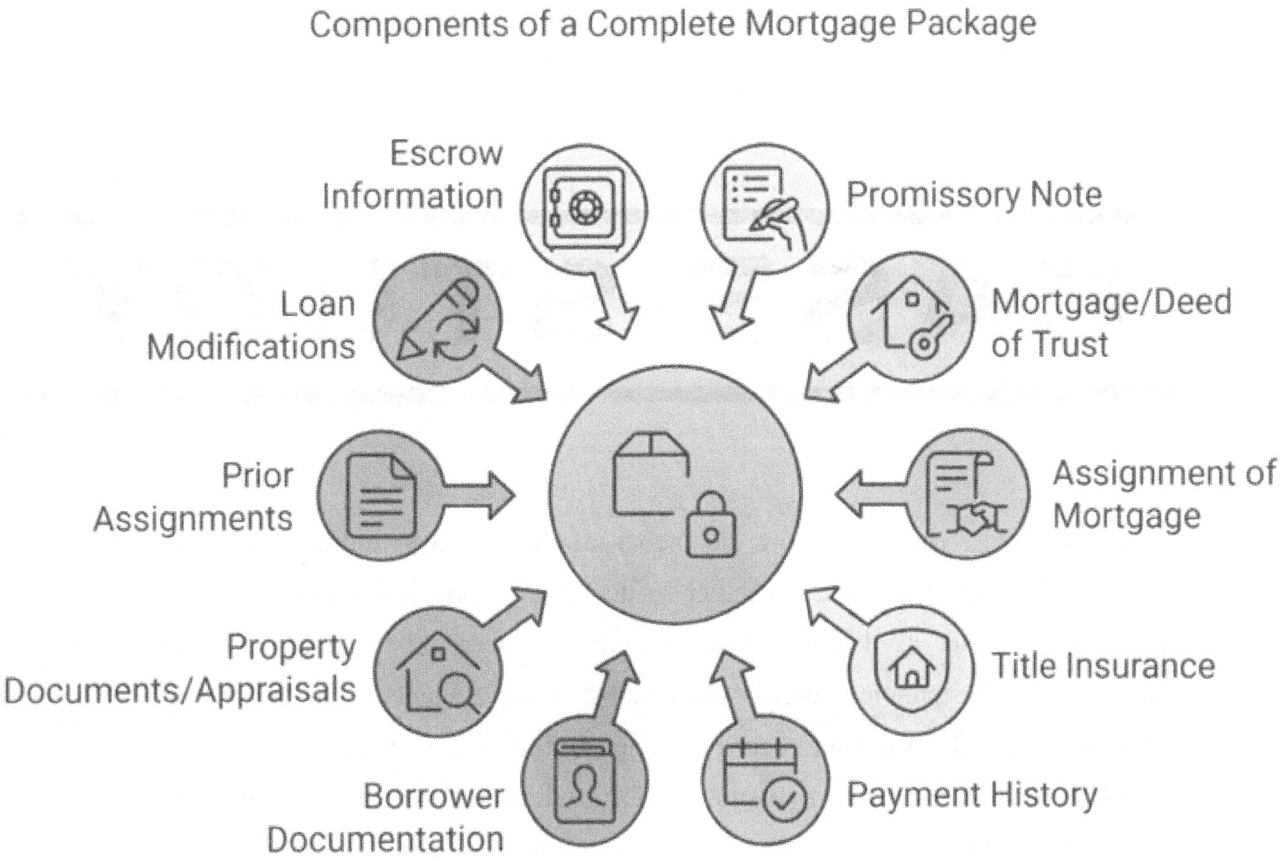
Components of a Complete Mortgage Package
Escrow Information
Promissory Note
Loan Modifications
Mortgage/Deed of Trust
Prior Assignments
Assignment of Mortgage
Property Documents/Appraisals
Title Insurance
Borrower Documentation
Payment History

CASE STUDY

Discovery allows you to support the theory of the case by finding evidence, While, evidence, refers to any material, whether written, oral, or physical, that is used to establish the truth of a fact in dispute. However, throughout my bankruptcy proceedings, I encountered a systematic pattern where substantive evidence was either considered "frivolous," excluded from the record or, when admitted, was inappropriately discounted or minimized. This pattern of dismissal occurred even though I presented extensive, credible documentation from authoritative sources, including:

Evidence of Mixed-Use Property Status

I provided definitive documentation proving the mixed-use nature of my properties, directly contradicting the creditors' claims that they were purely commercial:

- Deeds for both 367-371 Main Street and 511 Main Street in Laurel, Maryland
- Modification agreements for 367-371 Main Street and 511 Main Street
- Multiple City of Laurel Residential Renter's Licenses for multiple apartment units
- Six separate residential lease agreements for apartments within these properties
- Affidavits from two assistants confirming the residential usage
- Letters to Tenants Enforcing Commercial Deed by Hofmeister, Breza & Leavers

Proof of Loan Modifications and Payment History

I submitted conclusive evidence of loan modifications and payment compliance:

- Confirmation Order in my Bankruptcy Case
- Formal modifications for both properties (despite date errors)
- Letter from the Defendant's own Property Management Company
- Multiple emails between my attorney and the creditors' attorneys documenting the 5-year bankruptcy plan
- Comprehensive payment histories for both properties
- Letters to the defendant reflecting payments made

Expert Analysis and Regulatory Documentation

I presented expert analysis and regulatory evidence supporting my position:

- Affidavit and resume from a securitization expert serving as a fact witness
- Federal Reserve Board, FDIC, NCUA, and OCC interagency guidance on Troubled Debt Restructurings

- Written Agreement between Patapsco Bank, Federal Reserve Bank of Richmond, and Maryland Commissioner of Financial Regulation
- Task Force Report addressing relevant financial regulations

Chain of Title and Ownership Documentation

I provided extensive documentation showing problematic transfers and ownership issues:

- HUD-1 from refinance showing escrows
- Escrow statements and transfer documentation
- Deed of Appointment by Capital One Bank
- Certification of Ownership by Capital One Bank
- Order of Injunction
- Discounted Payoff reflecting Waterfall Victoria Master Fund LTD-NY
- Allonge and assignments showing potentially improper transfers
- List of Subsidiaries
- SEC filings related to the creditors
- 1098 Mortgage Interest Statement Showing Lehman Brothers

Despite the comprehensiveness, relevance, and authoritative nature of this evidence, much of it coming directly from the creditors themselves or from government regulatory bodies, the court deemed it "frivolous" and of "no benefit" to my case against the creditors. This dismissal of substantial documentary evidence raises significant questions about the fairness of the proceedings and suggests a prejudicial approach to evaluating my submissions compared to those of the institutional creditors.

This systematic devaluation of legitimate evidence effectively prevented me from establishing critical facts regarding the mixed-use nature of the properties, the existence of valid loan modifications, payment histories, and potential irregularities in the chain of title and ownership of my mortgage debt.

EVIDENCE

- Deed for 367-371 Main Street, Laurel, Maryland 20707
- City of Laurel Residential Renter's License for 369 Main Street, Two Units
- City of Laurel Residential Renter's License for 369 Main Street, Two Units
- Residential Lease – Apt. 1
- Residential Lease – Apt. 2
- Deed for 511 Main Street, Laurel, Maryland 20707
- City of Laurel/ Residential Renter's License for Apt. B
- City of Laurel/ Residential Renter's License for Apt. C
- City of Laurel/ Residential Renter's License for Apt. D
- Residential Lease – Apt. B
- Residential Lease – Apt. C
- Residential Lease – Apt. D
- Affidavit from Kecia L. Herrera – Assistant to Plaintiff
- Affidavit from Charles Phil Victor – Assistant to Plaintiff
- Confirmation Order in Bankruptcy Case
- Modification for 511 Main Street – Date is an Error
- Modification for 367 Main Street – Date is an Error
- Letter from Defendant's Property Management Company
- Email reflecting 5 Year Bankruptcy Plan – Plaintiff's Attorney to Defendant's Attorney
- Email by Plaintiff's Attorney agreement for 4 + 1
- Email by Plaintiff and Defendant's Attorney
- Email by Plaintiff and Defendant's Attorney

- Email by Plaintiff and Defendant's Attorney
- Email by Plaintiff and Defendant's Attorney
- Email by Plaintiff and Defendant's Attorney
- Pay Histories

a. 367 Main Street

b. 511 Main Street

- Letters from Plaintiff to Defendant Reflecting Payments
- Affidavit by Securitization Expert – Fact Witness
- Resume for Securitization Expert
- Board of Governors of the Federal Reserve System, Federal Deposit Insurance Corporation, National Credit Union Administration, and the Office of the Comptroller of the Currency issued Interagency supervisory guidance addressing issues related to Troubled Debt Restructurings ("TDRS").
- Written Agreement with The Patapsco Bank, Federal Reserve Bank of Richmond and the Maryland Commissioner of Financial Regulation (the "Commissioner" Task Force Report
- Hud-1 from Refinance showing escrows
- Escrow Impound from Closing
- Escrow Statement from Lehman Brothers
- Transfer to Countrywide
- Deed of Appointment by Capital One Bank
- Certification of Ownership by Capital One Bank
- Order of Injunction
- Enter of Appearance by Capital One Bank
- Discounted Payoff reflecting Waterfall Victoria Master Fund LTD-NY
- Email reflecting Documents Attached
- Allonge
- Assignment of Deed of Trust

- Assignment of Leases
- Copy of Note
- Email Purchaser of Note
- Amended Proof of Claim 09-12469
- Order Granting Receivership
- Proof of Claim 14-25022
- CV For Expert Witness, Paula Rush
- Affidavit by Paula Rush
- S/11 A Filing with SEC Dated January 6, 2015
- Letters to Tenants Enforcing Commercial Deed by Hofmeister, Breza & Leavers

Chapter Nineteen

STANDING

IMPORTANT: The concept of "standing" assist with the identification of what creditor may or may not have the right to enforce a claim, potentially eliminating significant liabilities from their bankruptcy proceedings.

WHAT IS THIS THING called "standing"? Imagine you're at a boxing match. The referee steps into the ring, ready to start the fight, but before the bell rings, a random guy in the audience jumps in, throws on some gloves, and starts swinging. The referee stops everything. "Wait a minute," he says. "Who are you? Are you even supposed to be here?" That's what the courts should do when they check for standing, they make sure the right people are in the legal fight before it begins.

Standing: The Legal Right to Be in the Fight

Standing is the legal principle that determines who has the right to be in court arguing over a dispute. You can't just walk in and start demanding things unless you can prove you belong there. Just like a boxing match needs real contenders, a court case needs real parties with actual stakes in the outcome. To have standing, a party must show three key things:

1. Is there an injury-in-fact? You must have suffered a real, concrete injury. You can't be upset on someone else's behalf. If you weren't punched, you don't get to step into the ring.

2. Is the person or entity responsible for causing you harm? The harm you suffered must have been caused by the party you're suing. If you get knocked down by a stray punch from the crowd, but you're trying to sue the boxer in the ring, the referee (court) will throw you out.

3. Can the court make you whole? The court must be able to provide a remedy that fixes your harm. If the fight's already over and the trophy's been handed out, the referee can't change the past.

The Problem with Missing Proof

Now, let's bring this back to our distressed note purchaser. Imagine someone claims they should be in the ring fighting over a championship belt (a property), but they never actually showed their boxing license (the note), proper registration (assignments), or proof they belong in the match (allonges). The referee isn't going to let them step into the fight just because they say they should be there. They need to prove it.

Similarly, in bankruptcy court, a party must prove they have the legal right to be there before the judge lets them fight over assets. If they can't produce the note, the assignments, and the allonges, they might as well be the guy jumping into the ring from the crowd, hoping no one notices they don't belong there.

No Standing? No Fight.

Courts, like referees, won't waste time on people who shouldn't be in the ring. If a party can't prove they have the legal right to fight over a property, they don't belong in court at all. Before we even examine the evidence, we have to ask, does this party have standing, or are they just a spectator trying to sneak into the match?

WHEN DOES A MORTGAGE LENDER HAVE STANDING?

For a mortgage company/lender/credit to have the ability to enforce a mortgage note, a financial institution must meet several critical legal and procedural requirements:

1. Proper Chain of Title

- Must demonstrate a complete and unbroken chain of ownership from the original lender to the current claim holder
- Each transfer must be documented with proper legal assignments
- All transfers must be valid and properly executed

2. Physical Note Requirements

- Must possess the ORIGINAL promissory note
- The note must be properly endorsed or assigned
- Endorsements must be:
    - Completed at the time of transfer
    - Signed by an authorized representative
    - Physically attached to the original note (via an allonge)

3. Documentation Integrity

- All assignment documents must be:
    - Dated correctly
    - Signed by authorized parties
    - Reflecting actual ownership at the time of transfer
    - Verifiable through official records

4. Legal Compliance

- Must comply with:
    - Uniform Commercial Code (UCC) Section 3-412

  - State-specific mortgage transfer laws
  - Securitization trust formation requirements
  - SEC reporting regulations for securitized trusts

5. Proof of Ownership

- Must provide:
  - Original note with complete endorsement chain
  - All assignment documents
  - Proof of trust formation (for securitized notes)
  - Verified corporate records showing legitimate transfer

6. Timing and Authenticity

- Transfers must occur while all entities in the chain are legally active
- Cannot transfer notes from defunct or dissolved entities
- Cannot backdate assignments
- Must have contemporaneous documentation at each transfer point

CRITICAL DISQUALIFYING FACTORS

A mortgage company LACKS standing if:

- The original note is lost
- Endorsements are missing
- Transfers occurred after an entity was dissolved
- Assignments are backdated
- No certified copy of the original note exists
- The securitization trust does not exist or has been liquidated

The fundamental legal principle is that you cannot transfer or enforce a debt instrument that you do not legally own. Each link in the ownership chain must be legitimate, provable, and contemporaneously documented.

Document Package

Purchase Agreement

Entity Documentation

Title Verification

Bill of Sale

Esoppel Certificate

UCC Financing Statement

CASE STUDY

In that moment, I felt the ground shift beneath me. The judge, with a casual dismissiveness that still haunts me, turned to me and essentially declared that the mere presence of an attorney on a phone line was sufficient to validate an entire mortgage claim.

"Ms. Smith-Scott," the judge said, his tone suggesting this was the most obvious thing in the world, "the creditor has standing because they have legal representation present."

I was stunned. Speechless.

An attorney's phone connection was now equivalent to proof of ownership. This defied every principle of legal logic I understood. It reduced the complex requirements of mortgage note enforcement to a bureaucratic checkbox; a mere technological connection somehow magically transformed a potentially fraudulent claim into a legitimate one.

THIS WASN'T JUSTICE!

The evidence I had meticulously gathered, the expert witness reports, the missing documentation, the dissolved trust, the backdated assignments, all of it seemed to evaporate in that moment. Years of financial struggle, mountains of documentation proving systemic fraud, reduced to a telephonic appearance.

The court had just created a dangerous precedent: legal standing could be manufactured through the simple act of hiring an attorney and connecting to a courtroom phone line.

It was a moment that exposed the profound vulnerability of property owners against institutional manipulation. The system wasn't just broken, it was rigged.

The Nonexistent Trust

The Trustee nor the Court could remove the glaring problem with the issue of standing with the U. S. Bank, NA., as Indenture Trustees for Waterfall Victoria Mortgage Trust 2011-SBC3. My expert witness, Paula Rush, conducted an exhaustive investigation that revealed that Waterfall Victoria Mortgage Trust 2011-SBC3 was essentially a phantom entity. She discovered:

1. The trust did not exist on US Bank's investor reporting site
2. No SEC filings could be found for this trust
3. Sutherland Asset Management Corporation reported the trust was liquidated in 2011

Broken Chain of Title

The chain of ownership was nothing short of legal fabrication:

- The original note passed through multiple hands: Greenpoint Mortgage, Lehman Brothers, Countrywide

- Critical endorsements were missing, especially from Lehman Brothers
- Allonges (transfer documents) were not physically attached to the original note
- Assignments appeared to be backdated

Documentation Fraud

The documents presented were riddled with critical issues:

- No certified copy of the original note was ever produced
- Assignments lacked proper endorsements
- The trust claimed ownership two years after it was reportedly dissolved
- No evidence existed that Greenpoint owned the loan when making assignments

Legal Violations

The Uniform Commercial Code is crystal clear: a creditor must possess the properly negotiated original promissory note to enforce collection. In my case, every single requirement was violated.

The Court's Flawed Reasoning

The court's decision hinged on the most tenuous of legal threads, the mere presence of an attorney on a phone call. This defies every principle of legal standing:

- Presence of counsel does not equate to ownership of a debt
- An attorney cannot manufacture standing where no legal right exists
- The fundamental requirement of proving actual ownership was completely ignored

Systemic Corruption

What happened to me was not an isolated incident. It represents a systemic problem in mortgage securitization where:

- Financial institutions create complex, opaque structures
- Courts often default to protecting institutional interests
- Property owners are left vulnerable to legal manipulation

The most disturbing aspect is how easily the court dismissed concrete evidence of fraud. An attorney on a telephone call was somehow deemed more credible than:

- Extensive expert testimony
- Lack of verifiable documentation
- Clear violations of commercial law

The Broader Implications

This was never just about my property. It was about the fundamental integrity of our legal system. When courts can ignore clear evidence of fraudulent documentation, they undermine the very principles of justice and property rights.

My fight became about more than a mortgage. It became a stand against a system that prioritizes institutional racism and profit over legal truth.

The Waterfall Victoria Mortgage Trust 2011-SBC3 had no more right to my property than a fictional character. Yet, through a combination of legal maneuvering and judicial indifference, they succeeded in taking everything I had worked for.

This is not just my story. It is a warning.

Chapter Twenty

STANDING AND THE SECURITIES AND EXCHANGE COMMISSION

IMPORTANT: Evidence can be obtained by various regulatory agencies, including the U. S. Securities and Exchange Commission, to determine the true owner of a mortgage debt. By following the paper trail through SEC filings and financial records, debtors can challenge questionable claims, protect their assets, and prevent fraudulent or erroneous creditors from improperly asserting rights over their property.

THE CENTRAL QUESTION: WHAT IS TRUE?

DETERMINING THE RIGHTFUL OWNER of a debt obligation is crucial in any legal dispute, particularly in bankruptcy proceedings where standing plays a key role. Courts rely on verifiable evidence to determine whether an entity has a legitimate claim. In cases involving securitized mortgages, ownership often becomes obscured as loans are transferred multiple times between financial entities, trusts, and third-party investors. This makes it imperative to trace the paper trail to establish whether a claimant has the legal right to enforce a mortgage.

The Role of Evidence in Ownership Disputes

Evidence serves as the foundation for establishing the existence of a claim, validating statements, or disproving alleged facts. In mortgage and financial disputes, where complex corporate structures often conceal ownership, reviewing official financial records and government filings is essential. Many financial institutions operate under layers of parent companies and subsidiaries, requiring meticulous investigation to uncover the true holder of a debt.

Securities and Exchange Commission Filings: A Critical Verification Tool

SEC filings constitute a vital yet often overlooked resource in mortgage ownership disputes. Unlike many other documents in the financial industry, SEC filings are subject to stringent legal requirements, with many being certified as true under penalty of law. This certification adds to a critical layer of reliability that distinguishes these documents from potentially self-serving statements made in court proceedings.

The Securitization Process of Mortgage Trusts

Mortgage securitization typically follows a complex path that obscures ultimate ownership:

1. **Loan Origination**: The process begins when a borrower obtains a mortgage from an originating lender.
2. **Pooling**: Multiple loans are bundled together into a pool by a sponsor or seller, usually a large financial institution.
3. **Transfer to Depositor**: These loan pools are sold to a special-purpose entity called a depositor, creating a legal separation from the originator's assets.
4. **Trust Formation**: The depositor transfers the loans to a trust, typically structured as a Real Estate Mortgage Investment Conduit (REMIC) for tax advantages.
5. **Securities Issuance**: The trust issues mortgage-backed securities (MBS) that represent fractional ownership interests in the pooled loans.
6. **Sale to Investors**: These securities are sold to various investors, who receive payments derived from the underlying mortgage payments.
7. **Servicing Arrangement**: A designated servicer collects payments from borrowers, handles administrative tasks, and manages defaults, often creating confusion about who actually owns the debt.

This complex chain of transactions creates multiple opportunities for documentation failures, making SEC filings crucial for verification.

Essential SEC Documents for Verifying Mortgage Ownership

Thorough investigation of mortgage ownership claims requires examination of these SEC documents:

1. **Form 8-K Current Reports** - These disclose material events like acquisitions, bankruptcies, or significant asset transfers. When a trust acquires mortgage pools, these transactions often trigger 8-K filings that reveal the actual chain of ownership.

2. **Form 10-K Annual Reports** - These comprehensive reports often contain detailed information about a company's mortgage-backed securities, including specific trust identifications and asset compositions that may contradict claims made in court.

3. **Prospectus and Prospectus Supplements** - These documents precisely define which loans are included in specific trusts, detailing the exact mortgage pools and their characteristics.

4. **Trust Formation Documents** - These specify cut-off dates for including mortgages in a trust, which is crucial because many claimed transfers violate these established deadlines.

The certified true nature of these documents cannot be overstated. SEC filings are presented under penalty of perjury by corporate officers who face severe consequences, including criminal liability, for material misrepresentations.

Systematically cross-referencing SEC filings against court claims frequently reveal contradictions. Cases often emerge where an entity claims to own a mortgage in bankruptcy court while SEC filings conclusively demonstrate the loan belongs to an entirely different trust or has been written off years earlier.

These contradictions only become apparent when conducting thorough SEC research - a step many attorneys unfortunately skip, leading to incorrect determinations of standing and ultimately unjust outcomes for debtors facing foreclosure or bankruptcy.

CASE STUDY

In my case, U.S. Bank, as National Association, Indenture Trustee for Waterfall Victoria Mortgage Trust 2011 SBC3, appeared in my bankruptcy case, claiming to hold the mortgage debt tied to my property. This development followed repeated calls and emails from John H. Davenport, who stated that his company, AMS Commercial Real Estate, located at 210 Barton Springs Road, Suite 550, Austin, TX 78704, was the rightful owner of the mortgage note. Before this, Capital One Bank had asserted its own claim to enforce the debt during my confirmation hearing. The origins of the debt trace back to GreenPoint Mortgage, yet 1098 tax forms were issued under Lehman Brothers, raising significant questions about the true ownership of the loan.

Given the conflicting claims regarding my mortgage, I turned to the United States Securities and Exchange Commission (SEC) filings to examine the financial and legal standing of the entities involved. While some trusts are too small to require formal SEC registration, many larger trusts are legally obligated to disclose financial transactions, subsidiaries, and ownership structures. This meant that an in-depth review of SEC records could provide critical insights into the legitimacy of U.S. Bank's claims.

Sutherland Asset Management and the S-11/A Filing

Through my research, I discovered that Sutherland Asset Management submitted an S-11/A filing with the SEC on January 6, 2015. This filing was particularly significant because it was required due to structural changes within the company. In order to comply with SEC regulations, Sutherland Asset Management had to submit an audited, sworn statement listing its subsidiaries, financial holdings, and any business interests related to mortgage-backed securities. Within this filing, Waterfall Victoria Mortgage Trust 2011 SBC3 was explicitly identified as an entity owned by Sutherland Asset Management.

Key Findings That Contradict Ownership Claims

The SEC filing provided verifiable financial and legal information that directly contradicted the claim that Waterfall Victoria Mortgage Trust 2011 SBC3 was an active entity with the legal standing to enforce my mortgage. The most alarming inconsistencies include:

- Subsidiary Status: The S-11/A filing submitted by Sutherland Asset Management explicitly listed Waterfall Victoria Mortgage Trust 2011 SBC3 as a subsidiary, confirming that it was under the control of another financial entity rather than operating independently.

- Financial Status: Page 317 of 418 in the S-11/A filing revealed that as of September 30, 2014, Waterfall Victoria Mortgage Trust 2011 SBC3 reported:

- A Current Principal Value of $0.00
- A Weighted Average Interest Rate of 0%

These figures suggest that the trust had no remaining assets and was effectively inactive, making it questionable how it could still claim to hold an interest in my mortgage.

- Grantor Trust Status: Page 386 of 419 confirmed that Waterfall Victoria Mortgage Trust 2011 SBC3 was a grantor trust that had been completed in 2011. This means that its purpose had been fulfilled, and it should have ceased holding any assets or issuing claims beyond that date.

- Lack of Assets in Maryland: Page 386 of 416, under Note 8, provided a detailed list of real estate acquired through loan settlements. As of December 31, 2013, Waterfall Victoria Mortgage Trust 2011 SBC3 had not acquired any mortgage loans in the state of Maryland.

Based on these official, audited, and SEC-certified findings, I was left with three major questions:

1. If Waterfall Victoria Mortgage Trust 2011 SBC3 was a grantor trust that closed in 2011, long before my bankruptcy case, how can it claim to be the active holder of my mortgage debt?

2. If the trust had a reported value of $0.00 and an interest rate of 0%, what financial basis exists for asserting ownership over my mortgage?

3. If Waterfall Victoria Mortgage Trust 2011 SBC3 never acquired mortgage loans in Maryland, how can it appear before the Maryland court and claim to hold my mortgage debt?

The Impact on U.S. Bank's Standing

These inconsistencies raised serious doubts about the legitimacy of U.S. Bank's claim in my bankruptcy case. The very foundation of legal standing requires a claimant to prove actual ownership and an enforceable interest in the debt. However, if Waterfall Victoria Mortgage Trust 2011 SBC3 had no reported assets, no record of holding mortgage loans in Maryland, and was legally closed in 2011, how could it legally claim rights over my property?

Courts rely on documented proof, not mere assertions, when determining who has the right to enforce a debt. In this case, U.S. Bank's appearance as trustee for an inactive and asset-less trust raises significant concerns about the validity of their claim. These questions demanded close scrutiny, and the answers lay within the very financial documents filed with the SEC. Following the paper trail revealed the truth: U.S. Bank's claim had no documented support.

By highlighting these inconsistencies, I was able to challenge their standing, demonstrating that without proper evidence of ownership, an entity cannot enforce a debt or claim rights over a mortgage. This case exemplifies why it is critical to investigate financial institutions thoroughly, as corporate structures and financial maneuvering often serve to obscure the truth behind debt ownership claims.

Chapter Twenty-One

EVIDENCE AND S-11/A FILING SHOWING NO OWNERSHIP

IMPORTANT: This technical information provides the reader with specific SEC documents to request which may reveal discrepancies between claimed ownership of debt and legal reality, potentially invalidating major claims. SEC filings may be a powerful tool in determining whether a creditor has the legal right to enforce a mortgage debt because it can contain sworn financial disclosures, which may lead to a legal challenge of questionable claims and ensure that only legitimate creditors are allowed to participate in their bankruptcy case.

EVIDENCE REFERS TO THE documentation, testimony, and records presented to the court to support or challenge a claim. Evidence is critical in determining the validity of debts, the ownership of assets, and the standing of parties involved. Courts rely on evidence to ensure that only legitimate claims are enforced, and that the bankruptcy process is fair and transparent. In cases where a creditor's standing is questioned, evidence such as SEC filings, mortgage assignments, and financial disclosures may reveal that the entity attempting to collect does not have a legitimate claim.

Filings made in the United States Securities and Exchange Commission can serve as legitimate evidence in bankruptcy courts which relies upon publicly filed financial disclosures to determine a company's assets, liabilities, corporate structure, and the legitimacy of claims made by creditors or debtors. Since SEC filings are sworn statements submitted under penalty of perjury, they are considered reliable and can be used to support or challenge claims in bankruptcy proceedings.

How SEC Filings Are Used as Evidence in Bankruptcy Court

One of the primary ways SEC filings become relevant in bankruptcy cases is when creditors or debtors dispute ownership of financial instruments, loans, or corporate assets. If a company or trust claims to own a mortgage, loan, or other financial asset, but an SEC filing contradicts that claim, the court may question the standing of the claimant. For example, if an entity files a Proof of Claim in a bankruptcy case but its name does not appear in an S-11/A or other SEC disclosure showing ownership of the debt, the debtor may argue that the creditor lacks the legal right to collect.

SEC filings also serve as evidence of corporate relationships and financial transactions. In many cases, especially those involving mortgage-backed securities, ownership of loans is transferred between multiple entities. When an SEC filing, such as an S-11/A, 10-K, or 8-K, lists a trust or investment firm as the owner of a debt portfolio, it can confirm whether the entity filing a claim in bankruptcy court is actually the rightful holder of the debt.

Conversely, if an SEC filing states that a trust was dissolved, had no assets, or did not acquire certain loans, this can undermine a creditor's claim in bankruptcy court.

Examples of SEC Filings and Lawsuits

First, a creditor's standing can be challenged. Suppose a bank files a claim in bankruptcy court asserting that it owns a mortgage debt. However, an SEC filing from a publicly traded REIT or investment firm shows that the debt was securitized and sold to another entity. The debtor can introduce the SEC filing as evidence that the bank does not have standing to enforce the debt because it was transferred elsewhere.

Second, it can prove fraudulent transfers or misrepresentations, if a debtor argues that a loan was improperly assigned or transferred without proper documentation, an SEC filing may reveal that the alleged transfer never occurred or was not recorded properly. This could be used to challenge the validity of the assignment and question whether the claimant owns the debt.

Third, it establishes a Trust's Ownership Structure which are mortgage-backed securities owned by real estate investment trusts (REITs) or securitization trusts, which must report their holdings to the SEC. If a creditor claims to own a loan but does not appear in SEC filings listing the trust's actual assets, this can be strong evidence that the creditor is not the rightful owner.

Fourth, it demonstrates a Company's Financial Condition, if a debtor files for bankruptcy but an SEC filing (such as a 10-Q or 10-K) shows that the company has undisclosed assets or recent financial activity inconsistent with insolvency, this can be used to challenge the debtor's need for bankruptcy protection or to argue for different treatment of creditors.

Limitations and Challenges

While SEC filings are strong evidence, they are not always conclusive proof of ownership or debt obligations. In some cases, entities involved in securitizations do not disclose every individual asset in their filings, so just because a loan is not specifically listed does not necessarily mean it was never acquired. Additionally, some filings contain forward-looking statements or estimates that may not reflect final ownership records.

Despite these limitations, SEC filings remain valuable tools in bankruptcy litigation. They provide a third-party, legally mandated record of corporate transactions, ownership structures, and financial conditions, making them persuasive evidence in disputes over standing, fraudulent conveyances, or misrepresented debt claims.

An S-11/A filing is an amended version of Form S-11, which is a registration statement that must be submitted to the United States Securities and Exchange Commission (SEC) by companies primarily engaged in real estate investment, real estate trusts (REITs), or mortgage-backed securities issuers. This type of filing is required when a real estate company wants to offer securities to the public, such as stocks or bonds, under the Securities Act of 1933.

The purpose of an S-11/A filing is to update or revise the information initially provided in the original Form S-11. Amendments to this filing may be necessary for a variety of reasons, including changes in financial conditions, structural modifications within the company, updated risk factors, or additional disclosures required by the SEC. Companies engaged in real estate investments and securities must maintain transparency with investors, and the SEC mandates these filings to ensure that the public has access to accurate and current financial information before making investment decisions.

A company submitting an S-11/A filing must disclose detailed information about its operations, financial standing, management structure, business strategies, and intended use of funds raised from investors. This filing serves as a critical tool for investor protection by allowing potential shareholders to review important data regarding the company's real estate holdings, revenue streams, liabilities, and associated risks. If there are significant changes between the original S-11 filing and the S-11/A amendment, the company must clearly outline those updates to maintain compliance with federal securities laws.

The significance of an S-11/A filing extends beyond regulatory compliance. Investors and financial analysts often scrutinize these filings to assess whether a company's financial standing remains stable or if new risks have emerged that could impact the viability of its real estate investments. In some cases, an amended filing may indicate internal restructuring, new acquisitions, asset liquidations, or changes in debt obligations, all of which can influence an investor's decision to buy, hold, or sell securities associated with the company.

For example, if Sutherland Asset Management files a S-11/A, it is updating investors and regulatory bodies about a shift in its business structure, a new acquisition, or a change in the valuation of its real estate holdings. If the filing references entities such as Waterfall Victoria Mortgage Trust 2011-SBC3, this inclusion would confirm that the trust is either owned, controlled, or financially linked to Sutherland Asset Management. This information is highly relevant in legal and financial disputes, particularly when determining which entity holds actual ownership of mortgage-backed securities or real estate assets.

In situations where mortgage-backed securities are being contested, an S-11/A filing can provide key evidence regarding the rightful ownership of a debt instrument. For example, if a company claims to own a mortgage note but fails to appear in an S-11/A filing submitted by a parent company, this omission could suggest that the entity lacks proper legal standing to enforce the debt. Investors, attorneys, and financial analysts frequently use these filings as evidentiary support in cases involving loan ownership disputes, fraudulent conveyances, and questionable debt transfers.

Ultimately, an S-11/A filing is an essential component of financial transparency in the real estate sector. It ensures that investors receive accurate and timely information about a company's financial health, while also serving as a regulatory safeguard against misleading or incomplete disclosures. Any company seeking to raise capital through publicly traded real estate securities must adhere to the stringent reporting requirements established by the SEC, and failure to do so can lead to regulatory penalties, loss of investor confidence, and legal challenges regarding ownership claims.

CASE STUDY

In my bankruptcy case, I encountered a troubling situation where highly credible evidence, specifically audited financial statements filed with the Securities and Exchange Commission (SEC), was disregarded by both the Trustee and the Bankruptcy Court. This evidence directly contradicted claims made by a purported creditor.

Waterfall Victoria Mortgage Trust-2011 SBC3, a subsidiary of Sutherland Asset Management Corporation, was represented by U.S. Bank, NA as Indenture Trustee in my bankruptcy proceedings. This entity made several claims regarding a mortgage on my property at 10 Stanley Drive, including filing Proof of Claim #6 asserting I owed $1,912,000.

However, Sutherland Asset Management Corporation's own Pre-Effective Amendment to Registration Statement (S/11-A) filed with the SEC on January 6, 2015, directly contradicted these claims in multiple material ways:

1. The SEC filing stated on page 385/419 that as of December 31, 2013, the company held 27 properties in its consolidated taxable REIT subsidiary—yet none were in Maryland, contradicting their claim to hold a mortgage on my Maryland property.

2. The filing confirmed on page 386/419 that "Waterfall Victoria Mortgage Trust 2011-SBC3 is a grantor trust securitization completed by the Company in 2011." This timeline makes it impossible for them to have received valid assignments in 2012 and 2013, as they claimed in court.

3. Most critically, the filing explicitly stated on page 317/419 that "as of September 30, 2014, the current principal balance is zero and the weighted average interest rate is zero." This directly contradicts their $1,912,000 claim in my bankruptcy case.

4. The SEC filing acknowledged at line 6,561 that "In the event of the bankruptcy of a mortgage loan borrower, the mortgage loan to such borrower will be deemed to be secured only to the extent of the value of the underlying collateral at the time of bankruptcy," yet their Proof of Claim #6 ignored this principle.

5. The document confirmed at multiple points (lines 38,109 and 38,643) that this securitization was completed in 2011, making any 2013 assignments logically impossible.

6. When I requested the securitization agreement documents during discovery, the creditor obtained a protective order and motion to quash discovery, preventing examination of documents that would have clarified these contradictions.

The Bankruptcy Court and Trustee should have given substantial weight to these SEC filings, as they represent certified, audited statements made under penalty of perjury to federal regulators. These are not merely allegations or theories, but official corporate disclosures with serious legal implications for false reporting.

By disregarding these official SEC filings, the Bankruptcy Court effectively privileged unsubstantiated claims by the purported creditor over federally filed, audited financial statements. This represents a serious failure in the truth-finding function of the bankruptcy process and raises significant questions about whether my case received proper judicial consideration of all relevant evidence.

The contradiction between their zero-balance report to the SEC and their $1.9 million claim in bankruptcy court should, at minimum, have triggered additional scrutiny and discovery rather than being summarily dismissed.

Chapter Twenty-Two

STANDING AND BACKDATED FINANCIAL INSTRUMENTS

IMPORTANT: Backdated financial documents and missing loan transfer records can raise serious legal questions about a creditor's right to enforce a debt. By identifying discrepancies in assignment dates and ownership claims, a filer can challenge the legitimacy of a creditor's standing in court, potentially preventing improper debt collection or foreclosure actions.

AN ILLUSION EXISTS IN mortgage documentation that often goes unnoticed by most homeowners. Consider a typical mortgage title that appears straightforward at first glance: "U. S. Bank, NA, as Indenture Trustee for Waterfall Victoria Mortgage Trust – 2011, SBC3."

This simple title reveals a nuanced legal structure. It's not a single entity as many might assume, but rather a complex arrangement involving multiple parties. The title explicitly identifies two distinct elements:

1. The Agent/Representative: U. S. Bank, NA, serving as the Indenture Trustee
2. The Underlying Entity: Waterfall Victoria Mortgage Trust – 2011, SBC3

What appears to be a straightforward property ownership designation is a legal mechanism where a bank acts in a fiduciary capacity, representing the interests of a specific mortgage trust. This subtle distinction can have significant implications for understanding the true nature of mortgage ownership and administration.

INDENTURE TRUSTEE

An indenture trustee typically acts as a legal representative for bondholders or note investors in a securitized trust. In this specific case, U.S. Bank was purportedly acting as the trustee for the Waterfall Victoria Mortgage Trust 2011-SBC3.

Claimed Responsibilities:

- Manage the trust's assets
- Represent the interests of investors
- Collect and distribute payments
- Enforce legal rights related to the mortgage notes, including hiring legal representatives

An indenture trustee is like a professional financial manager that banks provide to help organize and oversee complicated financial arrangements, particularly for things like mortgage-backed securities. The bank should have serious financial credentials, for example, national or state-chartered, with tons of resources and a proven track record.

While it might sound complicated, being an indenture trustee is just a specialized banking service. The bank is selling its expertise in managing complex financial arrangements, and companies pay good money for that expertise. It's not a public service or a charitable act, but a professional business offering that requires incredible attention to detail, technological sophistication, and deep understanding of financial regulations.

MORTGAGE TRUST

Imagine you're playing a complicated game of financial musical chairs. That's basically what mortgage trusts and funds are all about!

Let's break it down in a way that makes sense. When someone wants to buy a house, they usually don't have all the money upfront. So, they go to a bank and get a mortgage, basically a loan that lets them buy the house and pay it back over time.

Now, here's where things get interesting. Banks don't just want to sit on these loans. They want to make more money and reduce their risk. So, they created this clever system called mortgage trust.

Think of a mortgage trust like a big piggy bank where banks collect lots of different home loans. Instead of keeping all these loans to themselves, they package them up and sell pieces of these loans to investors. It's kind of like how you might trade baseball cards, but with home loans.

A mortgage fund is similar but imagine it more like an investment club. People pool their money together, and then they use that money to buy different types of home loans or invest in things related to home loans.

The crazy part? These financial tools are supposed to help make home buying easier and spread out the risk. But sometimes, they can be used in tricky ways that aren't really fair.

In the case we've been looking at, the Waterfall Victoria Mortgage Trust looked like a legitimate financial vehicle. But when people started digging deeper, they discovered it was more like a magic trick. The trust claimed to own mortgage loans, but when investigators looked closely, they found out the trust didn't really exist!

It's as if you claimed to own a super cool bike, but when someone asked to see it, you couldn't show them the bike or prove you ever bought it in the first place. These financial instruments are supposed to help the economy by:

- Letting banks free up money to make more loans
- Giving investors a way to invest in real estate without buying a whole house
- Spreading out financial risk

But they can also be dangerous. Some companies try to use these complicated financial structures to trick people or hide what they're really doing.

THE ILLEGALITY OF BACKDATED MORTGAGE DOCUMENTS

The illegality of backdating mortgage documents stems from fundamental principles of contract law, fraud prevention, and the integrity of financial transactions. Courts have consistently held that backdating documents can constitute several serious legal violations, with profound implications for both civil and potential criminal proceedings.

In the landmark case of In re Taylor (U.S. Bankruptcy Court, Southern District of New York, 2012), the court definitively established that backdating mortgage documents represents a form of fraudulent misrepresentation. The court emphasized that such actions intentionally obscure the true timeline of financial agreements, potentially misleading borrowers, investors, and judicial systems about the actual sequence of events.

The legal framework condemning backdating is rooted in multiple statutes and judicial precedents. The Sarbanes-Landmark Act of 2002 specifically criminalizes the manipulation of financial records, with severe penalties for intentional document falsification. Moreover, the Truth in Lending Act (TILA) and the Real Estate Settlement Procedures Act (RESPA) mandate complete transparency in mortgage documentation, making backdating a direct violation of federal consumer protection laws.

In Countrywide Financial Corporation Securities Litigation (Central District of California, 2010), the court elaborated on how backdating constitutes a material misrepresentation. The ruling explained that such actions can invalidate the entire mortgage instrument, potentially leaving the lender without legal recourse to collect on the debt. This judicial perspective underscores that backdating is not merely a technical irregularity but a fundamental breach of legal and ethical standards.

The legal consequences of backdating extend beyond potential document invalidation. In Wells Fargo Bank v. Miller (Ohio Supreme Court, 2014), the court outlined how backdated documents could trigger:

- Complete dismissal of foreclosure proceedings
- Potential criminal fraud charges

- Significant monetary sanctions against the lending institution
- Professional disciplinary actions against individual actors involved in the backdating

From an evidentiary standpoint, backdated documents violate the Federal Rules of Evidence, specifically Rule 602, which requires that testimony be based on personal knowledge. When a document is intentionally backdated, it creates a false narrative that cannot be substantiated by actual contemporaneous knowledge.

The financial crisis of 2008 brought unprecedented scrutiny to mortgage documentation practices. In numerous class-action lawsuits and regulatory investigations, backdating emerged as a systematic issue that undermined the entire mortgage securitization process. The Department of Justice and state attorneys general have repeatedly prosecuted financial institutions for such practices, viewing them as deliberate attempts to circumvent legal and regulatory requirements.

Practically speaking, backdating creates a presumption of intentional misrepresentation. Courts interpret such actions as an admission that the original documentation was insufficient or improper, instantly casting doubt on the entire transaction's legitimacy.

Importantly, illegality is not merely about the act of changing a date, but about the intentional misrepresentation of material facts. When a mortgage document is backdated, it suggests an attempt to create a fictional narrative about the timing of agreement, ownership, or financial terms that did not exist at the purported time of execution.

FINANCIAL FRAUD

Financial fraud is rarely a simple act of theft. In the world of mortgage trusts, it's a sophisticated dance of legal manipulation, carefully crafted documents, and intentional obstruction that can destroy lives while appearing perfectly legitimate.

Imagine a criminal enterprise that doesn't need to break into homes but instead uses paperwork as its weapon of choice. Backdating documents is the primary tool in this arsenal of financial deception. This isn't just about changing a date on a piece of paper. It's a calculated strategy of creating an entirely false narrative of ownership, generating assignment documents that fabricate a chain of ownership that never actually existed.

Fraudulent conveyance becomes an art form in these scenarios. Entities transfer mortgage notes through a variety of corporate structures designed to confuse and misdirect. They create paper trails that lead nowhere, generating complex corporate networks that obscure the true ownership of debt. It's like a shell game where the pea is never under any of the shells.

In the specific case of Waterfall Victoria Mortgage Trust 2011-SBC3, the fraud was particularly brazen. The trust was already dissolved, yet it continued to file claims. The audited financials showed that the trust owned no real estate in Maryland. And the value of the trust was zero. Assignments were backdated with surgical precision, and critical endorsements simply vanished from the chain of titles.

The judicial system becomes an unwitting accomplice in this process. Courts are bombarded with documentation so complex that even trained legal professionals struggle to unravel the truth. Fraudsters exploit this complexity, presenting documents that look official but lack any substantive legal backing. They count on the system's tendency to defer to apparent complexity.

The mechanics of fraud follow a predictable pattern. First, identify a vulnerable mortgage. Then, create a web of corporate entities so intricately that tracking true ownership becomes nearly impossible. Generate backdated documentation that creates an illusion of legitimate transfer. File claims using these fabricated documents. Finally, rely on the legal system's reluctance to deeply scrutinize complex financial instruments.

For homeowners, the human cost is devastating. Each fraudulent document represents more than just a piece of paper. It's a potential loss of home, savings, and financial security. The complexity of these schemes is intentional, designed to overwhelm and intimidate individuals, making it nearly impossible to challenge the fraudulent claims.

Courts, financial regulators, and homeowners must develop a more critical eye. Understanding these mechanisms requires looking beyond the surface, questioning every document, challenging every claim of ownership. The financial world is not always as transparent as it appears, and the most dangerous criminals wear suits and carry briefcases, not masks and weapons.

CASE STUDY

In my case, the Trustees and the Court were given the following document, the Assignment of the Deed of Trust, allegedly from Greenpoint Mortgage Funding, Inc., to Waterfall Victoria Master Fund, Ltd. This is the most important document because from this document flowed the ownership of the note pursuant to U. S. Bank, NA, as Indentured Trustee, for Waterfall Victoria Mortgage Trust, 2011- SBC3.

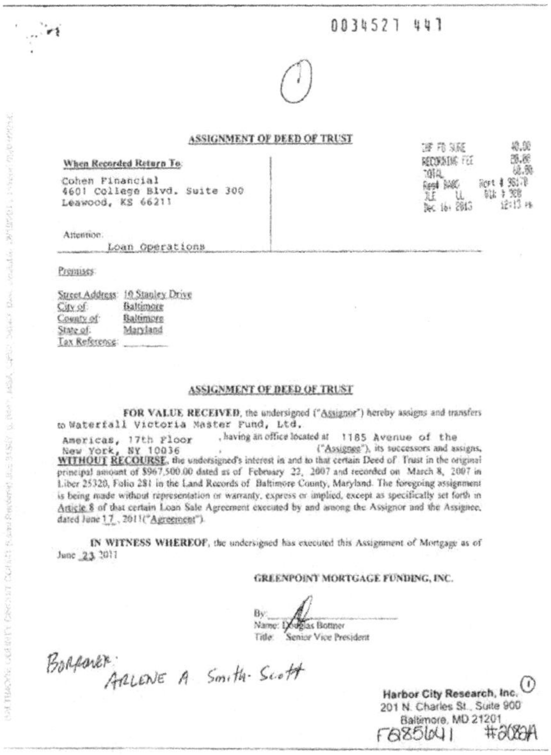

0034521 441

ASSIGNMENT OF DEED OF TRUST

When Recorded Return To:
Cohen Financial
4601 College Blvd. Suite 300
Leawood, KS 66211

Attention: Loan Operations

Premises:

Street Address: 10 Stanley Drive
City of: Baltimore
County of: Baltimore
State of: Maryland
Tax Reference: ________

ASSIGNMENT OF DEED OF TRUST

FOR VALUE RECEIVED, the undersigned ("Assignor") hereby assigns and transfers to Waterfall Victoria Master Fund, Ltd., having an office located at 1185 Avenue of the Americas, 17th Floor New York, NY 10036 ("Assignee"), its successors and assigns, **WITHOUT RECOURSE**, the undersigned's interest in and to that certain Deed of Trust in the original principal amount of $967,500.00 dated as of February 22, 2007 and recorded on March 8, 2007 in Liber 25320, Folio 281 in the Land Records of Baltimore County, Maryland. The foregoing assignment is being made without representation or warranty, express or implied, except as specifically set forth in Article 8 of that certain Loan Sale Agreement executed by and among the Assignor and the Assignee, dated June 17, 2011("Agreement").

IN WITNESS WHEREOF, the undersigned has executed this Assignment of Mortgage as of June 23, 2011

GREENPOINT MORTGAGE FUNDING, INC.

By: ________
Name: Douglas Bottner
Title: Senior Vice President

Borrower: ARLENE A Smith-Scott

Harbor City Research, Inc.
201 N. Charles St., Suite 900
Baltimore, MD 21201
F885641 #2080A

Backdated Assignment of Deed of Trust

Critical Questions as to Backdated Mortgage Assignments

1. The likelihood of a coincidence that three assignments be recorded on the same day. It is statistically improbable that multiple assignments on the same property would be filed simultaneously which suggest systematic document manipulation rather than genuine, independent transactions.

2. If the Assignment of Deed was not backdated, why is the date and the party's name for Assignor appeared to be typed in using a different font and character type? Typographical inconsistencies are a classic marker of document

alteration. Different fonts, character spacing, or text alignment often indicate digital manipulation or post-facto document reconstruction.

3. Assignment from Greenpoint Mortgage Funding, Inc. to Waterfall Victoria Master Fund, Ltd. This transfer lacks documented evidence of a legitimate loan sale agreement. Without a clear, traceable transaction record, the assignment appears manufactured to create an artificial ownership chain.

4. Assignment of Leases and Rents from Greenpoint Mortgage Funding, Inc. to Waterfall Victoria Master Fund, Ltd. The simultaneous assignment of both the mortgage and leases/rents further suggests a coordinated effort to retroactively construct a seemingly legitimate transfer, rather than a genuine, arms-length transaction.

5. Assignment from Waterfall Victoria Master Fund, Ltd. to U. S. Bank, NA, as Indentured Trustee for Waterfall Victoria Mortgage Trust-2011 SBC3. This transfer is particularly suspicious given the subsequent revelations about the trust's status. The assignment appears to be a mechanism for creating a legal fiction of ownership.

6. The 1098 Mortgage Statement showed Lehman Brothers as Owner after the ownership of mortgage by Greenpoint Mortgage Funding, Inc. This discrepancy reveals a critical break in the claimed ownership chain. Lehman Brothers' appearance as the owner contradicts the subsequent assignments, suggesting multiple, potentially conflicting claims of mortgage ownership.

7. Capitol One Bank, NA, certified they were the owners and appeared in the bankruptcy court after ownership of mortgage by Greenpoint Mortgage Funding, Inc. Multiple, competing claims of ownership from different institutions is a significant indicator of documentary fraud. The presence of

Capital One in bankruptcy proceedings further complicates the purported ownership narrative.

8. Transferred from Waterfall Victoria Master Fund, Ltd to Waterfall Victoria Mortgage Trust 2011-SBC3 after the S/11A filing with the SEC stated the trust was completed in 2011. The timing of the transfer relative to the trust's completion date raises serious questions about the legitimacy of the assignment. A transfer after the trust's formal completion suggests a retroactive attempt to assign assets.

9. Transferred from Waterfall Victoria Master Fund, Ltd to Waterfall Victoria Mortgage Trust 2011-SBC3 after the S/11A filing with the SEC stated the trust never held a real estate interest in Maryland. A trust claiming to hold a mortgage in a jurisdiction where it is legally documented as having no real estate interest represents a fundamental legal impossibility.

10. Transferred from Waterfall Victoria Master Fund, Ltd to Waterfall Victoria Mortgage Trust 2011-SBC3 after the S/11A filing with the SEC stated the trust had a value of -0-. A trust with zero financial values purporting to hold a mortgage is legally nonsensical. This suggests the transfer is a purely paper transaction with no underlying economic substance.

11. Is "D" the signature for Douglass Bottner and was he an authorized signatory for Greenpoint Mortgage Funding, Inc.? Without verifiable documentation confirming Bottner's authorization, the signature raises significant authentication concerns. An unverified signature on a critical legal document is a major red flag for potential forgery.

12. What Cohen Financial relationship to Waterfall Victoria Mortgage Trust 2011 SBC3 and their agent, U. S. Bank, NA. The unexplained involvement of Cohen

Financial suggests an additional layer of opacity in an already complex and suspicious ownership chain when Cohen Financial represented that they purchased the note at a discount.

13. Why are the following items missing:

- Loan Sale Agreement
- Corporate Governance of Trust
- Allonges
- Chain of Title

Response: The absence of these critical documents is perhaps the most damning evidence of documentary manipulation. Each missing document represents a crucial piece of evidence that would normally substantiate a legitimate property transfer. Their collective absence suggests an intentional effort to obscure the true nature of the transaction.

These questions collectively expose a document that appears to be a meticulously constructed legal fiction. The Assignment of Deed does not represent a genuine transfer of property rights but rather seems to be an elaborate attempt to create an illusion of legitimate mortgage ownership through systematic documentary fraud.

LACK OF AUTHORITY AND AUTHENTICITY

If Waterfall Victoria Mortgage Trust 2011 SBC3 did not legally own the debt at the time it claims, then it had no standing to enforce it. This means that the trust did not have the legal authority to assert ownership over the property.

The Impact of Missing Documents on Ownership Claims

The legitimacy of Waterfall Victoria Mortgage Trust 2011-SBC3's claim is further weakened by several missing key documents that would be necessary to establish its legal standing. The lack of should have raised serious concerns about whether the trust ever had a valid claim to the mortgage at all.

No Governance Documents for Waterfall Victoria Mortgage Trust 2011-SBC3

For a trust to claim ownership of a mortgage, it must have formal governance documents that outline who control the trust, who benefits from it, and what powers it has. In this case, no such documents exist, meaning there is no proof that Waterfall Victoria Mortgage Trust 2011-SBC3 was properly formed or had the authority to hold mortgage debt.

Missing Loan Sale Agreement

A Loan Sale Agreement is a critical document that proves how a mortgage was transferred from one entity to another. In this case, there is no Loan Sale Agreement showing that GreenPoint Mortgage Funding, Inc. legally transferred my loan to Waterfall Victoria Master Fund, Ltd. Without this document, there is no way to verify a loan transfer.

WHY THIS MATTERS IN COURT

When a company claims to own a mortgage but cannot provide proper documentation, it raises serious legal questions. The burden is on the entity claiming ownership to prove that they hold a valid interest in the debt. Missing documents, backdated assignments, and unverified transfers all undermine the legitimacy of a claim. If Waterfall Victoria Mortgage Trust 2011-SBC3 could not produce legally valid documents, then any attempt to enforce the mortgage should have been considered invalid.

Chapter Twenty-Three

STANDING AND THE 1098 MORTGAGE INTEREST STATEMENT

IMPORTANT: Understanding the significance of a 1098 Mortgage Interest Statement which can serve as a tax-record, and as evidence of the entity that legally owned and serviced the mortgage. If a different party later claims ownership without a properly documented transfer from the entity that issued the 1098 mortgage statement, the legal standing of the creditor may be challenged to invalidate a foreclosure or debt collection efforts.

A 1098 MORTGAGE INTEREST Statement is a tax document issued by the entity that legally owns or services the mortgage loan. It is used by borrowers to report the amount of mortgage interest paid during the year and is typically provided by the party that collects mortgage payments and has legal authority over the loan. A Form 1098 (Mortgage Interest Statement) and the actual ownership of the mortgage note are not necessarily connected, and this distinction is critically important in legal proceedings concerning mortgage standing.

What Form 1098 Actually Represents

Form 1098 is primarily a tax document that reports mortgage interest paid by a borrower during the tax year. The IRS requires the "recipient" of mortgage interest payments (typically the servicer) to issue this form if a borrower pays $600 or more in mortgage interest. However:

- The entity issuing Form 1098 is typically the mortgage servicer, not necessarily the legal owner of the mortgage note
- Servicers are often contracted third parties who collect payments on behalf of the actual note holder or trust
- The relationship is administrative rather than ownership-based

Why This Distinction Matters

This distinction becomes critically important in bankruptcy and foreclosure proceedings for several reasons:

1. **Standing Requirements**: Only the actual owner or holder of the note has legal standing to enforce the mortgage or file claims in bankruptcy

2. **Servicers vs. Owners**: A servicer sending a 1098 form may be acting merely as an agent with no ownership rights to the underlying debt

3. **Evidentiary Value**: Courts generally require much stronger documentation to prove ownership, such as:

    - The original promissory note
    - Complete chain of assignments and endorsements
    - Pooling and servicing agreements
    - Trust documents showing the mortgage were properly conveyed

Common Misconceptions

In legal proceedings, parties sometimes mistakenly rely on Form 1098 as evidence of ownership, but courts have consistently ruled that:

1. Tax reporting relationships do not establish legal ownership of debt instruments

2. Servicers routinely issue Form 1098s for loans owned by completely different entities

3. The mortgage servicing industry operates on a separation between servicing rights and ownership rights

Proper Verification of Ownership

To properly establish note ownership, one should examine:

1. SEC filings for securitized mortgages
2. County recording documents showing proper assignments
3. Pooling and Servicing Agreements showing proper and timely transfer into trusts
4. Custodial receipts demonstrating physical possession of original notes

A Form 1098 alone provides virtually no probative value in establishing who has the legal right to enforce a mortgage note or file claims based on it. This is why courts typically require much more substantial documentation when the ownership of a mortgage is in question.

When a Form 1098 Could Be Relevant Evidence

While a Form 1098 Mortgage Interest Statement isn't conclusive proof of mortgage note ownership, it can serve as relevant evidence in certain contexts:

Potential Evidentiary Uses of Form 1098

1. **Supporting Evidence in a Broader Chain**: A Form 1098 can corroborate other documentation by showing:
    - The existence of an ongoing lending relationship

- That payments were being made and accepted
- The identity of the entity servicing the loan
- Consistency (or inconsistency) with other claimed relationships

2. **Pattern of Dealing**: In some cases, courts may consider Forms 1098 as part of establishing a pattern of dealing between parties, particularly when:
    - The same entity has consistently issued these forms over multiple years
    - There's no conflicting documentation about who should be receiving payments
    - The parties have acted in reliance on the relationships indicated by the forms
3. **Inconsistency Evidence**: Form 1098s can be valuable when they contradict other claims:
    - If Entity A claims to own a mortgage but Entity B issues the 1098s
    - If multiple entities issue 1098s for the same loan in different years without documented transfers
    - When the issuing entity doesn't match courthouse records or SEC filings
4. **In Payment Dispute Cases**: When the issue is whether payments were made or properly credited (rather than who owns the note), 1098s can be relevant evidence of:
    - Payment amounts received

- Interest applied to the loan
- The recipient's acknowledgment of receiving payments

Limitations as Evidence

Even in these contexts, Form 1098 still has significant limitations:

1. It doesn't establish the legal right to enforce the note or mortgage
2. It cannot overcome defects in the chain of titles or assignments
3. It doesn't prove compliance with trust formation requirements for securitized loans
4. It's primarily an IRS tax reporting document, not a title document

Most Appropriate Uses

Form 1098s are most appropriately used as supplementary evidence rather than primary evidence of ownership. They might help establish:

- Who has been accepting payments
- When payments were made
- The amount of interest paid
- Inconsistencies in claimed ownership

In bankruptcy proceedings specifically, courts generally require more substantial documentation like original notes, recorded assignments, and pooling and servicing agreements to establish a creditor's standing to file claims or seek relief from the automatic stay.

CASE STUDY

In my specific case, I received three critical pieces of documentation that strongly suggest Lehman Brothers was more likely than not the holder of my mortgage note:

1. A formal letter notifying me of the transfer of my debt from GreenPoint Mortgage Funding to Lehman Brothers

2. A 1098 Mortgage Interest Statement issued directly by Lehman Brothers

3. An Escrow Statement from Lehman Brothers confirming their role in servicing my loan

My loan was originated by GreenPoint Mortgage Funding but was transferred to Lehman Brothers shortly after origination. This transfer aligns with the allegations made against GreenPoint in U.S. Bank's own legal filings, which stated that GreenPoint's standard practice was to table-fund loans or originate loans and sell the notes immediately.

The Significance of My Documentation

The 1098 statement I received constitutes meaningful evidence that Lehman Brothers was receiving my mortgage payments and had control over my loan for tax-reporting purposes. Based on these documents, Lehman Brothers was more likely than not the actual owner of my debt at that time.

The fact that Lehman Brothers, not GreenPoint, issued my 1098 statement and escrow documents indicates that GreenPoint did not retain ownership of my loan after its origination. With proper discovery and further documentation, it could have been definitively determined whether Lehman Brothers remained the noteholder or properly transferred the note to another entity.

For U.S. Bank or any other entity to establish legitimate standing in my foreclosure or bankruptcy proceedings, they would need to provide an authentic, verifiable assignment of my mortgage note from Lehman Brothers. Without thorough discovery of these transfer documents, their claim to ownership remains questionable at best.

How This Evidence Could Have Been Used

With appropriate legal discovery, these documents could have formed the foundation for challenging U.S. Bank's standing. The 1098 Mortgage Interest Statement from Lehman Brothers, the transfer notification, and the escrow documents create a reasonable presumption that Lehman was the true noteholder.

Further discovery could have revealed whether a legitimate chain of title existed from Lehman Brothers to any subsequent claimant. If U.S. Bank or another entity could not produce documentation showing proper transfers from the last known holder, Lehman Brothers, their standing to enforce my mortgage would be seriously undermined.

In my situation, these documents could have justified additional discovery in bankruptcy or foreclosure proceedings to determine definitively who held the legal right to enforce my mortgage note.

Chapter Twenty-Four

STANDING AND THE EXPERT WITNESS

IMPORTANT: This information helps the reader understand when expert testimony on banking practices, document authenticity, or securitization might be worth the investment to successfully challenge major creditor claims. By exposing missing documents, errors, or improper assignments, an expert witness can help a debtor prevent an invalid creditor from enforcing a debt, potentially protecting assets and financial interests.

AN EXPERT WITNESS IS someone who knows a lot about a special topic and helps the court understand complicated things. Unlike regular witnesses, who usually just tell the court what they saw or heard, an expert witness is allowed to give their opinion because they have training, education, or experience in a particular area. For example, if there was a big accident, a doctor might be an expert witness to explain how serious someone's injuries are. If there was a complicated money problem in a bankruptcy case, a financial expert might explain what all the numbers mean.

One of the ways an expert witness helps in court is during discovery, which is when both sides in a case gather information before the trial starts. Sometimes, one side might not be telling the full truth, or they might be mistaken about something important. An expert witness can look at all the evidence and point out mistakes or things that don't make sense. For example, if someone says that a property is worth a certain amount of money, but an expert in real estate looks at the records and says it's worth a lot more or less, that expert is helping to contradict (or challenge) what the first person said.

To prove that someone is a real expert and not just pretending, they need to have a CV, which stands for "curriculum vitae." This is like a detailed resume that shows all the schools they went to, the jobs they had, and any books or articles they've written. The CV helps the judge and lawyers decide if the person really knows what they are talking about.

Besides having a CV, an expert usually needs to write a report. This report explains their opinion on the case and shows how they reached their conclusions. For example, if a financial expert is trying to prove that a business is worth a lot of money, they will write a report with all the facts, calculations, and explanations so that everyone can understand their reasoning.

To officially call someone an "expert witness," they need to be designated as an expert. This means that one side in a case asks the court to recognize them as an expert in a certain field. The judge will look at their experience, education, and past work to decide if they are qualified to give expert opinions in court.

What Does the Daubert Rule Say?

For an expert witness to testify (give their opinion in court), their methods and knowledge must be:

1. Based on real science, it can't just be a guess or a personal opinion.
2. Tested and proven, other scientists should be able to check and agree with the expert's work.
3. Accepted by experts in the field, if no other scientist thinks it's real, the court won't either.
4. Using reliable methods, the way they studied or analyzed something has to be fair and logical.

Imagine you're in a courtroom, and someone is brought in as an expert witness to explain something really complicated, like whether a certain medicine is dangerous. But how do we know this expert is qualified and not just making things up?

That's where the Daubert v. Merrell Dow Pharmaceuticals, Inc., 509 U.S. 579 (1993) case comes in! This case set rules that courts must follow to decide if an expert's testimony (what they say in court) is trustworthy and based on real science.

Example in Real Life

Let's say a company is accused of polluting a river, and a scientist is called to testify that the water is unsafe. If that scientist just made up their research without real testing, the court won't allow their testimony because it doesn't follow the Daubert rule. However, if they used proper testing methods and other scientists agree with their findings, their testimony can be used in court. So, Daubert v. Merrell Dow Pharmaceuticals makes sure that expert witnesses only give information that is based on real facts and science, not just opinions or guesses!

Expert Witness and Pecuniary Interest

Having an expert witness can be important when talking about pecuniary interest, which is just a fancy way of saying "a financial interest in something." If a person is arguing that they might lose money because of something happening in a case, an expert can help prove that they really do have something to lose. For example, if a debtor (someone who owes money) is going through bankruptcy and their house is being sold, a real estate expert could be brought in to explain whether the house is being sold for a fair price or if the debtor will lose more money than they should.

Similarly, when asking the court for permission to sell real estate that belongs to a debtor, an expert might need to show why the sale is necessary and what the property is worth. This is important because selling a property at the wrong price could hurt the debtor or the people, they owe money to. The expert helps the court make a fair decision by providing facts and analysis.

In short, expert witnesses help courts understand difficult topics, make sure information is accurate, and provide expert opinions based on facts. Their knowledge can be the key to winning a case, especially when money, property, or financial interests are involved.

Expert Witness in a Bankruptcy Case

Expert witnesses are very important in bankruptcy cases, which happen when someone or a business owes more money than they can pay back. In these cases, a judge has to decide what happens to the money and property. Sometimes, a person who is in debt, might argue that a bank or lender does not have the legal right to collect money from them. To prove this, the debtor might hire an expert witness to study financial records and explain whether the lender actually owns the debt. If the lender cannot prove that they own the debt, they do not have standing, which means they are not allowed to be part of the case.

One case that shows how expert witnesses can help debtors in bankruptcy is *In re Varat Enterprises, Inc.*, 81 F.3d 1310 (4th Cir. 1996). In this case, the Fourth Circuit Court of Appeals ruled that an expert witness helped prove that a creditor (the person or business trying to collect money) did not have a valid claim because they could not show proper financial records. The court decided that expert testimony was important because it showed that the creditor was not legally allowed to demand payment. This case proves that when a debtor hires an expert, it can make a huge difference in whether a judge allows a lender to collect money.

Expert witnesses are also useful when a trustee, the person responsible for handling the debtor's money and property, makes a deal with creditors. Sometimes, these deals can cause big tax problems for the debtor. One example of this happened in *In re Merry-Go-Round Enterprises, Inc.,* 400 F.3d 219 (4th Cir. 2005). In this case, the trustee made a deal that resulted in a 1099-C form being issued, which meant that the debtor might have to pay extra taxes for "income" they never actually received. The expert witness in this case explained how this tax problem would hurt the debtor financially, and because of this testimony, the court agreed that the debtor had a pecuniary interest, which means they had a financial reason to challenge the deal. This case shows that expert witnesses can protect debtors from unfair financial consequences, like unexpected tax bills.

A real-life example of a debtor using an expert witness to challenge a creditor's standing happened in *In re Foreman*, No. 16-10554 (Bankr. D. Md. 2019). In this case, a debtor filed for bankruptcy, but a mortgage lender claimed they still had the right to collect money. The debtor hired a forensic mortgage expert, a person who specializes in studying loan records, to investigate the claim. The expert found that the lender did not have the correct paperwork to prove they owned the loan. Because of the expert's testimony, the judge ruled that the lender had no legal right to collect money from the debtor, and the case was dismissed. This case is important because it proves that expert witnesses can help debtors challenge mistakes made by banks or lenders.

REMEMBER: An expert witness can play a huge role in bankruptcy cases by helping the court understand complicated financial details. They can prove whether a lender has the right to collect money, show how a trustee's deal could hurt a debtor, and help debtors avoid unfair financial consequences. Real cases from the Fourth Circuit have shown that expert witnesses can change the outcome of a case, making sure that debtors are treated fairly and that creditors follow the law.

USING AN EXPERT TO CHALLENGE STANDING

In a bankruptcy case, a creditor must have "standing" to participate, which means they must prove they have a legal right to collect money from the debtor. If they cannot do this, they are not allowed to file claims, object to the bankruptcy process, or receive payments from the estate. Sometimes, debtors believe that a creditor does not actually own the debt or does not have proper paperwork to prove their claim. In these cases, a financial expert can be hired to carefully examine documents, track loan transfers, and challenge the creditor's right to collect.

What Does an Expert Look for When Challenging Standing?

An expert witness, such as a forensic accountant, real estate analyst, or banking specialist, can review financial records to find mistakes or missing information. They usually focus on:

a. Chain of Ownership Problems – Sometimes, debts are sold or transferred multiple times between banks, and important documents get lost. If a creditor cannot prove they actually own the debt, they lack standing to collect it.

b. Faulty Loan Assignments – A creditor must show a proper assignment (legal transfer) of the debt. If the paperwork is incorrect, missing, or backdated, it can mean that the creditor never legally received the right to collect.

c. Securitization Issues – Some loans are bundled together and sold to investors. If this happens, the original lender may no longer have any legal connection to the loan, meaning the creditor claiming to own the debt may actually have no rights.

d. Failure to Prove Debt Amount – A creditor must provide an accurate accounting of the debt, including all charges, interest, and payments made. If their records are inaccurate, their claim may be invalid.

Debtor Uses Expert to Challenge Standing

A great example of how an expert can challenge a creditor's standing is *In re Foreman*, No. 16-10554 (Bankr. D. Md. 2019). In this case, a debtor was fighting a mortgage lender who claimed they had the right to collect payments. The debtor hired a forensic mortgage expert, a specialist in tracking loan documents, to investigate the claim. The expert discovered that the lender did not have the correct loan assignment records, meaning they could not prove they owned the debt. Because of this expert testimony, the court ruled that the lender had no standing to demand payment from the debtor. This case shows that when an expert finds missing documents, errors in loan transfers, or false claims, a creditor's right to collect can be denied by the court.

REMEMBER: An expert witness can be a powerful tool in bankruptcy cases where a debtor believes a creditor does not have the legal right to collect. By examining financial records, exposing missing or fraudulent documents, and testifying in court, an expert can help prove that a creditor lacks standing, which can stop them from collecting any money. Real cases, such as *In re Foreman*, show how expert testimony can make or break a creditor's claim in bankruptcy court.

CASE STUDY

In my case, the court's refusal to allow Paula Rush to testify as an expert witness on my behalf represented a profound example of discriminatory treatment that undermined fundamental principles of due process and equal protection under the law.

The Discriminatory Nature of Excluding Expert Testimony

The exclusion of my expert witness, Paula Rush, an established professional with extensive credentials previously utilized by successful bankruptcy attorneys, represents discriminatory treatment in several critical ways:

1. Unequal Application of Evidentiary Standards: While financial institutions routinely present expert testimony to support their positions, my similarly qualified expert was barred without valid justification, creating an inherently unbalanced proceeding.

2. Selective Barrier to Evidence: The court erected a procedural barrier specifically against my case by rejecting expert testimony that would have provided technical analysis of complex financial transactions—testimony that is regularly permitted when offered by institutional creditors.

3. Disparate Treatment of Pro Se Litigants: The exclusion suggests a troubling pattern of holding self-represented litigants to different (and more stringent) standards than institutional parties represented by counsel.

The Critical Role of Expert Testimony in Modern Litigation

Courts rely on expert testimony in complex cases for several essential reasons:

1. Technical Interpretation: Experts translate specialized knowledge into understandable evidence for judges and juries, particularly crucial in cases involving complex financial transactions and securitization.

2. Objective Analysis: Qualified experts provide neutral assessment of technical facts beyond typical judicial expertise, helping courts reach informed decisions based on industry standards.

3. Evidentiary Context: Expert testimony establishes the framework for evaluating documentary evidence, particularly important when analyzing fragmented or incomplete documentation.

4. Industry Standard Verification: Courts depend on experts to determine whether actions conform to established industry practices and regulatory expectations.

The Devastating Impact of Expert Exclusion

The court's refusal to allow Paula Rush's testimony created severe consequences:

1. Evidentiary Void: Without expert interpretation, the court lacked proper context to evaluate the significance of:

- The complete absence of mandatory transfer documentation
- Backdated assignments recorded years after the purported transfers
- The SEC filing confirms the Trust never owned Maryland real estate

2. Technical Disadvantage: The court was deprived of professional analysis regarding the improper securitization attempt, fraudulent assignments, and violation of proper loan transfer protocols.

3. Truth Concealment: The exclusion effectively buried critical evidence about the Trust's SEC filing certifying zero value and no Maryland property interests.

4. Procedural Imbalance: While creditors could present their narrative unchallenged, my ability to present technical counterevidence was arbitrarily blocked.

The Expert's Critical Findings That Remained Unheard

Paula Rush's excluded expertise would have explained to the court:

1. The impossibility of proper securitization given the timeline between Greenpoint's origination (February 2007) and the subsequent collapse of both Greenpoint (Q3 2007) and Lehman Brothers (2008).

2. The fatal documentation gaps in the purported chain of title, with at least 15 mandatory transfer documents missing documents which were essential for valid note transfers.

- Original endorsed promissory note
- Original/recorded mortgage or deed of trust
- Assignment of mortgage document
- Title insurance policy
- Complete payment history
- Borrower information and documentation
- Property documents and appraisals
- Prior assignments showing complete chain of title
- Any loan modification documents
- Escrow information for taxes and insurance
- Purchase and Sale Agreement (PSA)
- Entity Documentation, if the buyer is a corporation, LLC, or trust.
- Chain of Title Verification with County Records
- Bill of Sale
- If applicable, Esoppel Certificate

3. The fraudulent nature of multiple backdated assignments suddenly recorded on December 16, 2013, years after the alleged transfers occurred.

4. The direct contradiction between Waterfall Victoria Trust's claim to hold my note and their own SEC certification that the Trust was completed in 2011 with zero Maryland property interests.

Broader Implications for Justice

This discriminatory exclusion of expert testimony:

1. Creates a dangerous precedent restricting access to justice for borrowers by challenging predatory or fraudulent mortgage practices.

2. Establishes an uneven playing field where financial institutions can operate with reduced accountability.

3. Undermines public confidence in judicial fairness when technically complex evidence favorable to individual litigants is systematically excluded.

The court's refusal to hear Paula Rush's expert testimony represents more than a mere evidentiary ruling, it constitutes a structural barrier to justice that preserved an unjust power imbalance and prevented the exposure of potential mortgage fraud that continues to impact my financial future to this day.

Chapter Twenty-Five

THE AUTOMATIC STAY IN BANKRUPTCY

IMPORTANT: Understanding what an automatic stay is and how it provides immediate relief from collection actions, foreclosures, and lawsuits, which allows breathing room to reorganize finances and develop a recovery strategy.

IMAGINE YOU'RE PLAYING A game of Dodgeball, and you're getting hit from every direction. Every time you turn around, someone throws a ball at you, bam! A bill collector calls. Bam! A foreclosure notice arrives. Bam! A lawsuit is filed against you. It's overwhelming, and you can't catch a break.

Now, imagine you shout "TIME-OUT!" and, just like that, all the balls freeze in mid-air. No one can throw another ball at you until the referee figures out what's fair. That, my friends, is what the automatic stay does in bankruptcy. It's like a legal pause button that stops creditors from coming after you the moment you file your case.

WHAT IS THE AUTOMATIC STAY?

The automatic stay is a powerful legal protection found in Section 362 of the U.S. Bankruptcy Code. Immediately after you file for bankruptcy, whether Chapter 7, Chapter 11, or Chapter 13, the automatic stay kicks in. It stops most lawsuits, foreclosures, garnishments, and collection calls immediately. Creditors can't harass you, take your wages, repossess your car, or kick you out of your home without first getting permission from the bankruptcy court.

Think of it like a magic shield. The moment your bankruptcy case is filed, this shield appears around you, and creditors must back off. They can't just keep coming after you like nothing happened; they have to respect the rules of the bankruptcy process.

Why Is the Automatic Stay Beneficial?

The automatic stay is like an oxygen mask for people drowning in debt. It gives you a chance to breathe. If your home is about to be foreclosed, the stay can stop the sale and give you time to catch up on payments or negotiate with your lender. If your wages are being garnished, the stay puts a halt to it, letting you keep your paycheck while figuring out your next steps.

Real-Life Example

Imagine Sarah, a single mom, struggling to keep up with her mortgage. She just got a foreclosure notice, and her bank is days away from selling her home. Desperate, she files for Chapter 13 bankruptcy. Instantly, the automatic stay stops the foreclosure, giving Sarah time to work out a repayment plan with her lender. Without the automatic stay, she would have lost her home.

Let's say you're behind on car payments, and the repo guy is lurking around your neighborhood, waiting to tow your car in the middle of the night. The second you file for bankruptcy, that repo guy has to put the tow truck in park and drive away, unless the lender gets special permission from the court (which we'll talk about later).

Another Real-Life Example

Mark lost his job and fell behind on car payments. His lender is about to repossess his vehicle, which he needs to get to job interviews. He files for Chapter 7 bankruptcy, and the automatic stay stops the repossession in its tracks. Mark now has time to negotiate with the lender or find another solution without suddenly losing his car.

When Are You NOT Eligible for an Automatic Stay?

The automatic stay is a great tool, but not everyone gets one. If you've been playing "bankruptcy tag," filing multiple bankruptcy cases back-to-back to dodge creditors, the court may cut you off. Under Section 362(c)(3) and (c)(4) of the Bankruptcy Code:

(a) If you've filed one bankruptcy case in the past year that was dismissed, the stay only lasts 30 days unless you convince the court to extend it.

(b) If you've filed two or more cases in the past year and they were dismissed, you get no automatic stay at all. It's like showing up late to the game and finding out the referee won't let you call "time-out" anymore.

This rule exists to stop serial filers, people who keep filing bankruptcy over and over just to delay creditors without actually trying to fix their debt problems. Judges don't like it when people treat bankruptcy like a "get out of jail free" card instead of a serious financial reset.

What Happens When a Creditor Gets Permission to Lift the Automatic Stay?

The automatic stay isn't bulletproof. Creditors can go to court and ask the judge to "lift" the stay, meaning they can resume collection efforts. They do this by filing something called a "Motion for Relief from Stay." If they win, the shield disappears, at least for that specific creditor.

For example, if you're behind on your mortgage and your bank wants to foreclose, they might file a "Motion for Relief from Stay to Foreclose." If the judge agrees that you don't have a realistic way to catch up on payments, the bank gets permission to proceed with foreclosure.

Similarly, if your landlord is trying to evict you, they might file a "Motion for Relief from Stay to Evict." If you are months behind on rent and have no plan to catch up, the judge might allow the eviction to move forward.

Real-Life Example

John is renting an apartment but lost his job and couldn't pay rent for three months. His landlord files a motion to lift the stay, arguing that John has no ability to pay and is simply using bankruptcy to delay eviction. The judge agrees, and the landlord is allowed to proceed with eviction despite the bankruptcy filing.

Why Do Some Creditors Bother Filing These Motions?

Creditors don't just sit back and accept that they can't collect from you anymore. They file motions to lift the stay because they want to protect their interests. A bank doesn't want to wait months while your bankruptcy case drags on if they think they can get their money faster by repossessing and selling your car. A landlord doesn't want to let you stay rent-free while your case plays out in court.

If you're in a Chapter 7 bankruptcy (which wipes out debts quickly), creditors are more likely to file these motions because they know you probably won't be making payments. But if you're in Chapter 13 (which involves a repayment plan), creditors are less likely to get the stay lifted if your plan includes catching up on missed payments.

The Automatic Stay Is Powerful, But Not Invincible

The automatic stay is one of the biggest perks of filing for bankruptcy. It immediately stops creditor actions and gives you room to figure out your financial situation without constant harassment. It's like pressing "pause" on all the chaos. But it's not a permanent solution. Creditors can and do challenge it, and repeat bankruptcy filers may not get the benefit of the stay at all.

If you ever find yourself in financial trouble, understanding how the automatic stay works can be the difference between getting relief and getting steamrolled by creditors. And if a creditor files a motion to lift the stay, you'd better be ready to fight, or at least have a good plan for what comes next. Because in bankruptcy, just like in dodgeball, the game isn't over until the referee (or the judge) says so.

CASE STUDY

In my case, my creditor, Patapsco Bank (also known as Howard Bank), successfully obtained an order granting their motion to lift the automatic stay, they effectively removed themselves from the bankruptcy court's jurisdiction with respect to the specific property covered by that order. This legal principle is well-established in bankruptcy law under 11 U.S.C. § 362, which provides for relief from the automatic stay.

Once the stay was lifted, the creditor generally regains their right to pursue collection actions against the specific property in question through state court proceedings or other non-bankruptcy remedies. The purpose of lifting the stay is precisely to allow the creditor to exit the bankruptcy forum for that particular asset and pursue their rights elsewhere.

As the Supreme Court noted in Johnson v. Home State Bank, 501 U.S. 78 (1991), a bankruptcy court's jurisdiction over secured creditors is primarily exercised through the automatic stay. When that stay is lifted for a particular creditor regarding specific collateral, the bankruptcy court's control over those proceedings is substantially diminished.

Improper Return to Bankruptcy Court

After being faced with a complaint in the Circuit Court for Prince George's County alleging various claims, the state court Judge, Leo Green, requested proof that the property was mixed-use and not commercial. When the state court judge requested proof that the property was mixed-use rather than commercial (with the implication that an injunction might be granted if it were mixed-use), the bank's decision to "run back" to the bankruptcy court was legally questionable for several reasons:

1. The bank had already obtained relief from the automatic stay, effectively removing that property from the bankruptcy court's primary jurisdiction.

2. The proper venue for resolving the classification dispute (mixed-use vs. commercial) was the state court where the issue had been raised, not the bankruptcy court which had already released its hold on the property.

3. This approach subverts the orderly administration of justice by attempting to play one court against another after receiving an unfavorable indication from the state court.

4. The bankruptcy court should not have entertained matters related to property for which it had already granted relief from stay, absent extraordinary circumstances or clear evidence that the property remained necessary for reorganization.

This situation illustrates a common problem in parallel proceedings: a party seeking the most favorable forum rather than respecting jurisdictional boundaries. The proper approach would have been for Patapsco Bank to address the mixed-use versus commercial classification issue in the state court proceeding where it was raised, rather than attempting to reimpose bankruptcy court oversight on property that had been released from the automatic stay.

Unless the bank formally moved to reimpose the stay (which would require showing changed circumstances), which they failed to do, their return to bankruptcy court after the stay was lifted circumvented the proper judicial process and the state court's authority to determine the property classification issue.

Chapter Twenty-Six

UNDERSTANDING BANKRUPTCY BUY-OUTS

IMPORTANT: Buying out an estate provides an opportunity to retain valuable assets by negotiating a fair purchase with the bankruptcy trustee, potentially preserving businesses or personal property. Knowing the legal framework and procedural steps involved helps debtors navigate the process effectively while ensuring compliance with bankruptcy laws and court rulings.

WHAT IS A BANKRUPTCY BUY-OUT?

When someone files for bankruptcy, everything they own becomes part of their "bankruptcy estate." A buy-out happens when someone offers money to purchase assets from this bankruptcy estate. What makes it special is when the debtor (the person who filed bankruptcy) wants to buy back their own property.

Imagine you own a skateboard shop that's having money problems. You file for bankruptcy because you can't pay your suppliers and rent. Normally, the bankruptcy trustee would sell your store's inventory and equipment to pay your debts. But if you really love your business and want to keep it going, you might be able to buy it back from your own bankruptcy estate.

The Laws That Allow Buy-Outs

The U.S. Bankruptcy Code (Title 11) doesn't have one specific section called "debtor buy-outs," but several parts work together to make this possible. Section 363(b) is especially important because it states: "The trustee, after notice and a hearing, may use, sell, or lease, other than in the ordinary course of business, property of the estate." Even though it doesn't specifically mention debtors buying back their own stuff, judges have decided this is allowed if it helps pay the creditors.

For businesses trying to reorganize in Chapter 11 bankruptcy, Section 1123(a)(5)(D) specifically mentions that "sale of all or any part of the property of the estate" can be part of a bankruptcy plan. There's also something called the "new value exception" to the absolute priority rule that courts recognize, which allows business owners to keep ownership by contributing new capital.

How Courts Have Ruled on Buy-Outs

In the landmark Supreme Court case *Bank of America National Trust & Savings Association v. 203 North LaSalle Street Partnership* (526 U.S. 434, 1999), the Court decided that business owners can't have exclusive rights to buy back their company without market competition. The case involved owners of an office building who wanted to keep ownership by putting in new money. The Supreme Court said this wasn't fair unless other people got a chance to bid too.

In a more recent case, *In re Snyder* (967 F.3d 1080, 10th Cir. 2020), the court said that if someone who filed bankruptcy wants to buy back their property and they match an offer from someone else, the trustee should usually accept the debtor's offer. This helps people who really want to keep their personal belongings.

The principles for sales in bankruptcy, including buy-outs, were established in cases like *In re Abbotts Dairies of Pennsylvania, Inc.* (788 F.2d 143, 3d Cir. 1986), which said that all sales require both "good faith" and "fair value." This means there can't be any fraud or unfair advantage, and the price must be reasonable.

Buy-Outs in Different Types of Bankruptcy

In Chapter 7 bankruptcy (liquidation bankruptcy), buy-outs happen when the trustee finds non-exempt assets. In *In re Brown* (498 B.R. 486, Bankr. E.D. Pa. 2013), a debtor wanted to buy back her car from the bankruptcy estate. The court said this was okay as long as the purchase price was fair and in the best interest of the estate.

In Chapter 11 and Chapter 13 (reorganization bankruptcies), it works differently. In the 4th Circuit case *In re Martin* (91 F.3d 389, 4th Cir. 1996), the court addressed a Chapter 13 debtor's plan that proposed to pay unsecured creditors less than 100% while keeping non-exempt property. The court said for such a plan to be approved, it must pass the "best interests of creditors" test, meaning creditors must receive at least as much as they would in a Chapter 7 liquidation.

For business reorganizations, *In re DBSD North America, Inc.* (634 F.3d 79, 2d Cir. 2011) established stricter standards for debtors trying to buy out their own companies in Chapter 11. DBSD's reorganization plan proposed that existing shareholders would receive shares in the reorganized company in exchange for new capital contributions. The Second Circuit ruled this violated the absolute priority rule because it allowed existing equity holders to retain ownership before unsecured creditors were paid in full.

Creative Buy-Out Arrangements

Sometimes bankruptcy cases involve creative settlements. In *In re SPM Manufacturing Corp.* (984 F.2d 1305, 1st Cir. 1993), a secured creditor and unsecured creditors' committee agreed to share proceeds from the sale of assets. The court ruled that a secured creditor can share what it would have received with other creditors, even if that changes normal priority rules. This opened the door to more flexible buy-out arrangements when key stakeholders agree.

How Buy-Outs Work in Practice

When you want to buy back your assets in Chapter 7, you typically negotiate directly with the trustee. The trustee evaluates whether your offer represents the best recovery for creditors compared to other options, as established in numerous cases interpreting Section 363 of the Bankruptcy Code.

For Chapter 11 business reorganizations, the process involves the court approving your plan under Section 1129, which includes the "best interest of creditors" test in Section 1129(a)(7). This requires showing that creditors will receive at least as much under your plan as they would in liquidation.

If you can't pay the full buy-out amount immediately, courts might approve payment plans or allow financing, as long as creditors' interests are protected under the adequate protection standards of Section 361.

Why Buy-Outs Matter

Understanding bankruptcy buy-outs is important if you want to keep your possessions while going through bankruptcy. The cases we've discussed show that courts try to balance allowing debtors to keep important assets while ensuring creditors receive fair value. With proper planning and enough resources, you might be able to get a fresh financial start without losing the things that matter most to you, just as the debtors did in cases like In re Brown and In re Snyder.

How to Request a Buy-Out of your Estate

If you are considering a "Buy-Out" of your estate, take the following steps. First, you need to determine how much of your estate is not exempted pursuant to Schedule "C" nor encumbered by a lien or security interest pursuant to Schedule "D".

Second, make a list of exactly which items you want to keep and research what they're worth by checking prices on websites like eBay, Craigslist, Kelly Blue Book or Zillow. It may be necessary for you to get a written appraisal.

Third, contact your bankruptcy trustee directly by calling or emailing them to set up a time to discuss your interest in buying back specific assets. When you meet with the trustee, bring a written offer that clearly states: 1) which specific items you want to buy, 2) how much you're offering for each item, and 3) how you plan to pay (cash is best). Be ready to explain where you're getting the money from. It's important the funds aren't from hidden assets that should have been disclosed in your bankruptcy. If the trustee thinks your offer is too low, politely ask what price would be acceptable and try to negotiate.

Make your offer early in your case, before the trustee arranges an auction or sale. If the trustee accepts your offer, get the agreement in writing and ask if you need to submit it to the court for approval. Some trustees will file a "Notice of Intent to Sell" with the court, which gives creditors about 21 days to object to the sale.

Once approved, make your payment exactly as agreed (get a receipt!) and keep all paperwork showing you properly bought back these items. Remember that trustees want to minimize work while maximizing money for creditors, so explaining how your offer saves time and auction expenses might help convince them to accept it.

CASE STUDY

THE SIGNIFICANCE AND CONSEQUENCES OF THE REJECTED BUY-OUT OFFER

My approach to the Trustee with a $35,000 buy-out offer ($17,500 for each of the two Patapsco Bank properties) represented a critical attempt at efficient resolution within the bankruptcy process. This action holds substantial importance for several reasons:

Importance of the Buy-Out Attempt

1. Fair Market Valuation: The $35,000 offer likely represented a reasonable valuation considering the encumbrances and legal complications surrounding the properties.

CASE STUDY

The Significance and Consequences of the Rejected Buy-Out Offer

My approach to the Trustee with a $35,000 buy-out offer ($17,500 for each of the two Patapsco Bank properties) represented a critical attempt at efficient resolution within the bankruptcy process. This action holds substantial importance for several reasons:

Importance of the Buy-Out Attempt

1. Fair Market Valuation: The $35,000 offer likely represented a reasonable valuation considering the encumbrances and legal complications surrounding the properties.

2. Immediate Liquidity: The offer would have converted contested assets into cash for the bankruptcy estate, eliminating uncertainty and administrative costs of prolonged proceedings.

3. Good Faith Negotiation: My proactive offer demonstrated willingness to resolve matters through established bankruptcy settlement mechanisms rather than protracted litigation.

4. Preservation of Value: The buy-out would have protected the properties' value from deterioration during extended legal proceedings and avoided potential foreclosure devaluation.

Consequences of Rejection

The Trustee's rejection of this buy-out offer triggered several significant negative consequences:

1. Increased Administrative Expenses: Continued litigation and property management drained estate resources that could have benefited creditors.

2. Delayed Creditor Recovery: Creditors were forced to wait longer for potential distributions that would have been immediately available through the settlement.

3. Asset Vulnerability: With the automatic stay already lifted, the properties remained exposed to foreclosure actions, potentially resulting in complete loss of equity for the estate.

4. Judicial Resource Burden: The rejection necessitated continued involvement across multiple courts rather than an efficient resolution.

5. Lost Opportunity Cost: The $35,000 that could have been invested or distributed was effectively frozen in contested assets.

6. Procedural Inefficiency: The rejection contradicted bankruptcy system goals of maximizing value and minimizing costs through reasonable settlements.

The Trustee's decision to reject this settlement opportunity based on a questionable legal interpretation regarding multiple filings ultimately undermined the bankruptcy system's core purposes of efficient asset liquidation and maximized creditor recovery.

Chapter Twenty-Seven

BANKRUPTCY TRUSTEE: CLAIMS AND DEFENSES

IMPORTANT: When you file for bankruptcy, any lawsuits you've filed or could file become part of the bankruptcy estate, giving the Trustee control over whether to pursue, settle, or abandon them. While the Trustee has significant power over assets and legal claims, they must act in the best interests of all creditors and cannot unfairly waive your legal defenses or engage in improper carve-out agreements that undermine your rights.

IMAGINE YOU'RE THE MAIN character in a video game, and just as things start getting tough, bills piling up, lawsuits flying at you, you grab a "Bankruptcy Power-Up." Suddenly, a new player joins the game: the Trustee. But instead of being your sidekick, the

Trustee is like the referee who now controls part of your character, especially when it comes to lawsuits you're involved in.

What Power Does the Trustee Have Over a Debtor's Lawsuit?

When you file for bankruptcy, everything you own, including lawsuits you've filed or could file against someone, gets scooped up into a big legal basket called the "bankruptcy estate." Under 11 U.S.C. § 541, this estate includes not just your house and car but also any lawsuits you've filed or could have filed before bankruptcy.

Here's where it gets tricky. The Trustee becomes the new "boss" of that lawsuit. If you had a civil complaint against someone, maybe you were suing a company for unpaid wages, or maybe you had a personal injury claim, the Trustee now decides what happens to it. They can:

1. Take over the lawsuit and pursue it on behalf of your creditors. If you're suing someone and might win money, that money no longer belongs just to you, it belongs to your bankruptcy estate. The Trustee might settle the case or keep it going, but either way, they control it.

2. Abandon the lawsuit if they think it's worthless or won't bring in enough money to benefit creditors. If that happens, the lawsuit goes back to you, and you can keep fighting it on your own.

3. Sell the lawsuit to someone else (yes, lawsuits can be sold!). If a creditor or another party wants to buy your claim, the Trustee can cut a deal.

The key takeaway? Once you file bankruptcy, you don't automatically control your lawsuits anymore, the Trustee does.

Can the Trustee Waive Your Claims?

Yes, and this is where things can get a little scary. Under 11 U.S.C. § 554, the Trustee can abandon a claim if it's not valuable to the estate, but they can also choose to settle or waive certain claims, meaning they can give up the right to pursue them. For example, if you're suing a company for breach of contract and the Trustee thinks the lawsuit isn't worth much, they might agree to settle it for pennies on the dollar or just drop it altogether. This can be frustrating if you believe your lawsuit was worth a lot more. But unless the Trustee is clearly acting against the best interests of the creditors, the court usually lets them call the shots.

What About Defenses? Can the Trustee Waive Those Too?

Now, let's flip the situation. Instead of you suing someone, imagine someone is suing you, like a foreclosure case where your mortgage lender is trying to take your house. If the creditor gets permission from the court to lift the automatic stay (which we talked about before), can the Trustee waive your defenses and just let them take the house?

Not exactly. Here's why!

1. The Trustee's Main Job is to Handle Assets, Not Defenses. The Trustee's power mostly extends to things that can bring in money for creditors, like selling property or controlling lawsuits where the estate could win money. A defense in a lawsuit is not an asset in the same way.

2. You Still Have a Right to Fight Foreclosure or Other Claims. If a creditor files a lawsuit against you, and you have legal defenses (like saying the bank messed up your loan

paperwork or charged illegal fees), those are your personal rights to raise. The Trustee does not have the power to just say, "We give up!" unless the defense is tied to a money claim that belongs to the estate.

3. Exception: If the Defense is Related to an Estate Asset. If your defense is based on an argument that the Trustee controls—like if you're arguing that the foreclosure should be stopped because the mortgage is invalid due to fraud—the Trustee might step in and say, "Nope, we're not fighting that." But if you're making a standard legal argument about why you should keep your home, the Trustee usually can't waive those defenses for you.

The Illegal Carve-Out Agreement: When the Trustee and Lender Make a Deal Behind Your Back

Now, let's talk about a sneaky trick some creditors pull when they don't get what they want in state court. Let's say a lender files a Motion to Lift Stay so they can foreclose on your home. But instead of letting the court decide fairly, the lender encounters resistance, maybe you have defenses that could stop the foreclosure.

So what does the lender do? They go around you and strike a secret deal with the Chapter 7 Trustee. This deal is called a carve-out agreement, where the Trustee agrees to sell your home and give a portion of the proceeds to creditors, even if you had a valid defense to stop the foreclosure.

Why This Could Be Illegal

1. The Trustee Has a Duty to Act in the Best Interest of the Estate, Not Creditors Alone.

• Under 11 U.S.C. § 704, the Trustee's job is to collect and liquidate assets for the benefit of all creditors—not just to serve one powerful lender's interest.

• If the Trustee makes a carve-out deal that benefits only one creditor while ignoring your legal defenses, they could be violating their duty to the bankruptcy estate.

2. Bad Faith and Abuse of Process

• Courts have ruled that carve-out agreements can be a form of bad faith if they strip debtors of legal rights unfairly. In *In re KVN Corp.*, 514 B.R. 1 (9th Cir. 2014), the court warned against carve-out deals that benefit only trustees and secured creditors while providing no meaningful benefit to unsecured creditors or the debtor.

• If the Trustee is not maximizing value for all creditors, instead just handing over your home to the lender, this could be challenged in bankruptcy court.

3. Violates the Debtor's Right to a Fresh Start

• One of the main goals of bankruptcy is to give debtors a fresh start. Under *Marrama v. Citizens Bank of Massachusetts,* 549 U.S. 365 (2007), the Supreme Court emphasized that bankruptcy laws are designed to protect honest debtors from being steamrolled by creditors.

• If a carve-out deal is just a sneaky way for a lender to get around your defenses, that goes against the spirit of bankruptcy law.

What Can You Do If This Happens?

If you suspect a carve-out deal is being made behind your back, you can:

• File an objection in bankruptcy court, arguing that the Trustee is not acting in the best interests of all creditors.

• Request an investigation into whether the Trustee is favoring one creditor unfairly.

• Ask the court to allow you to litigate your defenses in state court, ensuring that you get a fair chance to fight the foreclosure.

The Trustee is Like a Chess Master (But You're Still in the Game)

The Trustee is not just some paperwork-pushing bureaucrat, they wield serious power over your lawsuits and assets in bankruptcy. But they must follow the law and act in the best interests of all parties, not just side deals with powerful creditors. Bankruptcy law is supposed to protect you from unfair creditor tactics, not enable them. And in this high-stakes game, knowing the rules can make all the difference.

CASE STUDY

I was deeply troubled by the Chapter 7 Bankruptcy Trustee in my case. The Trustee entered into agreements with the two creditors who I had claims against in separate civil litigation, one filed after the conversion to a Chapter 7 bankruptcy and after the creditor received an order granting their motion to lift stay. The Trustee received buyouts, monies, from these creditors, creating what appeared to be a concerning financial arrangement.

What happened next was even more disturbing. The Trustee quickly intervened in my ongoing civil cases against these creditors and argued that I no longer had "standing" to pursue my legitimate claims. The Trustee then moved to dismiss my cases, effectively stripping me of my right to defend myself against what I believe were predatory and possibly fraudulent practices.

This maneuver completely undermined my ability to challenge the creditors' claims and to present evidence regarding the questionable ownership of my mortgage note. By asserting that only the Trustee had standing to pursue these claims, and then promptly abandoning them after receiving payments, the system effectively denied me access to justice.

What troubles me most is how this arrangement undermines the credibility of the bankruptcy court system. The Bankruptcy Code was designed to provide debtors with a fresh start while ensuring fair treatment of legitimate creditors, not to create a mechanism where trustees can profit by aligning with creditors against debtors. When a Trustee can receive financial benefits from the very entities a debtor is suing and then use that position to terminate the debtor's right to pursue justice, it creates an appearance of impropriety that damages public faith in the judicial system.

I was effectively silenced and prevented from presenting evidence that could have challenged the very foundation of the creditors' claims. This undermines not just my individual rights, but the integrity of a system that should protect vulnerable debtors from abusive practices, not facilitate them.

Chapter Twenty-Eight

DEFAMATION AND THE BANKRUPTCY TRUSTEE

IMPORTANT: Understanding the potential for defamation in bankruptcy court, for example, who said, "what," "when," "where," and about "whom." Are the statements offered as a fact? Are the statements true? Knowing the legal standards and the consequences of defamatory statements may help to protect legal rights and ensure that the bankruptcy process remains fair and just.

DEFAMATION IS WHEN SOMEONE says or writes something false about another person that harms their reputation. It's like if a kid at school spreads a false rumor about you that made everyone think badly of you, and as a result, you lost friends, got bullied, or were punished unfairly. In the legal world, defamation happens when false statements cause real harm, and the person making those statements didn't have proof to back them up.

In court, defamation usually comes in two forms: libel, which is when false statements are written, and slander, which is when false statements are spoken. To prove defamation, a person must show that someone made a false statement, shared it with others, caused harm, and didn't have a legal excuse for doing it.

Now, you might think, "Well, people lie all the time. Isn't that just freedom of speech?" Not exactly. The law protects people's right to speak freely, but it does not allow someone to make damaging, false statements that can ruin another person's reputation or career, especially when they do it recklessly or on purpose.

DEFAMATION IN BANKRUPTCY COURT

In the United States Bankruptcy Court, defamation can take on a special meaning. The court is supposed to be a place where people tell the truth so the judge can make fair decisions. When a bankruptcy trustee, the person assigned to manage a debtor's case, makes false or unsupported claims in legal documents, they are not just harming the debtor's reputation, but they are also undermining the entire court process.

For example, imagine a debtor named Lisa files for bankruptcy because she lost her job and has too much debt. The trustee, in trying to take away Lisa's assets, files a court document saying, "Lisa has been hiding money in secret bank accounts." But here's the problem, the trustee doesn't provide any proof, no bank records, no sworn affidavit, no reliable source for this accusation. Instead, they just throw the statement into the court record without evidence.

This is dangerous for many reasons. First, the judge might believe the statement, even though there's no proof, and rule against Lisa unfairly. Second, Lisa's reputation could be ruined, because once something is written in a court document, it becomes public record. Imagine if future employers, banks, or even landlords see that someone accused her of hiding money, even if it was never proven. Third, the entire bankruptcy process loses credibility if trustees can simply make claims without evidence, forcing debtors to prove their innocence rather than requiring trustees to prove guilt.

The Legal Standard for Defamation in Bankruptcy

In regular defamation cases, the law says that the false statement must be published to others, be about the person suing, being false, and cause harm. But in bankruptcy court, defamation can be even more damaging because it happens in an official legal setting.

In the Fourth Circuit, the case of *Trantham v. Tate,* No. 22-2263 (4th Cir. 2024), although not directly about defamation, underscores the importance of adhering to proper legal procedures in bankruptcy cases. The court emphasized that deviations from established protocols could lead to unjust outcomes, highlighting the necessity for trustees to base their actions on solid evidence.

In *In re Rome*, 162 B.R. 872 (Bankr. D. Colo. 1993), the court ruled that statements made in legal pleadings must have some factual basis. A trustee cannot simply make wild claims without any supporting evidence. If a trustee knowingly makes a false statement in court filings, it can be considered reckless disregard for the truth, which is one of the legal standards for defamation.

Another example is *In re Miller*, 247 B.R. 704 (Bankr. N.D. Ohio 2000), where the court found that false statements in bankruptcy filings damaged the debtor's reputation and could not be ignored. This case highlights why trustees and creditors must be careful with their words, if they accuse a debtor of wrongdoing, they need evidence to back it up.

Why False Statements by a Trustee Are Especially Harmful?

When a trustee files pleadings with false statements, it creates a ripple effect that is hard to undo. The bankruptcy judge might make decisions based on false claims, creditors might demand more money, and the debtor could face unnecessary legal battles trying to correct the record. The damage doesn't stop once the case is over, either. If the false statement is on public record, it could follow the debtor for years, affecting their ability to get jobs, loans, or even housing.

Imagine Lisa's case again. If the trustee falsely accuses her of hiding money, the judge might refuse to discharge her debts, leaving her stuck with bills she should have been freed from. Even if Lisa later proves the claim was false, the damage is already done. She might lose trust in the court system, struggle to repair her reputation, and face even more financial hardship.

The Bankruptcy Court's Duty to Prevent Defamation

Bankruptcy courts have a duty to ensure that all parties, debtors, trustees, and creditors, act in good faith. If a trustee files a pleading full of unsupported accusations, the debtor has the right to challenge those statements and demand evidence. The court should also hold trustees accountable for reckless or false allegations. If a debtor believes a trustee has defamed them through false pleadings, they may be able to file a motion to strike the statements from the record, ask for sanctions against the trustee, or even consider a separate lawsuit for defamation if the statements were made maliciously.

At its core, the bankruptcy system is built on fairness, and when trustees abuse their power by making false claims without proof, they hurt not just the debtor but the integrity of the entire court system.

CASE STUDY

During my bankruptcy proceedings, I was repeatedly defamed by the Chapter 7 Trustee and his attorney, Orbie Shively, who made multiple false statements about me in court. These defamatory remarks directly influenced the judge's perception of me and led to severe consequences.

First, Shively falsely claimed I had shut off electricity to intimidate tenants, when in reality the utility was disconnected for nonpayment while the bank was collecting rents. The BGE invoice proves this, and the tenant leases clearly stated tenants were responsible for their own electric bills.

Second, Shively misrepresented that I failed to disclose a lawsuit on my bankruptcy schedules, when the complaint against Howard Bank was filed nine months after my bankruptcy filing and five months after conversion to Chapter 7. This lawsuit was legitimate - I was challenging the bank's violation of Maryland real property laws regarding residential properties.

Third, Shively falsely described my office as "dark" to justify breaking in and changing the locks, when his own photographs later showed a clearly visible glass-fronted storefront with visible furniture and equipment inside.

Fourth, Shively falsely claimed I intended to use "aggressive tactics" based on an email that, when challenged and reviewed in court, did not actually contain such statements.

Fifth, Shively repeatedly claimed issues had been "litigated and re-litigated" when in fact the Trustee had merely intervened in my legitimate cases against creditors, declaring himself the "real party of interest," and then dismissed my claims with prejudice, denying me any opportunity to present my defenses.

These defamatory statements directly led Judge Schneider to threaten me with incarceration, stating: "Do you understand that you are going to be asked, not asked, told to vacate the premises? And if you don't do that, you're going to be subject to sanctions, and those sanctions might include incarceration."

The Trustee profited from deals with the very creditors I was challenging while using false statements to strip me of my legal rights and intimidate me with threats of imprisonment.

Chapter Twenty-Nine

PECUNIARY INTEREST AND BANKRUPTCY ESTATE

IMPORTANT: A prospective bankruptcy filer should understand "pecuniary interest" because it gives them the right to challenge creditor claims, especially when doing so, which could result in more money coming their way. This concept helps ensure that any surplus funds from a trustee sale or bankruptcy process are properly allocated, allowing debtors to protect their financial interests.

AH, THE JOYS OF financial jargon! "Pecuniary interest" is just a fancy way of saying you have skin in the game when it comes to money. If a financial decision can make you richer (or, let's be honest, less broke), congratulations, you have a pecuniary interest!

In the world of bankruptcy, pecuniary interest is crucial. It determines whether a debtor (the person who owes money) can challenge financial moves in their case. Imagine someone claiming they deserve a slice of your already shrinking financial pie, if kicking them out of the bakery means you might get some leftover crumbs, then you've got a solid reason to object.

Pecuniary Interest in Bankruptcy Cases

Over the years, courts have made it clear that debtors have the right to object to creditor claims, especially when those objections could lead to actual cash in their pockets. Let's take a quick trip through bankruptcy history:

In Re Povill (1939), a debtor successfully objected to a creditor's claim when it was the only one against their estate. No claim? More money for the debtor. Simple math!

In Re Kieffer-Mickes, Inc. (1998), the court ruled that if rejecting certain claims leaves a surplus in the estate, the debtor has a pecuniary interest.

In Re Toms (1999), even if there's no surplus, a debtor might still have the right to object if the claim isn't dischargeable (meaning they'd still owe it even after bankruptcy).

In Willemain v. Kivitz (1985), the court confirmed that debtors can object if there's a possibility of leftover funds. Because who doesn't want leftover funds?

The Connection Between Pecuniary Interest and Trustee Sales

A trustee sale is when a bankruptcy trustee sells off a debtor's property to pay creditors. If the sale generates more money than needed to pay off debts, the surplus should go back to the debtor. That's where pecuniary interest kicks in, if there's money left on the table, the debtor has every right to challenge questionable claims.

The debtor is contesting a claim from U.S. Bank, NA, arguing that it shouldn't be enforced. Why?

• The assignments were backdated. (Sketchy.)

• Important documents were missing. (Uh-oh.)

• The entity allegedly didn't exist when the sale happened. (Ghost creditors?)

• Financial audits showed the trust had a zero balance and never invested in real estate. (Red flag!)

If the court agrees with the debtor and disallows the claim, the surplus remains intact, meaning more money in their pocket.

The Role of 1099 and 1098 Forms After a Trustee Sale

When a bankruptcy trustee sells a property, tax forms may start appearing like uninvited guests. Two of the most common are:

a. 1099-C (Cancellation of Debt Form): If a lender forgives part of the debt, the IRS may treat it as taxable income. Because apparently, financial misery needs the company.

b. 1098 (Mortgage Interest Statement): Shows mortgage interest paid, which can be useful for tax deductions (yay for small wins!).

Does a 1099 or 1098 Form Mean You Owe Taxes?

A dreaded 1099-C could mean a tax bill—but not always. There are exceptions:

(1) Insolvency Exclusion: If you were financially underwater (more debts than assets) before the debt was forgiven, you might be off the hook for taxes.

(2) Bankruptcy Exclusion: If the debt was canceled as part of your bankruptcy case, the IRS won't tax it. (Finally, some good news!)

So, if you get hit with a 1099-C, it's worth checking if you qualify for one of these exclusions before panicking.

Debtor's Right to Object and Sue for Wrongful Acts

If a debtor can prove they have a pecuniary interest, they can challenge creditor claims and even sue if they think the trustee mishandled things. At its core, pecuniary interest in bankruptcy is all about ensuring debtors get what they're entitled to.

In this case, the debtor has a strong argument because the trustee sold their property for more than the amount owed. They could receive a 1099-C, but they may avoid tax liability if the debt was discharged in bankruptcy.

In my case, the creditor's claim was questioned due to suspicious documentation and legal inconsistencies. Since I had a direct financial stake in the outcome, I had every right to fight for my money. And let's be honest, who wouldn't?

Bankruptcy law is here to ensure that when there's extra cash left after debts are paid, it doesn't just disappear into the void. So, if you ever find yourself in a similar situation, remember when it comes to money, always check who's got their hands in the cookie jar!

CASE STUDY

In my case, the court ruled that I had "no pecuniary interest" in the sale of my real properties which represented a deeply discriminatory application of bankruptcy law for several key reasons:

Fundamental Rights Violated

This ruling effectively stripped me of the most basic right of ownership, the right to have a voice at the disposition of my property. While bankruptcy naturally limits some property rights, eliminating my standing to participate in decisions about my assets goes far beyond reasonable limitations and singles me out for exceptional treatment.

Double Standard in Recognizing Financial Stakes

The ruling creates an inherently discriminatory double standard: other parties (creditors, trustees) were recognized as having legitimate financial interests in my property, while I, the actual owner with ongoing financial obligations connected to these properties, were deemed to have no such interest. This selective recognition of financial stakes treats similarly situated parties (those with financial connections to the property) unequally.

Tax Consequences Without Representation

Perhaps most egregiously, the ruling forced me to bear tax consequences from the property disposition while simultaneously denying I had sufficient interest in participating in the decisions creating those consequences. This creates a fundamentally discriminatory situation where I alone bear certain financial burdens while being uniquely excluded from the process determining those burdens.

Selective Application of Legal Principles

In standard legal practice, property ownership inherently creates standing regarding that property's disposition. The selective disregard of this principle in my case suggests discriminatory treatment, especially if such standing would have been recognized in non-bankruptcy contexts or for differently situated debtors.

Procedural Inequality

This ruling created fundamental procedural inequality by allowing other parties to fully participate in proceedings directly affecting their financial interests while denying me the same right. This unequal access to procedural protections represents a form of systematic discrimination against me as the debtor.

The court's position created a catch-22 situation that is inherently discriminatory: I was considered sufficiently connected to the property to bear its tax and legal consequences yet insufficiently connected to having any say in decisions affecting those consequences, a contradiction that singles me out for disadvantageous treatment not applied to other parties in the proceedings.

Chapter Thirty

PECUNIARY INTEREST AND THE SETTLEMENT AGREEMENT

IMPORTANT: Understanding the true impact of a settlement agreement and whether there is a financial consequence if a 1099-C or 1099-MISC will be issued by the creditor because these forms can adversely impact tax liability. Therefore, pecuniary interest may be present even when Trustee enters into a settlement agreement.

WHEN A BANK OR mortgage lender forgives a debt or cancels part of what someone owes, they might send a Form 1099-MISC or Form 1099-C (Cancellation of Debt) to the debtor. This could happen in bankruptcy, foreclosure, or a loan settlement. But what does this mean for someone in bankruptcy?

1. What Is a 1099-C (Cancellation of Debt)?

A 1099-C means that the lender has canceled or forgiven some of the debt. The IRS usually treats canceled debt as taxable income because it's like receiving free money. However, if the person is in bankruptcy, they usually do NOT have to pay taxes on the canceled debt. Under 26 U.S.C. § 108(a)(1)(A), debt discharged in bankruptcy is not taxable income.

In *In re Porter,* 932 F.3d 282 (4th Cir. 2019), the court explained that debts discharged in bankruptcy do not count as taxable income for the debtor. This means that if a lender sends a 1099-C after bankruptcy, it might be a mistake, or at least something that shouldn't lead to extra taxes.

2. What Is a 1099-MISC and Why Does It Matter?

A 1099-MISC is different. Instead of canceled debt, it usually means the debtor received income, like extra money from a legal settlement or a business deal. If a lender wrongly sends a 1099-MISC for a forgiven debt, the IRS might think the debtor got income that they should pay taxes on, even though it was just a canceled loan. In *In re Piccadilly Cafeterias, Inc.,* 484 F.3d 1299 (4th Cir. 2007), the court stressed that tax issues in bankruptcy must be handled properly so that debtors aren't wrongly taxed on something that should be protected.

3. How Does This Affect the Debtor's Bankruptcy Estate?

A bankruptcy estate is like a pool of money and assets that the bankruptcy court controls. If a debtor gets money or assets, it could belong to the estate and be used to pay creditors.

But if a lender sends a 1099-C, it usually means the debtor does not actually receive money, just that a debt is wiped out. This means:

• If a 1099-C is issued correctly, it usually does not create a pecuniary interest (meaning the debtor doesn't gain money that can be used to pay creditors).

• If a 1099-MISC is issued incorrectly, it could wrongly make it look like the debtor has extra income, which could cause problems with the bankruptcy estate.

In *In re Andrews*, 80 F.3d 906 (4th Cir. 1996), the court explained that not all money-related transactions affect a bankruptcy estate, especially when they involve things that don't actually put cash in the debtor's hands. Also, in *In re Murphy*, 474 F.3d 143 (4th Cir. 2007), the court ruled that bankruptcy laws protect debtors from unfair tax burdens on debts that were legally canceled.

REMEMBER: A 1099-C after bankruptcy is usually not taxable, but a 1099-MISC can cause problems if issued incorrectly. Courts in the 4th Circuit have repeatedly ruled that debt canceled in bankruptcy shouldn't be taxed or treated as income. If a debtor gets one of these forms, they should act fast to make sure they don't end up paying taxes on something they don't owe.

WHAT HAPPENS WHEN A DEBTOR GETS A 1099-C - AFTER A NONDISCHARGEABLE CHAPTER 7 BANKRUPTCY?

When a debtor finishes Chapter 7 bankruptcy but later receives a 1099-C (Cancellation of Debt), it can cause serious financial and legal consequences, especially if the debt was ruled nondischargeable.

Generally, if the bankruptcy court ruled that the debts are nondischargeable, the debtor is still legally responsible for it. Just because a debtor gets a 1099-C doesn't always mean the debt is legally canceled. Some courts say a 1099-C is just a tax form, not proof that the lender actually forgave the debt. In *In re Reed,* 492 B.R. 261 (Bankr. E.D. Tenn. 2013), the court ruled that issuing a 1099-C does not automatically mean the debt is gone, it depends on the lender's actual intent. Also, in *In re Zilka,* 407 B.R. 684 (Bankr. W.D. Pa. 2009), the court found that creditors can still try to collect the debt even after sending a 1099-C, unless they formally release the debtor from liability.

Others have argued that the IRS must determine whether the Debtor is insolvent. Under 26 U.S.C. § 108(a)(1)(B), a debtor does not have to pay taxes on canceled debt if their liabilities exceed their assets at the time of cancellation. The debtor must file IRS Form 982 to claim this exclusion. In *In re Marrs-Winn Co.,* 103 F.3d 584 (7th Cir. 1996), the court ruled that debt forgiveness can be excluded from taxable income if the debtor is insolvent at the time of cancellation.

REMEMBER: If a debtor gets a 1099-C after a nondischargeable bankruptcy, they may still owe the debt AND could be taxed on it unless they qualify for the insolvency exclusion. The best course of action is to confirm whether the debt is truly canceled and take steps to avoid unnecessary taxes.

DOES A 1099-C FORM AMOUNT TO PECUNIARY INTEREST

The existence of a pecuniary interest in a bankruptcy case where the trustee enters into an agreement with a lender to issue a 1099-C (Cancellation of Debt form) depends on whether the resulting tax liability creates a direct financial impact on the debtor or the bankruptcy estate.

General Rule: Pecuniary Interest and Tax Liabilities in Bankruptcy

The pecuniary interest doctrine holds that an entity has standing in bankruptcy proceedings if it has a direct financial stake in the outcome. Typically, tax liabilities resulting from cancellation of debt (COD) are considered a personal obligation of the debtor, not the bankruptcy estate. Under IRS rules, discharged debts may be treated as income, unless an exception applies (e.g., insolvency or bankruptcy exclusion under 26 U.S.C. § 108(a)) as stated above.

Since the tax burden of a 1099-C issuance does not directly affect the bankruptcy estate's assets or creditor distributions, courts often find that it does not create a pecuniary interest in the estate. However, there are circumstances in which a 1099-C issuance creates a pecuniary interest.

i. The trustee's agreement with the lender changes the distribution of the estate's assets.

ii. The debtor is personally liable for taxes that alter creditor recoveries.

iii. The IRS challenges the discharge and asserts a tax claim against the estate.

Specifically, a trustee's agreement can alter creditor distributions in various ways. For example:

- Recharacterizing claims (e.g., treating an unsecured claim as secured).

- Prioritizing certain creditors over others.

- Entering settlements that affect the total assets available for distribution.

- Granting tax benefits (or burdens) that shift estate assets.

If a trustee's actions reduce or increase the funds available to creditors, this creates a pecuniary interest because it directly impacts the bankruptcy estate's value. Both a creditor and a Debtor's pecuniary interest can be impacted.

**A debtor has a pecuniary interest in a settlement agreement if:

• The settlement creates a new financial burden (e.g., Cancellation of Debtor income tax liability).

• The settlement reduces the debtor's exempt assets.

• The settlement releases third-party claims that could financially benefit the debtor.

In the case of *Bernstein v. Wells Fargo Bank, N.A.*, 958 F.3d 946 (4th Cir. 2020), the court ruled that a settlement that resulted in a tax burden to the debtor could be challenged on pecuniary interest grounds. The Fourth Circuit emphasized that even though a debtor's tax liability is separate from the bankruptcy estate, it may impact the debtor's financial interest. If a settlement agreement results in a tax liability from debt cancellation, the debtor has a pecuniary interest.

In the case of *Peabody v. United States,* 774 F.3d 197 (4th Cir. 2015), the Fourth Circuit ruled that a debtor had standing to challenge a settlement agreement because it created tax liabilities that impacted the debtor's post-bankruptcy financial condition. The trustee's settlement altered the debtor's tax position, resulting in a pecuniary interest.

In *Williams v. Internal Revenue Service*, 558 F.3d 302 (4th Cir. 2009), the debtor objected to a trustee's settlement with creditors on the grounds that it would trigger IRS tax liabilities on canceled debt. The Fourth Circuit ruled that a tax consequence created by the settlement conferred pecuniary interest on the debtor.

And, in *Williams v. IRS*, 67 Temple L. Rev. 201 (4th Cir. 1994), a Trustee abandoned certain assets, leading to IRS-imposed tax obligations on the debtor. The court ruled that a debtor has a pecuniary interest if a trustee's actions create tax burdens.

REMEMBER: The Fourth Circuit has repeatedly ruled that a debtor has a pecuniary interest if a trustee's settlement agreement creates tax consequences, such as:

• COD income resulting in a 1099-C.

• IRS-imposed tax burdens from abandoned assets.

• Post-bankruptcy financial harm caused by a trustee's settlement.

A Debtor can have a pecuniary interest in specific circumstances.

CASE STUDY

In my case, the Judge ruled I did ot have a pecuniary interest. However, by its standard legal meaning, pecuniary interest exists when a party would experience financial consequences from a proceeding's outcome. I received 1098 – Cancellation of Debt forms from two of my purported mortgage creditors who entered agreements with the Chapter 7 Trustee.

The tax implications from the settlement agreement establishes a pecuniary interest beyond any reasonable doubt. Yet the court ruled that I had no financial stake in proceedings that were generating actual tax liabilities in my name. This created the absurd situation where I was deemed to have insufficient interest in participating in proceedings that were simultaneously deemed significant enough to create tax obligations for me.

The Strategic Silencing

The denial of my pecuniary interest served a clear strategic purpose: to eliminate my voice from proceedings where I might have raised legitimate challenges. By declaring I had no financial stake, the court manufactured a justification to:

1. Prevent me from questioning the validity of the claimed debts

2. Block my challenges to the amounts being negotiated

3. Eliminate my ability to dispute improper procedures

4. Silence objections to agreements made between the Trustee and creditors

The Broader Injustice

To rule that I had no pecuniary interest did more than simply disadvantage me procedurally, it fundamentally corrupted the truth-seeking function of the bankruptcy process. My participation and my expert's participation would have introduced relevant facts and perspectives that might have led to different outcomes. By excluding our testimony based on a demonstrably false premise, the court ensured these perspectives would never be heard.

The claim that I lacked pecuniary interest stands as perhaps the most transparent fiction employed throughout the proceedings, a procedural sleight of hand that allowed the court to ignore the direct and substantial financial consequences being imposed upon me while simultaneously denying me any opportunity to address them.

Chapter Thirty-One

CONVERSION IS A BIG STICK

IMPORTANT: Understanding what strategies and/or arguments that should be made when a creditor attempts to convert a Chapter 11 or Chapter 13 re-organization case into a Chapter 7 liquidation case, which can lead to the loss of assets despite the debtor's efforts to reorganize. Knowing how to challenge such a motion, by proving good faith compliance, disputing creditor claims, and demonstrating that reorganization benefits all parties, can be critical in protecting one's financial future.

A BANKRUPTCY CONVERSION REPRESENTS a significant shift in a debtor's journey through the bankruptcy process, marking the transition from one chapter of the Bankruptcy Code to another. This procedural mechanism allows cases to adapt to changing circumstances, whether initiated by the debtor or imposed by the court system.

VOLUNTARY CONVERSION

Voluntary conversion occurs when debtors themselves decide that their current bankruptcy chapter no longer serves their best interests. A common scenario involves conversion from Chapter 13 to Chapter 7. This typically happens when debtors realize they cannot maintain their Chapter 13 payment plan due to deteriorating financial circumstances. Perhaps their income has become unstable or decreased substantially, making it impossible to fulfill the three-to-five-year repayment plan that Chapter 13 requires. In such situations, debtors may conclude that liquidation under Chapter 7 represents a more realistic path forward.

Conversely, debtors sometimes voluntarily convert from Chapter 7 to Chapter 13. This often occurs when they wish to protect non-exempt assets that would otherwise be liquidated under Chapter 7. Some debtors experience improved financial stability after initially filing for Chapter 7 and determine they can now manage a structured repayment plan. Others may convert to address specific debts that aren't dischargeable under Chapter 7, such as recent tax obligations or certain types of student loans. In some cases, debtors convert to Chapter 13 when facing a motion to dismiss their Chapter 7 case for abuse of the bankruptcy system.

The process for voluntary conversion typically requires filing a notice or motion with the bankruptcy court, paying any required conversion fees, submitting additional documentation specific to the new chapter, and attending any newly required meetings or hearings. While administratively straightforward, the decision to convert voluntarily should be made carefully, with full consideration of how it affects both the debtor's immediate situation and long-term financial recovery.

INVOLUNTARY CONVERSION

Involuntary conversion presents a more challenging scenario for debtors, as it represents the court's determination that a case should proceed under a different chapter, regardless of the debtor's wishes. When a case converts from Chapter 13 to Chapter 7 involuntarily, it typically results from the debtor's failure to make required plan payments, concealment of assets, fraudulent activity, or violations of court orders. In essence, the court determines that the Chapter 13 case cannot feasibly proceed as structured.

Involuntary conversion from Chapter 7 to Chapter 13 generally occurs when the court finds the debtor has sufficient disposable income to repay creditors, making liquidation inappropriate. This often stems from the means test indicating that allowing the debtor to proceed under Chapter 7 would constitute an "abuse" of the bankruptcy system. The United States Trustee frequently initiates these conversions after reviewing the debtor's financial information and determining that creditors would receive more if the debtor entered a payment plan.

The process for involuntary conversion involves a motion filed by a trustee, creditor, or the U.S. Trustee, followed by a hearing where the debtor can present arguments against conversion. If the court grants the motion, an order mandates the conversion, establishing new deadlines and requirements under the new chapter. For debtors, this can feel like having the rules changed midstream, often adding complexity and frustration to an already difficult process.

Legal and Financial Implications

When a bankruptcy case converts from one chapter to another, numerous legal and financial shifts occur simultaneously. A new trustee may be appointed, bringing different perspectives and priorities to the case. The bankruptcy estate, the collection of assets potentially available to creditors, gets redefined as of the conversion date. This timing can significantly impact what property remains subject to the bankruptcy proceeding.

New deadlines emerge for objections and claims, potentially disadvantaging creditors who were proceeding on the original timeline. Different exemption rules may apply depending on when property was acquired, creating complex questions about what assets the debtor can protect. For debtors who converted involuntarily, these changes often feel punitive rather than rehabilitative.

The implications of conversion extend beyond the technical aspects of the bankruptcy process. Financially, conversion can either provide relief or impose new burdens on the debtor, depending on their circumstances and whether they initiated the conversion. Psychologically, an involuntary conversion often creates additional stress during an already challenging time, as debtors must adapt to unexpected changes in how their financial future will unfold.

For creditors, conversions can either enhance or diminish the likelihood of recovery. A Chapter 7 liquidation might provide immediate partial payment, while a Chapter 13 plan might ultimately yield more substantial returns over time. When courts order involuntary conversions, they typically do so with creditors' interests in mind, believing the new chapter will better serve the collective interests of those owed money.

In the landscape of bankruptcy law, conversions serve as important adaptive mechanisms, allowing cases to respond to changing circumstances and realities. Whether voluntary or involuntary, these transitions fundamentally alter the trajectory of a bankruptcy case, reshaping the debtor's path toward financial recovery and the creditors' expectations for repayment.

CASE STUDY

In my case, the Court converted my Chapter 11 Reorganization to a Chapter 7 Liquidation, despite my submission of a Disclosure Statement and Chapter 11 Plan demonstrating a strong probability of success. I had used a proven template that had previously led to successful confirmation. Previously, my case was confirmed without additional streams of income, where now, I had income from my law practice, as well as the rental income of about $20,000 per month. Unfortunately, this made no difference.

Reversing a bankruptcy conversion is nearly impossible. Let me share the story of a family I represented after their Chapter 13 Bankruptcy was converted to Chapter 7. Previously, we discussed Bankruptcy Trustees, their role, and how financial interests influence the bankruptcy process. I want to add that Bankruptcy Trustees operate under the supervision of the United States Trustee Program. In Maryland, that office was led by Gerard Vetter. I had minimal interaction with him until I represented this family in their attempt to reverse a conversion.

I did not know about this family beforehand, nor did I recall who referred them to me, my assistant simply scheduled the appointment. When I met with them, a husband and wife from the Caribbean and their American military officer son-in-law, they were desperate and afraid. They explained that they had hired Brett Weiss to help reorganize their debt. He initially filed a Chapter 13 Bankruptcy for them but later converted it to Chapter 7. They had fallen behind on their mortgage payments, but their financial situation had improved since their daughter and son-in-law moved in.

They had initially filed a "bare-bones" bankruptcy (one without all required documentation and schedules) due to concerns that their total residential debt might exceed the Chapter 13 secured debt limit, which at the time was approximately $1,257,850. If their debt exceeded this threshold, they would have been ineligible for Chapter 13 and forced to file for Chapter 11 reorganization or Chapter 7 liquidation.

Brett Weiss charged $5,000 for Chapter 7 bankruptcy but required a $20,000 retainer at approximately $400 per hour for Chapter 11. The family opted for Chapter 13, which required $5,000 down, with the balance payable through their bankruptcy plan over 36–60 months. They filed a "bare-bones" Chapter 13, hoping the creditor's Proof of Claim would confirm their debt was below the Chapter 13 limit, as their mortgage statement suggested the figures were close.

As I recall, the creditor did file a Proof of Claim showing their debt was below the limit, meaning they were eligible to remain in Chapter 13. However, Brett Weiss, apparently unaware of this (having neither checked the figures nor contacted the mortgage company to verify the debt), had them convert to Chapter 7.

The problem with Chapter 7 is that it grants the Trustee the "power to sell" or liquidate assets, including those that are free and clear. In this case, the family owned two investment properties. The Chapter 7 Trustee, seeing the financial opportunity, refused to allow a conversion back to Chapter 13. There was simply too much money at stake.

Knowing the difficulty of opposing another attorney, I worked with the family to attempt a reversion to Chapter 13. They had nothing to lose, remaining in Chapter 7 meant losing everything.

As expected, the Chapter 7 Trustee provided multiple reasons to keep the case in Chapter 7, though he never mentioned the financial gains he and his associates (real estate agents, law firms, title companies, etc.) would receive from liquidating the properties. Brett Weiss testified that the family had signed documents consenting to the Chapter 7 conversion. The key question remained: why did Weiss have them sign Chapter 7 paperwork when the Proof of Claim and mortgage statement confirmed their debt was within the Chapter 13 limit?

The case was never converted back to Chapter 13. Gerard Vetter was present in the courtroom, quietly observing from the back. The family was ultimately forced out of their home, and all their assets were sold.

Chapter Thirty-Two

DEFENDING AGAINST A MOTION TO CONVERT

IMPORTANT: This information helps the reader maintain control over their preferred bankruptcy path (such as Chapter 11 reorganization versus Chapter 7 liquidation), preserving their business operations and long-term recovery prospects. Understanding what strategies can be employed when defending against a motion to convert.

A BANK MIGHT WANT to change a Debtor's bankruptcy from Chapter 11 reorganization to a Chapter 7 liquidation, where everything may be sold off, even if the Debtor is making payments. That might sound strange, but here's why:

1. The Bank Wants Its Money Faster

• Chapter 11 takes time because the company is working on a plan to pay its debts slowly.

• Chapter 7 would sell everything quickly, and the bank might get its money right away instead of waiting for years for payments.

2. The Bank Is in Trouble with the Law

• If the state attorney general found that the bank broke the law, it might have to follow special rules or sell its business.

• The bank might not want to wait around for slow payments; it may need to clean up its finances fast.

3. The Bank Is Selling Its Loans

• Sometimes, banks sell loans to other companies. If the bank is trying to sell, it might want the bankruptcy case to be finished quickly so the new owner doesn't have to deal with it.

• A Chapter 7 case would close things faster than a long Chapter 11 process.

4. The Bank Wants to Avoid More Problems

• If the company in bankruptcy is saying, "Hey, this bank treated us unfairly!" and is thinking about suing, the bank might not want to deal with that.

• A Chapter 7 trustee (a person who sells off the company's things) takes over the case, and the company has less power to fight the bank.

5. The Bank Doesn't Want the Loan Changed

• In Chapter 11, the company might get the court to change the loan, lower the amount owed, reduce the interest rate, or give more time to pay.

• The bank might want to stop this from happening and push for Chapter 7 instead, where the company's stuff is just sold off to pay debts.

6. The Bank Wants to Protect Its Reputation

• If the bank was caught doing something wrong, it might not want to be in a long, public fight with a company in bankruptcy.

• Ending the case quickly with Chapter 7 might help the bank move on and avoid bad press.

Remember, even if a Debtor is paying its debt, a bank might still want to switch to Chapter 7 so it can get its money faster, follow legal rules, avoid lawsuits, sell its loans, or protect its reputation. It's not always about the company's ability to pay, it's often about what's best for the bank.

DEFENDING A MOTION TO CONVERT FROM CHAPTER 11 TO CHAPTER 7

When a creditor files a motion to convert a Chapter 11 bankruptcy case to a Chapter 7 liquidation, the debtor must act promptly and strategically to demonstrate the feasibility of reorganization. Effectively opposing such a motion involves submitting a comprehensive disclosure statement, a proposed plan of reorganization, and timely monthly operating reports. These documents collectively provide the court with a detailed view of the debtor's financial health, operational stability, and ability to successfully reorganize under Chapter 11. Each serves a critical role in persuading the bankruptcy court to deny conversion and allow the debtor to continue restructuring.

The Disclosure Statement

The disclosure statement is a pivotal document in a Chapter 11 case, mandated under 11 U.S.C. § 1125. Its primary purpose is to furnish creditors with adequate information to evaluate the feasibility of the debtor's reorganization plan. The bankruptcy court must approve the disclosure statement before the plan can be submitted for creditor voting.

A well-prepared disclosure statement typically includes:

• A history of the debtor's business and the events leading to bankruptcy.

• A detailed analysis of assets, liabilities, and current financial condition.

• An explanation of how the reorganization plan will be executed.

• A comparison of creditor recoveries under Chapter 11 versus Chapter 7 liquidation.

By filing a robust disclosure statement, the debtor demonstrates transparency and a commitment to reorganization. This informs the court that the debtor has a clear strategy for repaying creditors, rather than opting for liquidation, which often results in diminished recoveries for unsecured creditors. In *In re Varat Enterprises, Inc*., 81 F.3d 1310 (4th Cir. 1996), the Fourth Circuit emphasized the importance of full disclosure to creditors to ensure informed decision-making during the reorganization process.

The Proposed Plan of Reorganization

The proposed plan of reorganization outlines how the debtor intends to restructure its debts while maintaining business operations. Governed by 11 U.S.C. § 1123, this document must contain specific elements to be considered confirmable by the court. A strong reorganization plan should include:

- Classification of creditor claims and treatment of each class.
- A feasible payment schedule demonstrating the debtor's ability to meet obligations.
- Identification of funding sources for plan execution.
- Provisions for the continuation of operations and potential growth strategies.
- Any necessary changes to management or business structure to enhance profitability.

The proposed plan serves as a direct rebuttal to a creditor's claim that conversion to Chapter 7 is necessary. It presents a structured and legally sound path for repayment, showing that liquidation is not in the best interest of creditors or the debtor. In *In re Maharaj,* 681 F.3d 558 (4th Cir. 2012), the Fourth Circuit highlighted that a feasible and comprehensive reorganization plan is central to the debtor's ability to continue under Chapter 11.

Monthly Operating Reports (MORs)

Monthly operating reports (MORs) are required under the U.S. Trustee guidelines and provide ongoing financial updates during the Chapter 11 process. These reports give the court a clear and current picture of the debtor's financial status, demonstrating whether the business remains viable. MORs typically include:

• Income and expenses for the reporting period.

• Cash flow statements showing liquidity.

• Accounts receivable and payable reports.

• Bank account reconciliations.

• Evidence of tax compliance and payroll obligations.

By submitting MORs, the debtor provides tangible proof of operational viability. Regularly filed MORs that reflect positive cash flow and the ability to meet financial obligations significantly weaken the creditor's argument that conversion is necessary. In *In re Superior Siding & Window, Inc.*, 14 F.3d 240 (4th Cir. 1994), the Fourth Circuit noted that compliance with reporting requirements and evidence of financial stability are critical factors in determining the appropriateness of conversion.

LEGAL JUSTIFICATIONS AGAINST CONVERSION

Under 11 U.S.C. § 1112(b), a court may convert a Chapter 11 case to Chapter 7 if it finds that the debtor is unable to effectively reorganize or is engaging in gross mismanagement.

However, conversion is not automatic, and the burden is on the moving party to establish cause. Courts have denied conversion when debtors show:

• A reasonable likelihood of successfully executing their reorganization plan.

• Sufficient cash flow to maintain operations and make payments under the plan.

• Compliance with reporting and procedural requirements.

• A better return to creditors under Chapter 11 than under Chapter 7 liquidation.

In *In re Landmark Atlantic Hess Farm, LLC*, 448 B.R. 707 (Bankr. D. Md. 2011), the court denied a motion to convert, emphasizing that the debtor's compliance with reporting requirements and the potential for successful reorganization weighed against conversion.

Impact of a Prior Chapter 11 Filing

A debtor who previously filed a Chapter 11 bankruptcy and had their plan confirmed despite insufficient income at the time may face heightened scrutiny in subsequent filings. However, if the debtor now has sufficient income to support a feasible plan, this change in circumstances is a strong argument against conversion. Courts will consider:

• Current income and financial stability: If the debtor can now support a Chapter 11 plan with sustainable revenue, this demonstrates an improved financial position.

• Lessons learned from the prior filing: If the debtor can show operational improvements and better financial management, this supports their ability to successfully complete reorganization.

• Creditor treatment comparison: If creditors receive a better recovery under Chapter 11 compared to Chapter 7, conversion is not in their best interest.

In *In re Timbuk* II, LLC, 452 B.R. 919 (Bankr. E.D.N.C. 2011), the court ruled that where a debtor has demonstrated improved financial stability and an ability to execute a feasible plan, a prior unsuccessful Chapter 11 does not automatically justify conversion. Similarly, in *In re Springfield Contracting Corp.*, 154 B.R. 214 (Bankr. E.D. Va. 1993), the court found that a debtor's demonstrated ability to manage finances more effectively in a second filing weighed against conversion.

REMEMBER: Creditors favor conversion to Chapter 7 when they believe that liquidation will maximize their recovery, shorten their time, allow them to take strategic steps, prevent further losses, and eliminate mismanagement. Courts weigh these concerns against the debtor's ability to propose a viable plan, ensure fairness to creditors, and meet obligations under Chapter 11.

CASE STUDY

In my bankruptcy, my goal was clear, to reorganize my debts, confirm a plan, and make structured monthly payments. I wasn't looking for a handout. I wasn't trying to escape my obligations. I was using the system exactly as it was designed, to restructure and rebuild.
But then came Patapsco's Bank motion to convert my Chapter 11 bankruptcy into a Chapter 7 liquidation, a move that would strip me of the real properties I had fought so hard to keep. This wasn't just a technicality; it was a deliberate attack on my efforts to regain control over my finances. If the motion was granted, I would lose everything. My properties would be seized and sold off; my years of investment wiped out in an instant.
So, the question became: What were my defenses? How could I oppose the conversion and fight to retain my assets?

Building a Defense Against Conversion

To oppose the motion, I had to demonstrate that I was actively progressing through the Chapter 11 process and that conversion would not benefit creditors. My defenses included:

1. Demonstrating Feasibility of the Plan – I had already obtained plan confirmation once, showing my ability to meet structured payments. There was no justifiable reason to claim I was incapable of following through.

2. Challenging the Creditor's Standing – Who were these alleged noteholders? Had they properly perfected their claims? Could they legally enforce the debt? In many cases, creditors pushing for conversion had questionable documentation at best.

3. Showing Good Faith Efforts to Reorganize – I had negotiated with creditors, made payments, and complied with court requirements. There was no pattern of delay or misconduct, only efforts to retain control over my assets.

4. Proving That Chapter 7 Would Yield Less Value – If my properties were liquidated under Chapter 7, the proceeds would barely cover secured debts, leaving little for unsecured creditors. A structured repayment plan in Chapter 11 was a better financial outcome for all parties.

5. Highlighting Procedural Deficiencies – Had the motion been filed correctly? Were there errors or inconsistencies in the creditor's claims? Often, procedural missteps could weaken their case.

The Fight for Control

This wasn't just a legal battle, it was a fight for my future, my investments, and the ability to dictate my own financial recovery. The push to convert my case wasn't about fairness or justice, it was about power and control.

QUESTIONS RAISED

I raised two questions. The first question was what was the correct date of maturity based on the loan modifications for both, 367 and 511, when (a) there is a clerical issue on the modification documents as to the wrong maturity date, March 30, 2014, versus the correct maturity date of March 30, 2015; and when (b) the modification documents contain the correct length of time "four (4) years" plus one (1) year.

It would be normal to ask, how did such an error occur? The confirmed plan dated March 11, 2011, contained the error and it was transferred throughout the documents. Below you will find the terms as set forth in the modification and I want to see if you can determine the error, even after being told.

"The Term of the Loan is extended for four (4) years such that the Loan will mature on March 30, 2014, subject, however to an "Extension Right" as hereafter provided. Provided that the Borrower timely and fully complies with terms, conditions and covenants contained in the Loan Documents, this Agreement and the Loan Documents associated with this Loan modification, the Borrower shall be provided with the right to extend the term of this modified loan for an additional (1) year period such that the maturity date will be extended through April 1, 2015 (the "Extension Right"), without the payment of any extension fee." The modification reflects a specific time of four (4) years plus (1)."

HOW SHOULD ERROR BE CORRECTED?

As a rule, courts apply specific legal principles to interpret and resolve inconsistencies. The goal is to determine the intent of the parties at the time of contracting and uphold the enforceability of the agreement. Below are the key principles used in such cases:

1. The Hierarchy of Contract Terms

When faced with contradictory terms, courts prioritize specific terms over general terms. If a contract includes both a broad general term and a more specific term that contradicts it, the specific term prevails because it represents the more precise intent of the parties (Restatement (Second) of Contracts § 203(c)). Handwritten or typed terms prevail over pre-printed terms. Courts give greater weight to manually added or specially typed terms rather than standardized, boilerplate language (UCC § 2-208(2)).

2. The Principle of Contra Proferentem

If ambiguity remains, courts interpret the contract against the drafter. This rule is especially relevant in adhesion contracts or agreements where one party had significantly more control over drafting the terms (Restatement (Second) of Contracts § 206). Courts will resolve ambiguities in favor of the non-drafting party.

3. The Parol Evidence Rule and Exceptions

Generally, extrinsic evidence (outside evidence such as oral agreements) is not allowed to alter a written contract. However, exceptions exist (a) to clarify ambiguity. If the contract language is unclear, courts may admit extrinsic evidence to establish what the parties intended at the time of contracting (UCC § 2-202). And (b) to show trade usage or prior dealings. Customary practices or past transactions between the parties can help clarify the meaning of contradictory terms (UCC § 1-303).

4. Course of Performance, Course of Dealing, and Trade Usage

When interpreting contradictory terms, courts consider how the contract has been performed in practice:

i. Course of Performance: How the parties have acted under this specific contract.

ii. Course of Dealing: How the parties have interacted in prior contracts.

iii. Trade Usage: Industry standards that may explain ambiguous terms (UCC § 1-303).

5. Good Faith and Fair Dealing

Every contract includes an implied duty of good faith and fair dealing (Restatement (Second) of Contracts § 205). If contradictory terms create confusion, courts will favor an interpretation that aligns with fairness and reasonableness.

SUPPORTING EVIDENCE TO SHOW INTENT

To determine what the parties intended when signing a contract, courts may consider:

• Negotiation history (emails, letters, drafts).

• Industry standards (evidence of how similar contracts are interpreted).

• Prior performance (how parties have acted under the contract).

• Testimonies or affidavits from parties involved.

When contract terms conflict, courts use hierarchy rules, extrinsic evidence, trade usage, and good faith principles to resolve contradictions. The goal is to uphold the agreement's enforceability while honoring the parties' intent at the time of contracting.

EVIDENCE

In my case, I relied on a series of emails exchanged between my attorney and the lender's attorney to demonstrate that there was a mutual understanding and a binding agreement. These emails provide a clear record of negotiations, confirmations, and expectations regarding the modification of my loan terms. Please see the following:

A. Email dated September 23, 2010 – My attorney informed me that the creditor's attorney acknowledged our proposal and indicated that, while he had not yet reviewed it, he was not ignoring us. My attorney also noted that the plan anticipated a five-year Chapter 11 period, during which we would work toward refinancing post-discharge.

B. Email dated November 2, 2010 – Subject line: "Lender agrees to 4 + 1." This email confirmed that the lender's attorney had agreed to the proposed terms, with a follow-up email from the lender's attorney expected to confirm the agreement.

C. Email dated November 2, 2010 – My attorney stated that he would need to prepare an Amended Plan incorporating all agreed-upon terms, reinforcing that an agreement had been reached.

D. Email dated December 2, 2010 – The lender's attorney contacted my attorney to follow up on the Third Amended Disclosure Statement, indicating an expectation that the modifications were moving forward.

E. Email dated February 2, 2015 – My attorney confirmed receipt of two ballots from Patapsco Bank, both accepting the plan as an impaired class, which indicated that the lender had agreed to modified terms under the Chapter 11 framework.

F. Email dated March 6, 2011 – The lender gave my attorney explicit permission to speak on their behalf at the confirmation hearing. This authorization suggests a clear mutual understanding of the agreement and an acknowledgment that my attorney trusted to convey its terms.

G. Email dated June 30, 2011 – The lender's attorney sent modification documents to my attorney, explicitly stating that they contained the previously agreed-upon terms included in the confirmed Disclosure Statement.

These emails provide compelling evidence that there was a meeting of the minds, a fundamental requirement for contract enforceability. The lender's consistent acknowledgment and participation in the negotiation process supports the position that the agreed-upon terms were binding and should have been upheld.

REPUTATION OF CREDITOR, PATAPSCO BANK AKA HOWARD BANK

Patapsco Bank, later purchased by Howard Bank, had a deeply troubled history. Their financial practices were so questionable that they were forced to sign a written agreement with the Federal Reserve Bank of Richmond and the Maryland Commissioner of Financial Regulations, committing to reform their operations to comply with banking laws. This agreement wasn't voluntary, it came after a Task Force Report exposed a series of discrepancies, complaints, and regulatory concerns surrounding the lender's activities.

Regulatory agencies, including the Board of Governors of the Federal Reserve System, the Federal Deposit Insurance Corporation (FDIC), the National Credit Union Administration, and the Office of the Comptroller of the Currency, issued interagency supervisory guidance specifically addressing Troubled Debt Restructurings (TDRs), a major issue for this lender. Their financial mismanagement was so severe that the bank was ultimately deemed unfit to continue operations independently and was slated for sale.

Chapter Thirty-Three

CARVE-OUTS IN BANKRUPTCY: ARE THEY BRIBES?

IMPORTANT: Understanding a "carve-out" also known as a "Trustee Bribe." When Trustees enter into settlement agreements for a fee and how those arrangements create conflicts of interest that prioritize trustee and attorney fees over fair asset distribution. Recognizing how carve-outs impacts the process help protect rights, negotiate effectively, and challenge unfair practices that could undermine financial recovery.

BANKRUPTCY IS MEANT TO be a fair process where debtors can either restructure their debts or liquidate assets to pay creditors. At its core, the system relies on objectivity, ensuring that all parties, the debtor, creditors, and trustee, work toward a resolution that is just and transparent. However, carve-outs, which allow money to be set aside for attorneys, trustees, and other professionals, introduce serious conflicts of interest that can distort the process.

Carve-outs can function in ways that resemble a bribe because they incentivize trustees and law firms to prioritize their own financial gain over the best interests of creditors and debtors. When a trustee controls key aspects of a case, acting as both legal counsel and a decision-maker, while hiring appraisers and real estate agents they have financial ties to, the bankruptcy process becomes less about fairness and more about profit. This manipulation can reduce payouts to creditors, prevent debtors from fairly buying back their own assets, and undermine trust in the system.

HOW CARVE-OUTS DISTORT THE BANKRUPTCY PROCESS

A bankruptcy trustee is supposed to be a neutral party, ensuring that assets are managed properly and fairly distributed. However, when trustees have financial relationships with the law firms, appraisers, and real estate agents involved in the case, objectivity is compromised. Trustees who direct legal work to their own firms or approve real estate sales handled by business associates are not truly independent. Instead, they stand to personally benefit from the very decisions they are making, which creates a clear conflict of interest.

Appraisals, which play a critical role in determining the value of a debtor's assets, can also be manipulated. If an appraiser undervalues a business or property, it can be sold at a price far lower than its true worth. This benefits the buyer, often a firm or individual with connections to the trustee, but harms creditors and debtors. By controlling the appraisal process, trustees can create a situation where the estate's assets are sold cheaply while still ensuring that legal fees are paid first through carve-outs.

For example, if a debtor owns a business worth $1 million, but the trustee hires an appraiser who values it at only $500,000, the business can be sold at a discount. The trustee's law firm and other professionals still receive their carve-out payments, but creditors receive far less than they should. Meanwhile, the debtor, who might have been willing to buy back their business at a fair price, is shut out of the process entirely.

How Carve-Outs Hurt Debtors Who Want to Buy Back Their Estate

In some bankruptcy cases, a debtor may wish to "buy out" their estate by paying creditors a fair price for their assets instead of having them liquidated. In theory, this can be a win-win situation, creditors get paid without the delays of asset sales, and the debtor can continue their business or keep their property. However, carve-outs make this process far more difficult, especially when a trustee and their firm have financial incentives to sell assets to third parties rather than back to the debtor.

If legal fees and trustee expenses are inflated through carve-outs, the amount that creditors receive is reduced, making it harder for a debtor to negotiate a buyout. Additionally, if an asset is deliberately undervalued, the debtor may be unable to match the artificially low price offered by an insider who benefits from the carve-out system. This turns bankruptcy into a rigged game, one where debtors are pushed out of reclaiming their assets, while trustees and law firms ensure they get paid first.

There have been cases where courts recognized this problem and intervened. In *In re Hotel Syracuse, Inc.*, 275 B.R. 679 (Bankr. N.D.N.Y. 2002), the court found that a trustee's law firm had charged excessive fees, reducing the money available for creditors. The judge rejected the fees, emphasizing that they were not in the best interests of the estate. Similarly, in *In re Kobra Properties*, 406 B.R. 396 (Bankr. E.D. Cal. 2009), the court ruled that manipulated appraisals led to undervalued sales, benefiting insiders while harming creditors. These cases illustrate how courts have pushed back against carve-outs that create conflicts of interest, but such abuses continue to occur because the incentives remain strong.

The Bigger Picture: How Carve-Outs Undermine Trust in the System

Bankruptcy depends on the idea that all parties act in good faith to resolve financial issues fairly. However, when carve-outs are misused, they create a system where lawyers and trustees profit while creditors and debtors suffer. If creditors believe that most of the estate will be eaten up by legal fees, they may stop negotiating in good faith. If debtors see that they have no realistic chance of buying back their own assets, they may avoid bankruptcy altogether, hiding assets or seeking alternative ways to escape the system.

The damage is not just financial; it is also a matter of perception. When bankruptcy cases appear to be dominated by self-serving professionals rather than a fair legal process, trust in the system erodes. Creditors lose confidence that they will receive fair treatment, and debtors feel powerless against a process that seems designed to enrich insiders at their expense.

The Need for Reform

Carve-outs were originally intended to ensure that legal professionals are paid for their work, but they have increasingly become a tool for self-enrichment. To restore fairness, reforms are needed. Trustees should not be allowed to hire their own law firms for bankruptcy cases they oversee, appraisals should be independently reviewed to prevent manipulation and carve-outs should be limited to ensure they do not drain estate funds before creditors receive their fair share.

Until such reforms take place, bankruptcy will continue to be a system where insiders win, creditors lose, and debtors have little chance of recovering fairly. The process should be about achieving justice, not maximizing profits for a select few. Only by addressing the inherent conflicts in carve-outs can the bankruptcy system regain its integrity and truly serve those it was designed to help.

CASE STUDY

My experience revealed how carve-out agreements can be weaponized to circumvent proper judicial process and deny fundamental rights to debtors. What transpired was not merely a legal maneuver but a systematic subversion of justice:

The Strategic Retreat

When my creditor initially sought to lift the automatic stay, they presented their case as requiring jurisdiction in the county state court. This is a standard request, until that court signaled it would likely grant me an injunction. What followed exposed the true nature of their strategy.

The Backroom Arrangement

Facing an unfavorable ruling in the state court, the creditors hastily abandoned their own argument about proper venue. Instead, they retreated to the bankruptcy court with a proposal that revealed their actual objectives: a carve-out agreement with the Trustee.

- They would pay a designated portion of the proceeds to the Trustee,
- In exchange, the Trustee would expedite the sale of my buildings, and
- The agreement explicitly blocked any meaningful defenses I might raise

As the culminating blow, it mandated the removal of my business from the premises.

The Corruption of Fiduciary Duty

This arrangement corrupted the purpose of the bankruptcy system. The Trustee, who should have been operating as a fiduciary for all parties including me as the debtor, effectively became a paid agent of my creditor. The carve-out payment functioned as compensation for the Trustee to adopt the creditor's objectives as his own.

The Judicial System Compromised

The most disturbing aspect of this arrangement was how it bypassed genuine judicial review. By securing the Trustee's cooperation, the creditor effectively neutralized the court as an independent arbiter. What should have been contested, issues requiring judicial determination were converted into "agreed orders" between the Trustee and creditor.

The Illusion of Process

While these actions maintained the outward appearance of legal procedure, they hollowed out its substance. The carve-out transformed what should have been an impartial process into a transaction, one where my rights and interests could be bargained away by parties who were supposed to ensure fair treatment under the law.

Chapter Thirty-Four

CONTEMPT IN BANKRUPTCY COURT

IMPORTANT: If you do not comply with the Judge's order, you can be found in contempt of court which may result in severe consequences, including fines, sanctions, or even jail time, jeopardizing the financial fresh start. Additionally, a finding of "contempt" can be misused to silence individuals who challenge unfair treatment while trying to protect their rights and navigate the legal system more effectively.

IMAGINE YOU'RE IN CLASS, and the teacher gives you a direct order: "Stop talking and turn in your homework." But instead of listening, you stand up, keep chatting, and toss your homework in the trash. What happens next? The teacher isn't just going to let that slide, you're probably getting detention, a call home, or worse.

Well, in bankruptcy court, if you ignore the judge's orders or refuse to follow the rules, the legal version of detention kicks in, it's called contempt of court. And trust me, contempt in bankruptcy court is no joke. It can lead to fines, sanctions, or even jail time.

What is Contempt in Bankruptcy Court?

Contempt happens when someone disrespects the authority of the court or disobeys a court order. This can apply to debtors (the person filing bankruptcy), creditors, attorneys, and even trustees. The court has the power to punish anyone who refuses to follow the legal process. There are two types of contempt:

1. Civil Contempt – This is like a teacher making you stay after school until you finish your missing homework. The goal is to force you to comply with the court's order. If a debtor refuses to turn over assets that the court ordered them to hand over, they could be held in civil contempt until they cooperate.

2. Criminal Contempt – This is much worse. Criminal contempt is like getting expelled instead of just detention. The court punishes you for disrespecting its authority, and the punishment can include fines or even jail time. If a debtor lies under oath, hides assets, or openly defies the court, they might face criminal contempt charges.

What Laws Give Bankruptcy Courts the Power to Hold You in Contempt?

While the Bankruptcy Code (Title 11, U.S. Code) doesn't specifically spell out contempt rules, bankruptcy courts rely on 28 U.S.C. § 157 and 11 U.S.C. § 105(a) to enforce orders and punish violations.

• 28 U.S.C. § 157 gives bankruptcy judges the power to issue orders in cases under their jurisdiction. If you don't follow those orders, they can hold you in contempt.

• 11 U.S.C. § 105(a) is like the "catch-all" rule. It allows bankruptcy judges to issue any order necessary to carry out the purpose of the bankruptcy process. If you're messing with that process, by hiding money, ignoring court rulings, or refusing to cooperate, the judge can use this section to punish you with contempt.

How Can Contempt Damage a Debtor?

If a debtor is held in contempt, the consequences can wreck their bankruptcy case and their financial future.

First, the court may deny the discharge of their debts, which means they remain stuck with all their unpaid bills. If the whole point of filing bankruptcy was to get a fresh start, contempt can slam that door shut and leave the debtor worse off than before.

Second, contempt can come with serious financial penalties. The judge can issue fines, order extra payments to creditors, or force the debtor to cover the other side's legal fees. If the debtor was hoping to get out of bankruptcy clean, contempt might leave them drowning in even more debt.

Third, and most extreme, jail time is possible. While it's rare, some debtors who repeatedly lie, hide assets, or ignore court orders have been thrown behind bars. It's one thing to have bad credit, but it's another whole problem when you're wearing an orange jumpsuit in federal lock-up.

CONTEMPT AND DISCRIMINATION

Now, imagine a debtor is trying to play by the rules and highlight wrongdoing by the bankruptcy court itself. Instead of being given a fair chance, they find themselves punished with contempt just for pointing out unfair treatment.

Let's say a debtor files for bankruptcy but notices that the court is treating them differently than other debtors in similar situations. Maybe the judge is refusing to grant legal protections that are normally available to debtors. Maybe they're being denied access to the same bankruptcy benefits as others. If this happens, the debtor may argue that they are being discriminated against and denied due process under the law.

Real-Life Example: When Bankruptcy Courts Go Too Far

Take the case of *In re Ruffalo*, 390 U.S. 544 (1968), where the Supreme Court ruled that a court's actions violated due process when they imposed severe punishment without giving the accused a fair chance to defend themselves. The lesson? Judges must follow the rules too, they can't use contempt as a weapon to silence debtors who challenge unfair treatment.

Or consider *Turner v. Rogers*, 564 U.S. 431 (2011), where the Supreme Court ruled that a person couldn't be jailed for failing to pay debts unless they were given proper legal protections. If a bankruptcy court jails a debtor without ensuring that their rights are respected, that could be unconstitutional.

Fighting Back Against Judicial Bias in Bankruptcy Court

If a debtor believes they are being unfairly targeted with contempt charges, they have legal tools to fight back:

1. Filing an Appeal – The debtor can take their case to a higher court, arguing that the judge abused their power.

2. Requesting a Recusal – If a judge appears biased, the debtor can request that the judge be removed from the case.

3. Challenging the Contempt Order – The debtor can argue that the contempt charge violates constitutional protections, such as due process under the Fifth and Fourteenth Amendments.

Don't be Fooled, Fighting Back is Hard!

Fighting back against judicial bias in the bankruptcy court is difficult for several reasons, even though legal tools exist. Here's why each of these options presents major challenges:

1. Filing an Appeal - The Burden of Proof is High

Appealing a judge's decision isn't as simple as saying, "Hey, this isn't fair!" A debtor must prove that the judge abused their discretion, a very high legal standard. Courts usually defer to the bankruptcy judge's decisions unless there is clear evidence of misconduct or legal error.

• Judicial discretion: Bankruptcy judges have broad authority in making rulings, and appellate courts rarely overturn their decisions unless they are clearly unreasonable.

• Time-consuming and costly: Appeals take months (or even years) and require extensive legal briefing, which can be expensive for a debtor already in financial distress.

• Limited success: Even if an appeal is granted, the higher court may simply send the case back to the same judge, meaning the debtor still must deal with the same biases.

2. Requesting a Recusal – Judges Rarely Step Aside

If a debtor believes the judge is biased, they can file a motion to recuse (remove) the judge. But here's the problem: judges decide their own recusal motions in most cases. That means the same judge accused of bias gets to rule on whether they should step aside.

• High burden of proof: The debtor must show actual bias, not just unfavorable rulings. Judges can argue that their decisions were legally justified, making it nearly impossible to prove bias.

• Reluctance to recuse: Judges often believe they are impartial, and they don't like setting a precedent of stepping aside just because a party feels they are unfair.

• Systemic protection of judges: Courts generally protect their own, meaning that higher courts are hesitant to criticize a bankruptcy judge unless the misconduct is extreme.

3. Challenging the Contempt Order – Legal Roadblocks

Contempt rulings can be challenged, especially if they violate due process under the Fifth and Fourteenth Amendments, but this is an uphill battle.

• Courts favor judges' authority: Contempt is meant to enforce compliance with court orders. Judges have wide discretion in using contempt powers, and higher courts tend to support these decisions unless there is clear evidence of abuse.

• Procedural traps: The debtor must file the correct motions and follow strict procedural rules, which can be overwhelming without a lawyer. If they miss a deadline or file the wrong paperwork, their challenge may be dismissed outright.

• Risk of retaliation: If the challenge fails, the judge could impose even harsher penalties, making the debtor's situation worse.

Challenging judicial bias in bankruptcy court is notably difficult, with few documented cases where debtors have successfully proven such bias. Allegations of bias often stem from adverse rulings, but courts typically require evidence of bias from an extrajudicial source, meaning bias arising outside of the judge's official actions and decisions. For instance, in a case from the United States Bankruptcy Court for the Eastern District of Wisconsin, debtors sought the recusal of a judge based on adverse rulings and statements made during hearings. The court denied the motion, emphasizing that adverse judicial decisions alone do not constitute valid grounds for claims of bias or partiality.

The scarcity of successful challenges highlights the judiciary's commitment to impartiality and the high threshold required to substantiate claims of judicial bias. Debtors considering such challenges should consult with legal professionals to assess the merits of their claims and navigate the complexities of the legal process.

Bankruptcy Judges Have Power, But Not Unlimited Power

Contempt in bankruptcy court is supposed to ensure that people follow the rules, not to punish debtors unfairly. When a judge uses contempt charges to silence a debtor who is simply asking for fair treatment, that crosses the line.

Bankruptcy laws exist to give people a fresh start, not to trap them in legal battles where the court picks favorites. If a debtor is being treated unfairly or denied access to bankruptcy protections, they have the right to challenge the system and ensure that the law is applied equally.

So, if a judge starts acting like a biased referee, calling penalties only against one side, the debtor doesn't have to just take it, they can fight back using the law and demand the fair treatment that bankruptcy was designed to provide.

But keep in mind that while it is possible to fight back against judicial bias in bankruptcy court, the reality is that the system heavily favors judges and creditors. Appeals are hard to win, recusal requests are usually denied, and contempt orders are difficult to overturn. Without strong legal representation, debtors often find themselves trapped in an unfair legal process with limited options for recourse.

CASE STUDY

In my case, the courtroom became a theater of humiliation rather than a forum for justice. What follows is my experience of being systematically silenced and demeaned throughout the proceedings:

A Pattern of Unsupported Accusations

The Trustee wielded allegations as weapons, making damaging claims without evidence. When he accused me of turning off the water to intimidate tenants, despite the creditor managing the property at that time, he did so without providing a single witness, document, or specific detail about who, when, or how this allegedly occurred. These baseless accusations were clearly designed to poison the court's perception of me while evading the burden of proof.

Systematic Dismissal of Valid Arguments

Any attempt I made to defend myself was immediately labeled "frivolous" by the Trustee. This dismissive categorization occurred regardless of the documentation or evidence I presented. This pattern created an impossible situation: my defense was dismissed before it could even be considered on its merits, establishing a pretense that I had nothing legitimate to contribute to my own case.

Hostile Questioning Techniques

The interrogation style employed against me was deliberately intimidating. Questions were delivered with contemptuous tones and accusatory language, creating an atmosphere where raising any objection or alternate perspective felt dangerous. This technique effectively suppressed my willingness to challenge their narrative, as each attempt was met with escalating hostility.

Selective Exclusion of Evidence

The court's refusal to hear my expert witness, who had traveled specifically to testify, revealed the proceedings' one-sided nature. This professional had come at considerable expense and inconvenience, yet their potentially case-altering testimony was summarily blocked, eliminating a crucial element of my defense.

Demonstrative Disrespect from the Bench

Perhaps most demoralizing was the Judge's physical manifestation of contempt. As I spoke, he would deliberately rotate his chair a full 180 degrees away from me and recline backward, a clear, non-verbal message that my words were unworthy of even the pretense of attention. This theatrical display of disinterest communicated to everyone present that my perspective had been rejected before it was even fully expressed.

Repeated Contempt Findings

The court found me in contempt three separate times, creating an escalating pattern of judicial censure that further undermined my standing. These contempt findings had a compounding effect, each one making it increasingly difficult to be heard as a credible party in my own case, effectively labeling me as obstinate rather than someone attempting to assert legitimate rights.

Jurisdictional Manipulation

What made this experience particularly devastating was the creditor's tactical manipulation of jurisdiction. After successfully requesting relief from the automatic stay to pursue their claims in another court, the creditor abruptly reversed course when that alternative jurisdiction appeared poised to grant me an injunction. They hastily retreated to the bankruptcy court, a forum they had previously claimed was inadequate, solely because the other venue seemed likely to rule in my favor. This blatant forum shopping was permitted without scrutiny, revealing how procedural rules were flexibly applied to benefit my opponents while being rigidly enforced against me.

Intimidation Through Force

The Judge's decision to summon U.S. Marshals immediately after ruling against me regarding the property sale transformed legal disagreement into threatening spectacle. This disproportionate response to a standard legal ruling conveyed that challenging the court's decisions, even through normal legal channels, would be met with the threat of force, creating an atmosphere of fear rather than procedural fairness.

These tactics collectively created an environment where I was not merely losing a case but being systematically stripped of dignity and the right to meaningful participation in proceedings that would determine my financial future.

Chapter Thirty-Five

WHAT IS AN EXPARTE COMMUNICATION?

IMPORTANT: Ex parte refers to communication or legal action taken by one party in a case without the other party being present or given a chance to respond. In bankruptcy court, ex parte communication between a judge and one side, such as the trustee or a creditor, can create an unfair advantage and undermine the debtor's right to a fair hearing.

IMAGINE YOU'RE PLAYING A game, and the referee pulls one team aside to whisper some secret game-changing rules, without telling the other team. Sounds unfair, right? That's exactly what ex parte communication is in the legal world.

Ex parte communication happens when a judge talks privately with one party in a case without the other party being present. This is a big no-no because it creates an unfair advantage and makes it seem like the judge is picking favorites instead of being neutral.

Why is Ex Parte Communication Important?

Courts are supposed to be fair and impartial, meaning they don't favor one side over the other. But when a judge has secret conversations with just one party, it raises serious questions like:

• Is the judge getting biased information?

• Is the judge making decisions based on what one side is saying, instead of looking at all the facts?

• Can the other party ever get a fair shot?

Even if the judge means well, just the appearance of favoritism destroys trust in the legal system. And if people can't trust the courts, then the whole system starts to crumble.

How Does Ex Parte Communication Affect a Defendant in a Bankruptcy Case?

Now, let's say a judge, the United States Trustee overseeing the bankruptcy case, and the attorney for the Chapter 7 trustee are having private conversations about your case without you or your lawyer being present. Here's why that's a disaster for the defendant:

1. Decisions Might Be Made Without Your Input

a. If they discuss legal strategies, case facts, or financial details without your side of the story, how can you trust the outcome?

b. The judge might be convinced of something that isn't true because they didn't hear your side.

2. You're Fighting a Rigged Game

a. If the judge has already heard and considered the trustee's arguments in private, then when you finally get your turn to talk, it might be too late.

b. The judge could have already made up their mind before you even enter the courtroom.

3. It Looks Corrupt

a. Even if the judge isn't actually favoring the other side, it looks bad.

b. People will assume the system is unfair, making it harder for anyone to believe in justice.

What Does the Law Say About Ex Parte Communication?

Ex parte communication isn't just unfair, it's illegal in many cases. Here are some key laws and court cases that address it:

1. 28 U.S.C. § 455 – This law requires judges to step aside (recuse themselves) from a case if their impartiality might reasonably be questioned.

(a) If a judge is caught having secret meetings with one side, this law gives the defendant a strong reason to demand a new judge or even a new trial.

2. Canon 3(A)(4) of the Code of Conduct for United States Judges – This rule explicitly forbids judges from having one-sided communications about a case unless both parties are present or given a fair chance to respond.

3. *In re Kensington Int'l Ltd.,* 368 F.3d 289 (3d Cir. 2004) – This case involved a judge having private meetings with government officials about a bankruptcy case.

i. The court ruled that these secret meetings created an appearance of bias and undermined confidence in the legal process.

ii. Translation: Ex parte communication wrecks fairness and trust in the courts.

WHY THIS MATTERS IN YOUR CASE

If the judge, the U.S. Trustee, and the Chapter 7 trustee's attorney are secretly discussing your bankruptcy case, then:

- You're not getting a fair trial because decisions might be made behind closed doors.
- The judge may already be biased before hearing your arguments.
- It violates federal law and judicial conduct rules, giving you strong grounds to object and possibly request a different judge.

Bottom Line

Ex parte communication isn't just a "small mistake." It's a serious violation that can destroy a defendant's chance of fairness. It creates the appearance of favoritism, which is just as damaging as actual bias. Courts are supposed to be neutral referees, but when judges have secret huddles with one team, the whole game is unfair.

CASE STUDY

Though one cannot definitively know what transpires in one's absence, certain moments create undeniable suspicion. The most telling instance occurred when the Judge entered the courtroom and, without preamble or context, immediately demanded: "Why aren't you letting people in the building?"

This question, loaded with accusation and presumed facts, was jarring precisely because it referenced matters never previously raised in open court. The query clearly built upon information the Judge had received through channels outside the formal proceedings, information to which I had no opportunity to respond.

The Architecture of Disadvantage

The nature of this question revealed several troubling elements:

1. It contained a presumption of misconduct ("aren't letting people in") that had never been established through testimony or evidence in my presence.

2. It demonstrated the Judge had formed opinions on disputed facts without my knowledge or participation.

3. It signaled that conversations about central issues in my case were occurring in settings where I could not defend myself.

4. It positioned me to respond to accusations whose origin, context, and supporting details remained hidden from me.

Beyond Coincidence

This was not merely a matter of the Judge having background knowledge. The specific phrasing, timing, and certainty with which the allegation was delivered suggested recent and detailed communication with parties adverse to my interests, communication from which I had been deliberately excluded.

The impossibility of knowing precisely what was said in these private exchanges only amplified their damaging effect. I was left to defend against shadows, fighting accusations whose full substance remained concealed.

Systemic Imbalance

Such moments transform theoretical concerns about judicial impartiality into concrete disadvantages. When a judge's understanding of key facts is shaped in private conversations with opposing parties, the foundation of adversarial justice, where both sides have equal opportunity to present their case, crumbles silently but completely.

Chapter Thirty-Six

DISCHARGEABLE VERSUS NON-DISCHARGEABLE DEBT

IMPORTANT: Not all debts are dischargeable. You must know which debts are and are not dischargeable since the primary reason for filing bankruptcy is to provide financial relief and get a fresh start by eliminating debts. This critical knowledge helps set realistic expectations about which debts will remain after bankruptcy, allowing better long-term financial planning and potential negotiation strategies.

IMAGINE YOUR LIFE IS like a video game, and you've hit a level where you're being chased by a swarm of monsters, in this case, a mountain of debt. You're overwhelmed, you can't move forward, and it seems like there's no escape. That's where bankruptcy, and specifically the idea of a "discharge," comes in.

A discharge in bankruptcy is essentially a legal "power-up" that wipes away most of your debts. It's like pressing a reset button, giving you a fresh start. When a judge grants a discharge, it means creditors can no longer legally pursue you for those debts. They can't call you, send you letters, or take you to court. It's as if those debts never existed. This is why people file bankruptcy. They want to get their debt discharge and escape the overwhelming pressure of their financial burdens.

For example, Sarah, a single mom, lost her job and faced mounting medical bills after a car accident. She tried her best, but the bills piled up, and she couldn't keep up. The constant calls from debt collectors were making her life miserable. So, she filed for Chapter 7 bankruptcy. After going through the process, the judge granted her a discharge, and those medical bills were gone. She could finally breathe again and focus on rebuilding her life.

The United States Bankruptcy Code, specifically 11 U.S.C. § 727 for Chapter 7 and 11 U.S.C. § 1328 for Chapter 13, outlines the conditions for obtaining a discharge. The idea is that honest debtors deserve a fresh start, a chance to recover from financial hardship.

NON-DISCHARGEABLE DEBT

However, not all debts are discharged. Certain categories of debts are expressly designated as non-dischargeable, meaning they survive the bankruptcy process and remain the debtor's responsibility. Foremost among non-dischargeable debts are domestic support obligations, encompassing child support, alimony, and other forms of spousal or child maintenance. These obligations are considered fundamental to the well-being of families, and courts prioritize their enforcement to ensure the financial security of dependents. The legal basis for this is found in 11 U.S.C. § 523(a)(5).

Debts arising from willful and malicious injury, as defined in 11 U.S.C. § 523(a)(6), also fall outside the scope of discharge. This provision prevents debtors from escaping liability for intentional harm inflicted upon others or their property. To establish non-dischargeability under this section, a creditor must demonstrate that the debtor intended to cause the injury, not merely that the injury resulted from the debtor's actions.

Similarly, debts obtained through fraudulent means, such as false pretenses, false representations, or actual fraud, are non-dischargeable under 11 U.S.C. § 523(a)(2). This protects creditors from debtors who obtain credit through deception. The Supreme Court case *Field v. Mans*, 516 U.S. 59 (1995), clarified the standard for "justifiable reliance" in fraud-based non-dischargeability actions, emphasizing the importance of a creditor's reasonable belief in the debtor's representations.

Certain tax obligations, particularly those related to fraudulent tax returns or recent tax liabilities, are also non-dischargeable. This reflects the government's strong interest in collecting taxes and prevents debtors from using bankruptcy as a means of evading these obligations.

Furthermore, federal and most private student loans are generally non-dischargeable. Congress has made it difficult to discharge student loans, reflecting concerns about potential abuse and the importance of educational debt. It is very difficult to discharge student loans, requiring a showing of "undue hardship".

Finally, debts related to criminal activity, such as fines, penalties, and restitution orders, are non-dischargeable. This ensures that individuals cannot escape the consequences of their criminal actions through bankruptcy.

It is important to understand that in many instances, creditors must initiate an adversary proceeding within the bankruptcy case to establish that a debt is non-dischargeable, and they bear the burden of proving that the debt falls within one of the designated categories.

PURPOSE OF THE BANKRUPTCY CODE

The Supreme Court has addressed the importance of a fresh start in cases like Local Loan Co. v. Hunt, 292 U.S. 234 (1934). In this case, the Court emphasized that bankruptcy is intended to provide a "new opportunity in life and a clear field for future effort, unhampered by the pressure and discouragement of preexisting debt." This highlights the fundamental purpose of discharge: to give debtors a chance to rebuild their lives.

Another example is a small business owner, John, who took out loans to expand his restaurant. When the economy took a downturn, his business failed, and he was left with huge debts. He filed for Chapter 13 bankruptcy, which allowed him to create a repayment plan. After completing his plan, the remaining eligible debts were discharged. He was able to close his failed business and start a new job, without the burden of the old debts.

This principle, codified in 11 U.S.C. § 523, serves to balance the debtor's right to a new beginning with the legitimate interests of creditors and the broader societal values that underpin the legal system.

RULING OF NONDISCHARGEABILITY AS PUNITIVE MEASURE

Remember, Chapter 7 Trustees are like the referee in a bankruptcy game. Their job is to make sure everyone plays by the rules and that the creditors get as much of their money back as possible from what the debtor owns.

Let's say a debtor, we'll call them Alex, discovered that two creditors and the Trustee were working together to commit fraud. Alex, being honest, blew the whistle and told the court. Now, instead of investigating the fraud, the Trustee tries to get all of Alex's debts declared non-dischargeable, meaning Alex will have to pay them back forever, even after bankruptcy.

This is where things get tricky. The Bankruptcy Code, which is like the rulebook for bankruptcy, has specific reasons why a debt can be non-dischargeable. These reasons are usually about protecting creditors from debtors who have done something wrong, like lying to get a loan or intentionally hurting someone.

However, if the Trustee tries to use non-dischargeability simply to punish Alex for telling the truth about fraud, that's not what the Bankruptcy Code is for. The code is not meant to be used as a weapon against honest people. When a court rules a debt nondischargeable, it must be because the facts of the case meet the rules of the bankruptcy code, such as those within 11 U.S.C. 523.

When a court rules a debt nondischargeable as a punishment, it is acting punitively, which is when a person, or in this case a court, tries to punish someone. This is not the point of bankruptcy court. The problem here is that the Trustee is abusing their power. They're using the law to punish someone who did the right thing, not to protect the system. This goes against the whole idea of bankruptcy, which is supposed to give honest people a fresh start.

It's important to remember that the law is supposed to be fair. Even if someone makes a mistake, they deserve a chance to fix it. But using the law to punish someone for being honest is never right. And that is what is happening when a Trustee uses non-dischargeability as a weapon against a whistleblower.

Now, imagine Alex has no money, no lawyer, and no way to fight back. The Trustee knows this and is counting on it. This is even more unfair. The system is supposed to protect everyone, not just those with money and power.

CASE STUDY

THE DISCRIMINATORY NATURE OF NON-DISCHARGEABILITY IN MY CASE

The Chapter 7 Trustee's decision to block the discharge of my debts represents a clear case of discriminatory retaliation with profound implications for both my financial recovery and the integrity of the bankruptcy system as a whole.

Discriminatory Nature

The Trustee's action was fundamentally discriminatory because it specifically targeted me for exercising my constitutional rights to due process and equal protection under the law. This discrimination manifested in several ways:

1. Selective Punishment: The Trustee applied non-dischargeability as a punitive measure against me for engaging in protected legal activities that other debtors routinely undertake without consequence.

2. Disparate Treatment: My legitimate challenges regarding Patapsco Bank's failure to honor its loan modification commitment and Waterfall Victoria Mortgage Fund's questionable standing were treated differently than similar challenges raised by debtors with different characteristics or circumstances.

3. Procedural Inequality: Despite following all prescribed legal procedures, filing appropriate motions, seeking recusal when necessary, requesting venue changes, and pursuing appeals, I faced extraordinary sanctions not typically imposed on similarly situated debtors.

Impact on Present and Future

The Present Impact:

1. Financial Devastation: The non-dischargeable status of my debts prevents me from achieving the "fresh start" that bankruptcy is designed to provide, leaving me in a state of perpetual financial distress.

2. Credit Rehabilitation Barriers: Without discharge, my ability to rebuild credit, secure housing, or obtain employment remains severely compromised.

3. Continued Legal Costs: The non-dischargeability forces me to continue addressing these debts through additional costly legal proceedings.

Future Impact

1. Chilling Effect: This punitive application of non-dischargeability creates a dangerous precedent that could discourage other debtors from asserting legitimate legal rights for fear of similar retaliation.

2. Systemic Inequality: If left unchallenged, this practice threatens to create a two-tiered bankruptcy system—one for compliant debtors and another for those who exercise their constitutional rights to challenge creditor misconduct.

3. Judicial Integrity: The bankruptcy system's reputation for fairness and equal application of law suffers when non-dischargeability is weaponized against protected legal advocacy.

Why It Was Wrong

The Trustee's action was wrong on multiple levels:

1. Legal Impropriety: Non-dischargeability provisions in bankruptcy law exist for specific circumstances like fraud or willful injury—not as punishment for legitimate legal challenges.

2. Constitutional Violation: Penalizing a debtor for exercising fundamental rights to petition courts and seeking judicial review violates core constitutional protections.

3. Abuse of Authority: The Trustee misused their discretionary power to achieve an improper purpose, suppressing legitimate legal advocacy rather than maximizing creditor recovery.

4. Contrary to Bankruptcy Purpose: This action fundamentally contradicts bankruptcy's dual purpose of providing debtors with a fresh start and ensuring equitable treatment of creditors.

5. Evidence Disregard: My substantiated claims regarding Patapsco Bank's broken promises and Waterfall Victoria's questionable standing were summarily dismissed without proper consideration.

This punitive application of non-dischargeability represents a dangerous distortion of bankruptcy law that undermines fundamental fairness and constitutional rights, setting a troubling precedent that threatens the integrity of the entire bankruptcy system.

Chapter Thirty-Seven

FEDERAL BAR ASSOCIATION VERSUS STATE BAR ASSOCIATION

I received a call from the attorney who had represented me before the Attorney Grievance Commission. He informed me that the state of Maryland had disbarred me. I was in shock. I had not expected this outcome. My bankruptcy proceedings were in the United States Bankruptcy Court, which falls under federal jurisdiction, not the state of Maryland. Furthermore, I had been representing myself, not a client, throughout the process.

After I received the attorney's call, a docket entry was uploaded to all my current and former bankruptcy clients, indicating that their attorney, me, was either suspended or disbarred as of that date. However, the statement itself failed to recognize the fundamental difference between the Maryland Bar and the Federal Bar. Maryland disbarment does not automatically affect an attorney's standing under the jurisdiction of the Federal court system.

In fact, approximately three weeks after the docket entry, I received a show cause order from the Federal Bar Association. To summarize the show cause order, it stated that it was their understanding that I was no longer a member of the Maryland Bar and if I could provide an explanation or details as to why my bar membership for the Federal Bar should not be terminated by the specified date given in February? One of their requirements was that I must be a member of a state bar to have membership with the Federal Bar.

This show cause order demonstrates that the Bankruptcy Court's docket entry was premature and misleading. It is critical to note that someone who did not identify themselves but had the authority and ability to enter information directly into the docket for all of my clients, entered the statement, "Attorney was suspended or disbarred." This was done with the clear motivation to publicly humiliate me rather than for any procedural necessity.

Therefore, the question arises as to "WHO" authorized a statement to be entered into the docket for all my clients that filed bankruptcies, when the jurisdiction rests in the Federal Court. Therefore, was the statement that was entered into the docket, accurate?

In fact, prior to the proceedings in the Maryland courts, there came time to renew my license for the Federal Bar, I was required to complete a questionnaire that inquired about various issues including the orders of contempt. I answered honestly and forthrightly. My Federal Bar license was renewed without issue. This was one of the reasons why I was surprised by the disbarment in the state of Maryland.

The fact that the Federal Bar renewed my bar license highlights a crucial distinction between the Maryland Bar and the Federal Bar. They operate as separate entities with independent authority over attorney admissions and disciplinary matters. Disbarment in one jurisdiction does not automatically lead to disbarment in another. Instead, the federal court typically conducts its own review before deciding whether reciprocal disciplinary action is warranted.

CASE STUDY

IN MY CASE, THE United States Trustee (UST), a critical component of the Department of Justice that oversees bankruptcy cases, exceeded its authority and engaged in improper actions that had serious legal and financial implications for both me and my clients.

The UST entered statements on all my clients' dockets incorrectly asserting that I was suspended or disbarred by the Federal Court, where bankruptcy court is located. This caused severe reputational harm, interfered with my ability to assist clients with a smooth transition, and led to financial losses when the UST subsequently refused to release earned compensation from confirmed bankruptcy plans.

What makes this particularly egregious is that while the Maryland Attorney Grievance Commission had initiated disbarment proceedings against me based on an "anonymous" complaint (likely from Orbie Shively, the Chapter 7 Trustee's attorney who was their only witness), the federal bar had taken no such action. The federal bar, which requires membership in the state bar, had issued a Notice to Show Cause on January 10, 2020, giving me until February 18, 2020, to respond as to why my federal bar membership should not be revoked based on the state disbarment. This reasonable time period to respond confirmed that no action has yet been taken against my federal bar status.

Despite this, Gerard Vetter from the UST's office contacted my attorney and confirmed he had already sent letters to all my bankruptcy clients incorrectly stating I was suspended or disbarred from federal practice. Vetter was fully aware of the distinction between state and federal bar status and knew that no federal action had yet been taken against me.

This misrepresentation constituted potential defamation, professional harm, and abuse of administrative power. The UST's actions violated due process protections under the Fifth Amendment, as the government must provide notice and an opportunity to respond before taking action that could impact an individual's rights. Additionally, the UST improperly withheld earned fees for confirmed plans without a valid legal basis, which may constitute an unlawful taking under the Takings Clause.

The impact on my clients was severe. Many experienced panic and confusion about their ongoing bankruptcy proceedings. Several faced delayed hearings as they scrambled to find new counsel, while others incurred additional legal fees to bring new attorneys up to speed. Some missed important filing deadlines during the transition period, potentially jeopardizing their bankruptcy proceedings.

To address these improper actions, I considered several legal remedies, including filing motions to correct the record, submitting complaints to the court and Department of Justice's Office of Professional Responsibility, and filing motions to compel payment of withheld fees. Several significant legal precedents support attorneys' rights to fair compensation in bankruptcy proceedings and establish that administrative misconduct affecting attorney compensation can be challenged through appropriate legal channels.

I was beaten and depressed.

PART TWO

Chapter Thirty-Eight

WHAT IS BANKRUPTCY?

BANKRUPTCY IS A LEGAL process that provides individuals and businesses overwhelmed by debt with a fresh financial start. It works by either eliminating (discharging) unsecured debts or creating a structured plan to reorganize and repay them.

The key elements of bankruptcy include:

- Debt discharge: Many unsecured debts can be eliminated completely
- Automatic stay: Immediate protection from creditor collection efforts
- Asset liquidation: In some cases, certain assets may be sold to pay creditors
- Debt reorganization: Creating manageable repayment plans for certain debts
- Fair distribution: Ensuring creditors receive payment according to legal priorities
- Fresh start: The opportunity to rebuild financial stability without crushing debt

Bankruptcy serves as a vital debt relief option for those genuinely unable to meet their financial obligations or who need a comprehensive financial reset.

Chapter Thirty-Nine

PREPARE TO FILE A BANKRUPTCY

BEFORE FILING FOR BANKRUPTCY, thorough preparation is essential. Take these important steps:

- Gather comprehensive creditor information from all available sources
- Document each creditor's full details: name, mailing address, phone number, account numbers, and specific debt type
- Calculate your household income according to required bankruptcy guidelines
- Organize all financial documents and records

Proper preparation creates the foundation for a successful bankruptcy process.

Chapter Forty

VOLUNTARY PETITION

THE VOLUNTARY PETITION (OFFICIAL Form 101) is the document used to formally begin bankruptcy proceedings. When filed, it immediately activates an automatic stay, a legal protection that stops most creditor collection activities.

This petition is a legally binding document. By signing it, you are certifying under penalty of perjury that all the information provided is accurate and complete.

Fresh Start. Survivor's Guide to Bankruptcy Practice

Fill in this information to identify your case:

United States Bankruptcy Court for the:

District of __________

Case number (If known): ____________________

Chapter you are filing under:
- ☐ Chapter 7
- ☐ Chapter 11
- ☐ Chapter 12
- ☐ Chapter 13

☐ Check if this is an amended filing

Official Form 101

Voluntary Petition for Individuals Filing for Bankruptcy

12/22

The bankruptcy forms use *you* and *Debtor 1* to refer to a debtor filing alone. A married couple may file a bankruptcy case together—called a *joint case*—and in joint cases, these forms use *you* to ask for information from both debtors. For example, if a form asks, "Do you own a car," the answer would be *yes* if either debtor owns a car. When information is needed about the spouses separately, the form uses *Debtor 1* and *Debtor 2* to distinguish between them. In joint cases, one of the spouses must report information as *Debtor 1* and the other as *Debtor 2*. The same person must be *Debtor 1* in all of the forms.

Be as complete and accurate as possible. If two married people are filing together, both are equally responsible for supplying correct information. If more space is needed, attach a separate sheet to this form. On the top of any additional pages, write your name and case number (if known). Answer every question.

Part 1: Identify Yourself

	About Debtor 1:	About Debtor 2 (Spouse Only in a Joint Case):
1. **Your full name** Write the name that is on your government-issued picture identification (for example, your driver's license or passport). Bring your picture identification to your meeting with the trustee.	______ First name ______ Middle name ______ Last name ______ Suffix (Sr., Jr., II, III)	______ First name ______ Middle name ______ Last name ______ Suffix (Sr., Jr., II, III)
2. **All other names you have used in the last 8 years** Include your married or maiden names and any assumed, trade names and *doing business as* names. Do NOT list the name of any separate legal entity such as a corporation, partnership, or LLC that is not filing this petition.	______ First name ______ Middle name ______ Last name ______ First name ______ Middle name ______ Last name ______ Business name (if applicable) ______ Business name (if applicable)	______ First name ______ Middle name ______ Last name ______ First name ______ Middle name ______ Last name ______ Business name (if applicable) ______ Business name (if applicable)
3. **Only the last 4 digits of your Social Security number or federal Individual Taxpayer Identification number** (ITIN)	XXX – XX – ___ ___ ___ ___ OR 9 XX – XX – ___ ___ ___ ___	XXX – XX – ___ ___ ___ ___ OR 9 XX – XX – ___ ___ ___ ___

Fresh Start. Survivor's Guide to Bankruptcy Practice

Debtor 1 ______________________________ Case number *(if known)*______________________
First Name Middle Name Last Name

	About Debtor 1:	About Debtor 2 (Spouse Only in a Joint Case):
4. **Your Employer Identification Number (EIN), if any.**	EIN __ __ – __ __ __ __ __ __ __ EIN __ __ – __ __ __ __ __ __ __	EIN __ __ – __ __ __ __ __ __ __ EIN __ __ – __ __ __ __ __ __ __
5. **Where you live**	______________________ Number Street ______________________ ______________________ City State ZIP Code ______________________ County **If your mailing address is different from the one above, fill it in here.** Note that the court will send any notices to you at this mailing address. ______________________ Number Street ______________________ P.O. Box ______________________ City State ZIP Code	**If Debtor 2 lives at a different address:** ______________________ Number Street ______________________ ______________________ City State ZIP Code ______________________ County **If Debtor 2's mailing address is different from yours, fill it in here.** Note that the court will send any notices to this mailing address. ______________________ Number Street ______________________ P.O. Box ______________________ City State ZIP Code
6. **Why you are choosing *this district* to file for bankruptcy**	*Check one:* ☐ Over the last 180 days before filing this petition, I have lived in this district longer than in any other district. ☐ I have another reason. Explain. (See 28 U.S.C. § 1408.) ______________________ ______________________ ______________________ ______________________	*Check one:* ☐ Over the last 180 days before filing this petition, I have lived in this district longer than in any other district. ☐ I have another reason. Explain. (See 28 U.S.C. § 1408.) ______________________ ______________________ ______________________ ______________________

Fresh Start. Survivor's Guide to Bankruptcy Practice

Debtor 1 ______________________________ Case number *(if known)* ______________________
First Name Middle Name Last Name

Part 2: Tell the Court About Your Bankruptcy Case

7. The chapter of the Bankruptcy Code you are choosing to file under

Check one. (For a brief description of each, see *Notice Required by 11 U.S.C. § 342(b) for Individuals Filing for Bankruptcy* (Form 2010)). Also, go to the top of page 1 and check the appropriate box.

- ❑ Chapter 7
- ❑ Chapter 11
- ❑ Chapter 12
- ❑ Chapter 13

8. How you will pay the fee

❑ **I will pay the entire fee when I file my petition**. Please check with the clerk's office in your local court for more details about how you may pay. Typically, if you are paying the fee yourself, you may pay with cash, cashier's check, or money order. If your attorney is submitting your payment on your behalf, your attorney may pay with a credit card or check with a pre-printed address.

❑ **I need to pay the fee in installments**. If you choose this option, sign and attach the *Application for Individuals to Pay The Filing Fee in Installments* (Official Form 103A).

❑ **I request that my fee be waived** (You may request this option only if you are filing for Chapter 7. By law, a judge may, but is not required to, waive your fee, and may do so only if your income is less than 150% of the official poverty line that applies to your family size and you are unable to pay the fee in installments). If you choose this option, you must fill out the *Application to Have the Chapter 7 Filing Fee Waived* (Official Form 103B) and file it with your petition.

9. Have you filed for bankruptcy within the last 8 years?

❑ No

❑ Yes. District ______________ When ________ Case number ______________
MM / DD / YYYY

District ______________ When ________ Case number ______________
MM / DD / YYYY

District ______________ When ________ Case number ______________
MM / DD / YYYY

10. Are any bankruptcy cases pending or being filed by a spouse who is not filing this case with you, or by a business partner, or by an affiliate?

❑ No

❑ Yes. Debtor ______________________ Relationship to you ______________

District ______________ When ________ Case number, if known ______________
MM / DD / YYYY

Debtor ______________________ Relationship to you ______________

District ______________ When ________ Case number, if known ______________
MM / DD / YYYY

11. Do you rent your residence?

❑ No. Go to line 12.

❑ Yes. Has your landlord obtained an eviction judgment against you?

- ❑ No. Go to line 12.
- ❑ Yes. Fill out *Initial Statement About an Eviction Judgment Against You* (Form 101A) and file it as part of this bankruptcy petition.

Fresh Start. Survivor's Guide to Bankruptcy Practice

Debtor 1 ______________________ First Name Middle Name Last Name Case number *(if known)* ______________________

Part 3: Report About Any Businesses You Own as a Sole Proprietor

12. **Are you a sole proprietor of any full- or part-time business?**

A sole proprietorship is a business you operate as an individual, and is not a separate legal entity such as a corporation, partnership, or LLC.

If you have more than one sole proprietorship, use a separate sheet and attach it to this petition.

- ☐ No. Go to Part 4.
- ☐ Yes. Name and location of business

____
Name of business, if any

____
Number Street

____

______________________ City ______ State ______ ZIP Code

Check the appropriate box to describe your business:

- ☐ Health Care Business (as defined in 11 U.S.C. § 101(27A))
- ☐ Single Asset Real Estate (as defined in 11 U.S.C. § 101(51B))
- ☐ Stockbroker (as defined in 11 U.S.C. § 101(53A))
- ☐ Commodity Broker (as defined in 11 U.S.C. § 101(6))
- ☐ None of the above

13. **Are you filing under Chapter 11 of the Bankruptcy Code, and are you a *small business debtor* or a debtor as defined by 11 U.S. C. § 1182(1)?**

For a definition of *small business debtor*, see 11 U.S.C. § 101(51D).

If you are filing under Chapter 11, the court must know whether you are a small business debtor or a debtor choosing to proceed under Subchapter V so that it can set appropriate deadlines. If you indicate that you are a small business debtor or you are choosing to proceed under Subchapter V, you must attach your most recent balance sheet, statement of operations, cash-flow statement, and federal income tax return or if any of these documents do not exist, follow the procedure in 11 U.S.C. § 1116(1)(B).

- ☐ No. I am not filing under Chapter 11.
- ☐ No. I am filing under Chapter 11, but I am NOT a small business debtor according to the definition in the Bankruptcy Code.
- ☐ Yes. I am filing under Chapter 11, I am a small business debtor according to the definition in the Bankruptcy Code, and I do not choose to proceed under Subchapter V of Chapter 11.
- ☐ Yes. I am filing under Chapter 11, I am a debtor according to the definition in § 1182(1) of the Bankruptcy Code, and I choose to proceed under Subchapter V of Chapter 11.

Fresh Start. Survivor's Guide to Bankruptcy Practice

Debtor 1 ______________________________ Case number *(if known)*______________________
First Name Middle Name Last Name

Part 4: Report if You Own or Have Any Hazardous Property or Any Property That Needs Immediate Attention

14. **Do you own or have any property that poses or is alleged to pose a threat of imminent and identifiable hazard to public health or safety? Or do you own any property that needs immediate attention?**

For example, do you own perishable goods, or livestock that must be fed, or a building that needs urgent repairs?

☐ No

☐ Yes. What is the hazard? ______________________________

____

If immediate attention is needed, why is it needed? ______________________________

____

Where is the property? ______________________________
Number Street

____

______________________________ ______ ______________
City State ZIP Code

Fresh Start. Survivor's Guide to Bankruptcy Practice

Debtor 1 ______________________________ Case number (*if known*) ______________________
First Name Middle Name Last Name

Part 5: Explain Your Efforts to Receive a Briefing About Credit Counseling

15. Tell the court whether you have received a briefing about credit counseling.

The law requires that you receive a briefing about credit counseling before you file for bankruptcy. You must truthfully check one of the following choices. If you cannot do so, you are not eligible to file.

If you file anyway, the court can dismiss your case, you will lose whatever filing fee you paid, and your creditors can begin collection activities again.

About Debtor 1:

You must check one:

☐ **I received a briefing from an approved credit counseling agency within the 180 days before I filed this bankruptcy petition, and I received a certificate of completion.**

Attach a copy of the certificate and the payment plan, if any, that you developed with the agency.

☐ **I received a briefing from an approved credit counseling agency within the 180 days before I filed this bankruptcy petition, but I do not have a certificate of completion.**

Within 14 days after you file this bankruptcy petition, you MUST file a copy of the certificate and payment plan, if any.

☐ **I certify that I asked for credit counseling services from an approved agency, but was unable to obtain those services during the 7 days after I made my request, and exigent circumstances merit a 30-day temporary waiver of the requirement.**

To ask for a 30-day temporary waiver of the requirement, attach a separate sheet explaining what efforts you made to obtain the briefing, why you were unable to obtain it before you filed for bankruptcy, and what exigent circumstances required you to file this case.

Your case may be dismissed if the court is dissatisfied with your reasons for not receiving a briefing before you filed for bankruptcy.

If the court is satisfied with your reasons, you must still receive a briefing within 30 days after you file. You must file a certificate from the approved agency, along with a copy of the payment plan you developed, if any. If you do not do so, your case may be dismissed.

Any extension of the 30-day deadline is granted only for cause and is limited to a maximum of 15 days.

☐ **I am not required to receive a briefing about credit counseling because of:**

☐ **Incapacity.** I have a mental illness or a mental deficiency that makes me incapable of realizing or making rational decisions about finances.

☐ **Disability.** My physical disability causes me to be unable to participate in a briefing in person, by phone, or through the internet, even after I reasonably tried to do so.

☐ **Active duty.** I am currently on active military duty in a military combat zone.

If you believe you are not required to receive a briefing about credit counseling, you must file a motion for waiver of credit counseling with the court.

About Debtor 2 (Spouse Only in a Joint Case):

You must check one:

☐ **I received a briefing from an approved credit counseling agency within the 180 days before I filed this bankruptcy petition, and I received a certificate of completion.**

Attach a copy of the certificate and the payment plan, if any, that you developed with the agency.

☐ **I received a briefing from an approved credit counseling agency within the 180 days before I filed this bankruptcy petition, but I do not have a certificate of completion.**

Within 14 days after you file this bankruptcy petition, you MUST file a copy of the certificate and payment plan, if any.

☐ **I certify that I asked for credit counseling services from an approved agency, but was unable to obtain those services during the 7 days after I made my request, and exigent circumstances merit a 30-day temporary waiver of the requirement.**

To ask for a 30-day temporary waiver of the requirement, attach a separate sheet explaining what efforts you made to obtain the briefing, why you were unable to obtain it before you filed for bankruptcy, and what exigent circumstances required you to file this case.

Your case may be dismissed if the court is dissatisfied with your reasons for not receiving a briefing before you filed for bankruptcy.

If the court is satisfied with your reasons, you must still receive a briefing within 30 days after you file. You must file a certificate from the approved agency, along with a copy of the payment plan you developed, if any. If you do not do so, your case may be dismissed.

Any extension of the 30-day deadline is granted only for cause and is limited to a maximum of 15 days.

☐ **I am not required to receive a briefing about credit counseling because of:**

☐ **Incapacity.** I have a mental illness or a mental deficiency that makes me incapable of realizing or making rational decisions about finances.

☐ **Disability.** My physical disability causes me to be unable to participate in a briefing in person, by phone, or through the internet, even after I reasonably tried to do so.

☐ **Active duty.** I am currently on active military duty in a military combat zone.

If you believe you are not required to receive a briefing about credit counseling, you must file a motion for waiver of credit counseling with the court.

Fresh Start. Survivor's Guide to Bankruptcy Practice

Debtor 1 ______________________________ Case number *(if known)* ______________________
First Name Middle Name Last Name

Part 6: Answer These Questions for Reporting Purposes

16. What kind of debts do you have?

16a. **Are your debts primarily consumer debts?** *Consumer debts* are defined in 11 U.S.C. § 101(8) as "incurred by an individual primarily for a personal, family, or household purpose."

- ☐ No. Go to line 16b.
- ☐ Yes. Go to line 17.

16b. **Are your debts primarily business debts?** *Business debts* are debts that you incurred to obtain money for a business or investment or through the operation of the business or investment.

- ☐ No. Go to line 16c.
- ☐ Yes. Go to line 17.

16c. State the type of debts you owe that are not consumer debts or business debts.

____

17. Are you filing under Chapter 7?

Do you estimate that after any exempt property is excluded and administrative expenses are paid that funds will be available for distribution to unsecured creditors?

- ☐ No. I am not filing under Chapter 7. Go to line 18.
- ☐ Yes. I am filing under Chapter 7. Do you estimate that after any exempt property is excluded and administrative expenses are paid that funds will be available to distribute to unsecured creditors?
  - ☐ No
  - ☐ Yes

18. How many creditors do you estimate that you owe?

☐ 1-49	☐ 1,000-5,000	☐ 25,001-50,000
☐ 50-99	☐ 5,001-10,000	☐ 50,001-100,000
☐ 100-199	☐ 10,001-25,000	☐ More than 100,000
☐ 200-999		

19. How much do you estimate your assets to be worth?

☐ $0-$50,000	☐ $1,000,001-$10 million	☐ $500,000,001-$1 billion
☐ $50,001-$100,000	☐ $10,000,001-$50 million	☐ $1,000,000,001-$10 billion
☐ $100,001-$500,000	☐ $50,000,001-$100 million	☐ $10,000,000,001-$50 billion
☐ $500,001-$1 million	☐ $100,000,001-$500 million	☐ More than $50 billion

20. How much do you estimate your liabilities to be?

☐ $0-$50,000	☐ $1,000,001-$10 million	☐ $500,000,001-$1 billion
☐ $50,001-$100,000	☐ $10,000,001-$50 million	☐ $1,000,000,001-$10 billion
☐ $100,001-$500,000	☐ $50,000,001-$100 million	☐ $10,000,000,001-$50 billion
☐ $500,001-$1 million	☐ $100,000,001-$500 million	☐ More than $50 billion

Part 7: Sign Below

For you

I have examined this petition, and I declare under penalty of perjury that the information provided is true and correct.

If I have chosen to file under Chapter 7, I am aware that I may proceed, if eligible, under Chapter 7, 11,12, or 13 of title 11, United States Code. I understand the relief available under each chapter, and I choose to proceed under Chapter 7.

If no attorney represents me and I did not pay or agree to pay someone who is not an attorney to help me fill out this document, I have obtained and read the notice required by 11 U.S.C. § 342(b).

I request relief in accordance with the chapter of title 11, United States Code, specified in this petition.

I understand making a false statement, concealing property, or obtaining money or property by fraud in connection with a bankruptcy case can result in fines up to $250,000, or imprisonment for up to 20 years, or both. 18 U.S.C. §§ 152, 1341, 1519, and 3571.

✘ ______________________________ ✘ ______________________________

Signature of Debtor 1 Signature of Debtor 2

Executed on ____________ Executed on ____________
MM / DD / YYYY MM / DD / YYYY

Fresh Start. Survivor's Guide to Bankruptcy Practice

Debtor 1 ______________________________ Case number (if known) ____________________
First Name Middle Name Last Name

For your attorney, if you are represented by one

If you are not represented by an attorney, you do not need to file this page.

I, the attorney for the debtor(s) named in this petition, declare that I have informed the debtor(s) about eligibility to proceed under Chapter 7, 11, 12, or 13 of title 11, United States Code, and have explained the relief available under each chapter for which the person is eligible. I also certify that I have delivered to the debtor(s) the notice required by 11 U.S.C. § 342(b) and, in a case in which § 707(b)(4)(D) applies, certify that I have no knowledge after an inquiry that the information in the schedules filed with the petition is incorrect.

✗ ______________________________ Date ____________
Signature of Attorney for Debtor MM / DD / YYYY

____
Printed name

____
Firm name

____
Number Street

____

____
City State ZIP Code

Contact phone ____________________ Email address ____________________

____
Bar number State

Fresh Start. Survivor's Guide to Bankruptcy Practice

Debtor 1 ______________________________ Case number *(if known)* ______________________
First Name Middle Name Last Name

For you if you are filing this bankruptcy without an attorney

If you are represented by an attorney, you do not need to file this page.

The law allows you, as an individual, to represent yourself in bankruptcy court, but **you should understand that many people find it extremely difficult to represent themselves successfully. Because bankruptcy has long-term financial and legal consequences, you are strongly urged to hire a qualified attorney.**

To be successful, you must correctly file and handle your bankruptcy case. The rules are very technical, and a mistake or inaction may affect your rights. For example, your case may be dismissed because you did not file a required document, pay a fee on time, attend a meeting or hearing, or cooperate with the court, case trustee, U.S. trustee, bankruptcy administrator, or audit firm if your case is selected for audit. If that happens, you could lose your right to file another case, or you may lose protections, including the benefit of the automatic stay.

You must list all your property and debts in the schedules that you are required to file with the court. Even if you plan to pay a particular debt outside of your bankruptcy, you must list that debt in your schedules. If you do not list a debt, the debt may not be discharged. If you do not list property or properly claim it as exempt, you may not be able to keep the property. The judge can also deny you a discharge of all your debts if you do something dishonest in your bankruptcy case, such as destroying or hiding property, falsifying records, or lying. Individual bankruptcy cases are randomly audited to determine if debtors have been accurate, truthful, and complete. **Bankruptcy fraud is a serious crime; you could be fined and imprisoned.**

If you decide to file without an attorney, the court expects you to follow the rules as if you had hired an attorney. The court will not treat you differently because you are filing for yourself. To be successful, you must be familiar with the United States Bankruptcy Code, the Federal Rules of Bankruptcy Procedure, and the local rules of the court in which your case is filed. You must also be familiar with any state exemption laws that apply.

Are you aware that filing for bankruptcy is a serious action with long-term financial and legal consequences?

- ☐ No
- ☐ Yes

Are you aware that bankruptcy fraud is a serious crime and that if your bankruptcy forms are inaccurate or incomplete, you could be fined or imprisoned?

- ☐ No
- ☐ Yes

Did you pay or agree to pay someone who is not an attorney to help you fill out your bankruptcy forms?

- ☐ No
- ☐ Yes. Name of Person______________________________.
  Attach *Bankruptcy Petition Preparer's Notice, Declaration, and Signature* (Official Form 119).

By signing here, I acknowledge that I understand the risks involved in filing without an attorney. I have read and understood this notice, and I am aware that filing a bankruptcy case without an attorney may cause me to lose my rights or property if I do not properly handle the case.

✘ ______________________	✘ ______________________
Signature of Debtor 1	Signature of Debtor 2
Date ________ MM / DD / YYYY	Date ________ MM / DD / YYYY
Contact phone ________	Contact phone ________
Cell phone ________	Cell phone ________
Email address ________	Email address ________

Official Form 101 **Voluntary Petition for Individuals Filing for Bankruptcy** page 9

Chapter Forty-One

Schedules A/B: Property

SCHEDULE A/B IS A comprehensive inventory that requires you to list ALL the assets you own at the time of filing bankruptcy. This detailed document is divided into two main sections:

Real Property (Schedule A)

- All real estate you own or have interest in
- Primary residence, vacation homes, rental properties
- Land, timeshares, and other real property interests
- Current market value of each property

Personal Property (Schedule B)

- Cash, bank accounts, and financial instruments
- Household goods, furnishings, and electronics
- Clothing, jewelry, and personal items
- Vehicles, boats, and other transportation
- Business-related assets and inventory
- Retirement accounts and investments
- Insurance policies with cash value
- Potential claims and lawsuits
- Tax refunds and other government benefits
- Intellectual property (patents, copyrights, etc.)

- Licenses, franchises, and other intangible assets
- Any other personal property not already listed

It's crucial to be thorough and accurate when completing Schedule A/B, as intentional omissions could constitute bankruptcy fraud. The trustee will review this document carefully to determine what assets might be available for liquidation to pay creditors or what might be protected through exemptions.

Each item must include:

- Description of the property
- Current market value
- Ownership interest (sole, joint, community)
- Location of the property

This schedule serves as the foundation of your bankruptcy case, as it establishes what assets you have that might be subject to the bankruptcy process.

Fresh Start. Survivor's Guide to Bankruptcy Practice

Fill in this information to identify your case and this filing:

Debtor 1 ______________________________
First Name Middle Name Last Name

Debtor 2 ______________________________
(Spouse, if filing) First Name Middle Name Last Name

United States Bankruptcy Court for the: District of ________

Case number ______________________________

❑ Check if this is an amended filing

Official Form 106A/B

Schedule A/B: Property

12/15

In each category, separately list and describe items. List an asset only once. If an asset fits in more than one category, list the asset in the category where you think it fits best. Be as complete and accurate as possible. If two married people are filing together, both are equally responsible for supplying correct information. If more space is needed, attach a separate sheet to this form. On the top of any additional pages, write your name and case number (if known). Answer every question.

Part 1: Describe Each Residence, Building, Land, or Other Real Estate You Own or Have an Interest In

1. **Do you own or have any legal or equitable interest in any residence, building, land, or similar property?**

❑ No. Go to Part 2.
❑ Yes. Where is the property?

1.1. ______________________________
Street address, if available, or other description

____

____
City State ZIP Code

____
County

What is the property? Check all that apply.

❑ Single-family home
❑ Duplex or multi-unit building
❑ Condominium or cooperative
❑ Manufactured or mobile home
❑ Land
❑ Investment property
❑ Timeshare
❑ Other ______________________

Who has an interest in the property? Check one.

❑ Debtor 1 only
❑ Debtor 2 only
❑ Debtor 1 and Debtor 2 only
❑ At least one of the debtors and another

Do not deduct secured claims or exemptions. Put the amount of any secured claims on Schedule D: Creditors Who Have Claims Secured by Property.

Current value of the entire property?	Current value of the portion you own?
$____________	$____________

Describe the nature of your ownership interest (such as fee simple, tenancy by the entireties, or a life estate), if known.

____

❑ **Check if this is community property** (see instructions)

Other information you wish to add about this item, such as local property identification number: ______________________

If you own or have more than one, list here:

1.2. ______________________________
Street address, if available, or other description

____

____
City State ZIP Code

____
County

What is the property? Check all that apply.

❑ Single-family home
❑ Duplex or multi-unit building
❑ Condominium or cooperative
❑ Manufactured or mobile home
❑ Land
❑ Investment property
❑ Timeshare
❑ Other ______________________

Who has an interest in the property? Check one.

❑ Debtor 1 only
❑ Debtor 2 only
❑ Debtor 1 and Debtor 2 only
❑ At least one of the debtors and another

Do not deduct secured claims or exemptions. Put the amount of any secured claims on Schedule D: Creditors Who Have Claims Secured by Property.

Current value of the entire property?	Current value of the portion you own?
$____________	$____________

Describe the nature of your ownership interest (such as fee simple, tenancy by the entireties, or a life estate), if known.

____

❑ **Check if this is community property** (see instructions)

Other information you wish to add about this item, such as local property identification number: ______________________

Debtor 1 ______ First Name Middle Name Last Name Fresh Start. Survivor's Guide to Bankruptcy Practice Case number (if known) ______

1.3. ______
Street address, if available, or other description

______

______
City State ZIP Code

______
County

What is the property? Check all that apply.

- ☐ Single-family home
- ☐ Duplex or multi-unit building
- ☐ Condominium or cooperative
- ☐ Manufactured or mobile home
- ☐ Land
- ☐ Investment property
- ☐ Timeshare
- ☐ Other ______

Who has an interest in the property? Check one.

- ☐ Debtor 1 only
- ☐ Debtor 2 only
- ☐ Debtor 1 and Debtor 2 only
- ☐ At least one of the debtors and another

Other information you wish to add about this item, such as local property identification number: ______

Do not deduct secured claims or exemptions. Put the amount of any secured claims on *Schedule D: Creditors Who Have Claims Secured by Property.*

Current value of the entire property?	**Current value of the portion you own?**
$______	$______

Describe the nature of your ownership interest (such as fee simple, tenancy by the entireties, or a life estate), if known.

______

☐ **Check if this is community property** (see instructions)

2. **Add the dollar value of the portion you own for all of your entries from Part 1, including any entries for pages you have attached for Part 1. Write that number here.** .... ➔ $______

Part 2: Describe Your Vehicles

Do you own, lease, or have legal or equitable interest in any vehicles, whether they are registered or not? Include any vehicles you own that someone else drives. If you lease a vehicle, also report it on *Schedule G: Executory Contracts and Unexpired Leases.*

3. **Cars, vans, trucks, tractors, sport utility vehicles, motorcycles**

- ☐ No
- ☐ Yes

3.1. Make: ______
Model: ______
Year: ______
Approximate mileage: ______
Other information:

Who has an interest in the property? Check one.

- ☐ Debtor 1 only
- ☐ Debtor 2 only
- ☐ Debtor 1 and Debtor 2 only
- ☐ At least one of the debtors and another

☐ **Check if this is community property** (see instructions)

Do not deduct secured claims or exemptions. Put the amount of any secured claims on *Schedule D: Creditors Who Have Claims Secured by Property.*

Current value of the entire property?	**Current value of the portion you own?**
$______	$______

If you own or have more than one, describe here:

3.2. Make: ______
Model: ______
Year: ______
Approximate mileage: ______
Other information:

Who has an interest in the property? Check one.

- ☐ Debtor 1 only
- ☐ Debtor 2 only
- ☐ Debtor 1 and Debtor 2 only
- ☐ At least one of the debtors and another

☐ **Check if this is community property** (see instructions)

Do not deduct secured claims or exemptions. Put the amount of any secured claims on *Schedule D: Creditors Who Have Claims Secured by Property.*

Current value of the entire property?	**Current value of the portion you own?**
$______	$______

Debtor 1 ______________________ First Name Middle Name Last Name Fresh Start. Survivor's Guide to Bankruptcy Practice Case number (if known) ______________________

3.3. Make: ______
Model: ______
Year: ______
Approximate mileage: ______
Other information:

Who has an interest in the property? Check one.
- ❑ Debtor 1 only
- ❑ Debtor 2 only
- ❑ Debtor 1 and Debtor 2 only
- ❑ At least one of the debtors and another

❑ **Check if this is community property** (see instructions)

Do not deduct secured claims or exemptions. Put the amount of any secured claims on *Schedule D: Creditors Who Have Claims Secured by Property.*

Current value of the entire property?	Current value of the portion you own?
$______	$______

3.4. Make: ______
Model: ______
Year: ______
Approximate mileage: ______
Other information:

Who has an interest in the property? Check one.
- ❑ Debtor 1 only
- ❑ Debtor 2 only
- ❑ Debtor 1 and Debtor 2 only
- ❑ At least one of the debtors and another

❑ **Check if this is community property** (see instructions)

Do not deduct secured claims or exemptions. Put the amount of any secured claims on *Schedule D: Creditors Who Have Claims Secured by Property.*

Current value of the entire property?	Current value of the portion you own?
$______	$______

4. **Watercraft, aircraft, motor homes, ATVs and other recreational vehicles, other vehicles, and accessories**
Examples: Boats, trailers, motors, personal watercraft, fishing vessels, snowmobiles, motorcycle accessories
- ❑ No
- ❑ Yes

4.1. Make: ______
Model: ______
Year: ______
Other information:

Who has an interest in the property? Check one.
- ❑ Debtor 1 only
- ❑ Debtor 2 only
- ❑ Debtor 1 and Debtor 2 only
- ❑ At least one of the debtors and another

❑ **Check if this is community property** (see instructions)

Do not deduct secured claims or exemptions. Put the amount of any secured claims on *Schedule D: Creditors Who Have Claims Secured by Property.*

Current value of the entire property?	Current value of the portion you own?
$______	$______

If you own or have more than one, list here:

4.2. Make: ______
Model: ______
Year: ______
Other information:

Who has an interest in the property? Check one.
- ❑ Debtor 1 only
- ❑ Debtor 2 only
- ❑ Debtor 1 and Debtor 2 only
- ❑ At least one of the debtors and another

❑ **Check if this is community property** (see instructions)

Do not deduct secured claims or exemptions. Put the amount of any secured claims on *Schedule D: Creditors Who Have Claims Secured by Property.*

Current value of the entire property?	Current value of the portion you own?
$______	$______

5. **Add the dollar value of the portion you own for all of your entries from Part 2, including any entries for pages you have attached for Part 2. Write that number here** .... ➔ $______

Debtor 1 ______ First Name Middle Name Last Name Fresh Start. Survivor's Guide to Bankruptcy Practice Case number (if known) ______

Part 3: Describe Your Personal and Household Items

Do you own or have any legal or equitable interest in any of the following items?

Current value of the portion you own? Do not deduct secured claims or exemptions.

6. **Household goods and furnishings**
Examples: Major appliances, furniture, linens, china, kitchenware
❑ No
❑ Yes. Describe......... $______

7. **Electronics**
Examples: Televisions and radios; audio, video, stereo, and digital equipment; computers, printers, scanners; music collections; electronic devices including cell phones, cameras, media players, games
❑ No
❑ Yes. Describe.......... $______

8. **Collectibles of value**
Examples: Antiques and figurines; paintings, prints, or other artwork; books, pictures, or other art objects; stamp, coin, or baseball card collections; other collections, memorabilia, collectibles
❑ No
❑ Yes. Describe.......... $______

9. **Equipment for sports and hobbies**
Examples: Sports, photographic, exercise, and other hobby equipment; bicycles, pool tables, golf clubs, skis; canoes and kayaks; carpentry tools; musical instruments
❑ No
❑ Yes. Describe.......... $______

10. **Firearms**
Examples: Pistols, rifles, shotguns, ammunition, and related equipment
❑ No
❑ Yes. Describe.......... $______

11. **Clothes**
Examples: Everyday clothes, furs, leather coats, designer wear, shoes, accessories
❑ No
❑ Yes. Describe.......... $______

12. **Jewelry**
Examples: Everyday jewelry, costume jewelry, engagement rings, wedding rings, heirloom jewelry, watches, gems, gold, silver
❑ No
❑ Yes. Describe.......... $______

13. **Non-farm animals**
Examples: Dogs, cats, birds, horses
❑ No
❑ Yes. Describe.......... $______

14. **Any other personal and household items you did not already list, including any health aids you did not list**
❑ No
❑ Yes. Give specific information. .... $______

15. **Add the dollar value of all of your entries from Part 3, including any entries for pages you have attached for Part 3. Write that number here** .... ➔ $______

Debtor 1 ______ First Name Middle Name Last Name Fresh Start. Survivor's Guide to Bankruptcy Practice Case number (if known) ______

Part 4: Describe Your Financial Assets

Do you own or have any legal or equitable interest in any of the following?

Current value of the portion you own?
Do not deduct secured claims or exemptions.

16. **Cash**
Examples: Money you have in your wallet, in your home, in a safe deposit box, and on hand when you file your petition

- ❑ No
- ❑ Yes .... Cash: .... $______

17. **Deposits of money**
Examples: Checking, savings, or other financial accounts; certificates of deposit; shares in credit unions, brokerage houses, and other similar institutions. If you have multiple accounts with the same institution, list each.

- ❑ No
- ❑ Yes .... Institution name:

	Institution name	
17.1. Checking account:	______	$______
17.2. Checking account:	______	$______
17.3. Savings account:	______	$______
17.4. Savings account:	______	$______
17.5. Certificates of deposit:	______	$______
17.6. Other financial account:	______	$______
17.7. Other financial account:	______	$______
17.8. Other financial account:	______	$______
17.9. Other financial account:	______	$______

18. **Bonds, mutual funds, or publicly traded stocks**
Examples: Bond funds, investment accounts with brokerage firms, money market accounts

- ❑ No
- ❑ Yes .... Institution or issuer name:

______ $______
______ $______
______ $______

19. **Non-publicly traded stock and interests in incorporated and unincorporated businesses, including an interest in an LLC, partnership, and joint venture**

- ❑ No
- ❑ Yes. Give specific information about them..........

Name of entity:	% of ownership:	
______	0% %	$______
______	0% %	$______
______	0% %	$______

Debtor 1 First Name Middle Name Last Name Fresh Start. Survivor's Guide to Bankruptcy Practice Case number (if known)

20. **Government and corporate bonds and other negotiable and non-negotiable instruments**

Negotiable instruments include personal checks, cashiers' checks, promissory notes, and money orders.
Non-negotiable instruments are those you cannot transfer to someone by signing or delivering them.

❑ No
❑ Yes. Give specific information about them...................... Issuer name:

$
$
$

21. **Retirement or pension accounts**

Examples: Interests in IRA, ERISA, Keogh, 401(k), 403(b), thrift savings accounts, or other pension or profit-sharing plans

❑ No
❑ Yes. List each account separately.

Type of account:	Institution name:	
401(k) or similar plan:		$
Pension plan:		$
IRA:		$
Retirement account:		$
Keogh:		$
Additional account:		$
Additional account:		$

22. **Security deposits and prepayments**

Your share of all unused deposits you have made so that you may continue service or use from a company
Examples: Agreements with landlords, prepaid rent, public utilities (electric, gas, water), telecommunications companies, or others

❑ No
❑ Yes.........................

	Institution name or individual:	
Electric:		$
Gas:		$
Heating oil:		$
Security deposit on rental unit:		$
Prepaid rent:		$
Telephone:		$
Water:		$
Rented furniture:		$
Other:		$

23. **Annuities** (A contract for a periodic payment of money to you, either for life or for a number of years)

❑ No
❑ Yes......................... Issuer name and description:

$
$
$

Debtor 1 ______ First Name Middle Name Last Name Fresh Start. Survivor's Guide to Bankruptcy Practice Case number (if known)______

24. **Interests in an education IRA, in an account in a qualified ABLE program, or under a qualified state tuition program.**
26 U.S.C. §§ 530(b)(1), 529A(b), and 529(b)(1).

❑ No
❑ Yes .... Institution name and description. Separately file the records of any interests.11 U.S.C. § 521(c):

______ $______
______ $______
______ $______

25. **Trusts, equitable or future interests in property (other than anything listed in line 1), and rights or powers exercisable for your benefit**

❑ No
❑ Yes. Give specific information about them.... $______

26. **Patents, copyrights, trademarks, trade secrets, and other intellectual property**
Examples: Internet domain names, websites, proceeds from royalties and licensing agreements

❑ No
❑ Yes. Give specific information about them.... $______

27. **Licenses, franchises, and other general intangibles**
Examples: Building permits, exclusive licenses, cooperative association holdings, liquor licenses, professional licenses

❑ No
❑ Yes. Give specific information about them.... $______

Money or property owed to you?

Current value of the portion you own?
Do not deduct secured claims or exemptions.

28. **Tax refunds owed to you**

❑ No
❑ Yes. Give specific information about them, including whether you already filed the returns and the tax years. ....

Federal: $______
State: $______
Local: $______

29. **Family support**
Examples: Past due or lump sum alimony, spousal support, child support, maintenance, divorce settlement, property settlement

❑ No
❑ Yes. Give specific information.............

Alimony: $______
Maintenance: $______
Support: $______
Divorce settlement: $______
Property settlement: $______

30. **Other amounts someone owes you**
Examples: Unpaid wages, disability insurance payments, disability benefits, sick pay, vacation pay, workers' compensation, Social Security benefits; unpaid loans you made to someone else

❑ No
❑ Yes. Give specific information.............. $______

Debtor 1 ______________________________ Fresh Start. Survivor's Guide to Bankruptcy Practice Case number (if known) ______________________
First Name Middle Name Last Name

31. **Interests in insurance policies**
Examples: Health, disability, or life insurance; health savings account (HSA); credit, homeowner's, or renter's insurance

☐ No
☐ Yes. Name the insurance company of each policy and list its value. ..

Company name:	Beneficiary:	Surrender or refund value:
		$
		$
		$

32. **Any interest in property that is due you from someone who has died**
If you are the beneficiary of a living trust, expect proceeds from a life insurance policy, or are currently entitled to receive property because someone has died.

☐ No
☐ Yes. Give specific information............. $______

33. **Claims against third parties, whether or not you have filed a lawsuit or made a demand for payment**
Examples: Accidents, employment disputes, insurance claims, or rights to sue

☐ No
☐ Yes. Describe each claim. .... $______

34. **Other contingent and unliquidated claims of every nature, including counterclaims of the debtor and rights to set off claims**

☐ No
☐ Yes. Describe each claim. .... $______

35. **Any financial assets you did not already list**

☐ No
☐ Yes. Give specific information............ $______

36. **Add the dollar value of all of your entries from Part 4, including any entries for pages you have attached for Part 4. Write that number here** .... ➔ $______

Part 5: Describe Any Business-Related Property You Own or Have an Interest In. List any real estate in Part 1.

37. **Do you own or have any legal or equitable interest in any business-related property?**

☐ No. Go to Part 6.
☐ Yes. Go to line 38.

Current value of the portion you own?
Do not deduct secured claims or exemptions.

38. **Accounts receivable or commissions you already earned**

☐ No
☐ Yes. Describe....... $______

39. **Office equipment, furnishings, and supplies**
Examples: Business-related computers, software, modems, printers, copiers, fax machines, rugs, telephones, desks, chairs, electronic devices

☐ No
☐ Yes. Describe....... $______

Debtor 1 ______ First Name ______ Middle Name ______ Last Name Fresh Start. Survivor's Guide to Bankruptcy Practice Case number (if known) ______

40. **Machinery, fixtures, equipment, supplies you use in business, and tools of your trade**

❑ No
❑ Yes. Describe....... $______

41. **Inventory**

❑ No
❑ Yes. Describe....... $______

42. **Interests in partnerships or joint ventures**

❑ No
❑ Yes. Describe....... Name of entity: % of ownership:

Name of entity	% of ownership	
______	____%	$______
______	____%	$______
______	____%	$______

43. **Customer lists, mailing lists, or other compilations**

❑ No
❑ Yes. **Do your lists include personally identifiable information** (as defined in 11 U.S.C. § 101(41A))?

❑ No
❑ Yes. Describe........ $______

44. **Any business-related property you did not already list**

❑ No
❑ Yes. Give specific information ....

______ $______
______ $______
______ $______
______ $______
______ $______
______ $______

45. **Add the dollar value of all of your entries from Part 5, including any entries for pages you have attached for Part 5. Write that number here** .... ➔ $______

Part 6: **Describe Any Farm- and Commercial Fishing-Related Property You Own or Have an Interest In. If you own or have an interest in farmland, list it in Part 1.**

46. **Do you own or have any legal or equitable interest in any farm- or commercial fishing-related property?**

❑ No. Go to Part 7.
❑ Yes. Go to line 47.

Current value of the portion you own?
Do not deduct secured claims or exemptions.

47. **Farm animals**

Examples: Livestock, poultry, farm-raised fish

❑ No
❑ Yes......................... $______

Debtor 1 ______ First Name Middle Name Last Name Fresh Start. Survivor's Guide to Bankruptcy Practice Case number (if known) ______

48. **Crops—either growing or harvested**

☐ No
☐ Yes. Give specific information. .... $______

49. **Farm and fishing equipment, implements, machinery, fixtures, and tools of trade**

☐ No
☐ Yes.......................... $______

50. **Farm and fishing supplies, chemicals, and feed**

☐ No
☐ Yes.......................... $______

51. **Any farm- and commercial fishing-related property you did not already list**

☐ No
☐ Yes. Give specific information. .... $______

52. **Add the dollar value of all of your entries from Part 6, including any entries for pages you have attached for Part 6. Write that number here** .... ➔ $______

Part 7: Describe All Property You Own or Have an Interest in That You Did Not List Above

53. **Do you have other property of any kind you did not already list?**
Examples: Season tickets, country club membership

☐ No
☐ Yes. Give specific information. .... $______ $______ $______

54. **Add the dollar value of all of your entries from Part 7. Write that number here** .... ➔ $______

Part 8: List the Totals of Each Part of this Form

55. **Part 1: Total real estate, line 2** .... ➔ $______

56. **Part 2: Total vehicles, line 5** $______

57. **Part 3: Total personal and household items, line 15** $______

58. **Part 4: Total financial assets, line 36** $______

59. **Part 5: Total business-related property, line 45** $______

60. **Part 6: Total farm- and fishing-related property, line 52** $______

61. **Part 7: Total other property not listed, line 54** + $______

62. **Total personal property.** Add lines 56 through 61. .... $______ Copy personal property total ➔ + $______

63. **Total of all property on Schedule A/B.** Add line 55 + line 62. .... $______

Chapter Forty-Two

SCHEDULE C: THE PROPERTY YOU CLAIM AS EXEMPT

SCHEDULE C IS A critical bankruptcy form where you list property that should be protected from liquidation during your bankruptcy case. This document is essential for preserving your essential possessions while seeking debt relief.

Purpose and Function

- Identifies specific assets you wish to keep through legal exemptions
- Prevents the trustee from selling these items to pay creditors
- Helps you maintain necessities for living and working after bankruptcy

Key Components of Schedule C

- Property Description: Must match exactly how items are listed in Schedule A/B
- Specific Exemption Laws: Federal or state exemption systems (depending on your state)
- Exemption Value: The dollar amount of protection claimed for each item
- Current Value: The fair market value of the property being exempted

Common Exemption Categories

- Homestead (primary residence) exemption
- Vehicle exemption (often limited to one vehicle of moderate value)
- Household goods and furnishings
- Clothing and personal effects
- Tools of trade/professional equipment
- Retirement accounts and pensions
- Life insurance policies
- Public benefits (Social Security, unemployment, etc.)
- Wildcard exemption (varies by state, can be applied to any property)

Strategic Considerations

- Some states allow choosing between state and federal exemption systems
- Exemption amounts vary significantly between jurisdictions
- Married couples filing jointly may double certain exemptions
- Non-exempt property may be liquidated to pay creditors
- Improperly claimed exemptions can be challenged by trustees or creditors

Schedule C requires careful planning and attention to detail, as properly claimed exemptions are the primary mechanism for protecting your assets during bankruptcy. Many debtors work closely with attorneys to maximize available exemptions under applicable law.

Fresh Start. Survivor's Guide to Bankruptcy Practice

Fill in this information to identify your case:

Debtor 1 ______ First Name / Middle Name / Last Name

Debtor 2 (Spouse, if filing) ______ First Name / Middle Name / Last Name

United States Bankruptcy Court for the: District of ______

Case number (If known) ______

❑ Check if this is an amended filing

Official Form 106C

Schedule C: The Property You Claim as Exempt

04/22

Be as complete and accurate as possible. If two married people are filing together, both are equally responsible for supplying correct information. Using the property you listed on *Schedule A/B: Property* (Official Form 106A/B) as your source, list the property that you claim as exempt. If more space is needed, fill out and attach to this page as many copies of *Part 2: Additional Page* as necessary. On the top of any additional pages, write your name and case number (if known).

For each item of property you claim as exempt, you must specify the amount of the exemption you claim. One way of doing so is to state a specific dollar amount as exempt. Alternatively, you may claim the full fair market value of the property being exempted up to the amount of any applicable statutory limit. Some exemptions—such as those for health aids, rights to receive certain benefits, and tax-exempt retirement funds—may be unlimited in dollar amount. However, if you claim an exemption of 100% of fair market value under a law that limits the exemption to a particular dollar amount and the value of the property is determined to exceed that amount, your exemption would be limited to the applicable statutory amount.

Part 1: Identify the Property You Claim as Exempt

1. **Which set of exemptions are you claiming?** *Check one only, even if your spouse is filing with you.*
   - ❑ You are claiming state and federal nonbankruptcy exemptions. 11 U.S.C. § 522(b)(3)
   - ❑ You are claiming federal exemptions. 11 U.S.C. § 522(b)(2)

2. **For any property you list on *Schedule A/B* that you claim as exempt, fill in the information below.**

Brief description of the property and line on *Schedule A/B* that lists this property	**Current value of the portion you own** Copy the value from *Schedule A/B*	**Amount of the exemption you claim** *Check only one box for each exemption.*	**Specific laws that allow exemption**
Brief description: ______ Line from *Schedule A/B:* ____	$______	❑ $______ ❑ 100% of fair market value, up to any applicable statutory limit	______
Brief description: ______ Line from *Schedule A/B:* ____	$______	❑ $______ ❑ 100% of fair market value, up to any applicable statutory limit	______
Brief description: ______ Line from *Schedule A/B:* ____	$______	❑ $______ ❑ 100% of fair market value, up to any applicable statutory limit	______

3. **Are you claiming a homestead exemption of more than $189,050?**
   (Subject to adjustment on 4/01/25 and every 3 years after that for cases filed on or after the date of adjustment.)
   - ❑ No
   - ❑ Yes. Did you acquire the property covered by the exemption within 1,215 days before you filed this case?
     - ❑ No
     - ❑ Yes

Debtor 1 ______ Fresh Start. Survivor's Guide to Bankruptcy Practice Case number (if known) ______
First Name Middle Name Last Name

Part 2: **Additional Page**

Brief description of the property and line on *Schedule A/B* that lists this property	Current value of the portion you own Copy the value from *Schedule A/B*	Amount of the exemption you claim *Check only one box for each exemption*	Specific laws that allow exemption
Brief description: ______ Line from *Schedule A/B*: ______	$______	☐ $______ ☐ 100% of fair market value, up to any applicable statutory limit	______
Brief description: ______ Line from *Schedule A/B*: ______	$______	☐ $______ ☐ 100% of fair market value, up to any applicable statutory limit	______
Brief description: ______ Line from *Schedule A/B*: ______	$______	☐ $______ ☐ 100% of fair market value, up to any applicable statutory limit	______
Brief description: ______ Line from *Schedule A/B*: ______	$______	☐ $______ ☐ 100% of fair market value, up to any applicable statutory limit	______
Brief description: ______ Line from *Schedule A/B*: ______	$______	☐ $______ ☐ 100% of fair market value, up to any applicable statutory limit	______
Brief description: ______ Line from *Schedule A/B*: ______	$______	☐ $______ ☐ 100% of fair market value, up to any applicable statutory limit	______
Brief description: ______ Line from *Schedule A/B*: ______	$______	☐ $______ ☐ 100% of fair market value, up to any applicable statutory limit	______
Brief description: ______ Line from *Schedule A/B*: ______	$______	☐ $______ ☐ 100% of fair market value, up to any applicable statutory limit	______
Brief description: ______ Line from *Schedule A/B*: ______	$______	☐ $______ ☐ 100% of fair market value, up to any applicable statutory limit	______
Brief description: ______ Line from *Schedule A/B*: ______	$______	☐ $______ ☐ 100% of fair market value, up to any applicable statutory limit	______
Brief description: ______ Line from *Schedule A/B*: ______	$______	☐ $______ ☐ 100% of fair market value, up to any applicable statutory limit	______
Brief description: ______ Line from *Schedule A/B*: ______	$______	☐ $______ ☐ 100% of fair market value, up to any applicable statutory limit	______

Chapter Forty-Three

SCHEDULE D: CREDITORS WHO HAVE CLAIMS SECURED BY PROPERTY

SHEDULE D IS A bankruptcy form requiring detailed information about all secured debts and obligations where creditors have legal claims (liens) against specific property you own. These secured interests serve as collateral that creditors can potentially claim if the debt remains unpaid.

What Must Be Included in Schedule D?

- All secured creditors: Every creditor who holds a lien or security interest in your property
- Property descriptions: Detailed information about the collateral securing each debt
- Claim amounts: The total amount owed to each secured creditor
- Lien information: Whether the lien is consensual (you agreed to it), statutory, or judicial
- Unsecured portions: Any portion of the debt that exceeds the value of the collateral
- Lien priority: Whether the creditor holds a first, second, or subsequent position

Common Types of Secured Debts

- Mortgage and home equity loans

- Auto loans and vehicle financing
- Secured credit cards
- Tax liens from government entities
- Judgment liens from court cases
- Purchase-money security interests on appliances or furniture
- Statutory liens (mechanic's liens, HOA liens, etc.)

Strategic Considerations

Accurately completing Schedule D is crucial because it affects how these debts will be treated during bankruptcy. In Chapter 7, you typically have three options for secured property: surrender it, redeem it (pay fair market value in one lump sum), or reaffirm the debt (continue paying under the original or modified terms).

The information in Schedule D also helps the bankruptcy trustee understand your financial situation and determines which secured creditors must receive notice of your bankruptcy filing. Failure to list secured creditors could result in those debts surviving bankruptcy, leaving liens intact against your property.

Any significant discrepancies between the value listed on Schedule A/B and the secured debt amount on Schedule D will be scrutinized by the trustee, as this indicates potential equity that might be available for unsecured creditors.

Fresh Start. Survivor's Guide to Bankruptcy Practice

Fill in this information to identify your case:

Debtor 1 ______________________________
First Name Middle Name Last Name

Debtor 2 ______________________________
(Spouse, if filing) First Name Middle Name Last Name

United States Bankruptcy Court for the: District of __________

Case number ______________________________
(If known)

❑ Check if this is an amended filing

Official Form 106D

Schedule D: Creditors Who Have Claims Secured by Property

12/15

Be as complete and accurate as possible. If two married people are filing together, both are equally responsible for supplying correct information. If more space is needed, copy the Additional Page, fill it out, number the entries, and attach it to this form. On the top of any additional pages, write your name and case number (if known).

1. **Do any creditors have claims secured by your property?**
   - ❑ No. Check this box and submit this form to the court with your other schedules. You have nothing else to report on this form.
   - ❑ Yes. Fill in all of the information below.

Part 1: List All Secured Claims

2. **List all secured claims.** If a creditor has more than one secured claim, list the creditor separately for each claim. If more than one creditor has a particular claim, list the other creditors in Part 2. As much as possible, list the claims in alphabetical order according to the creditor's name.

	Column A **Amount of claim** Do not deduct the value of collateral.	*Column B* **Value of collateral that supports this claim**	*Column C* **Unsecured portion** If any
2.1	$__________	$__________	$__________
2.2	$__________	$__________	$__________

2.1

Creditor's Name ______________________

Number Street ______________________

City State ZIP Code ______________________

Describe the property that secures the claim:

As of the date you file, the claim is: Check all that apply.
- ❑ Contingent
- ❑ Unliquidated
- ❑ Disputed

Who owes the debt? Check one.
- ❑ Debtor 1 only
- ❑ Debtor 2 only
- ❑ Debtor 1 and Debtor 2 only
- ❑ At least one of the debtors and another

❑ **Check if this claim relates to a community debt**

Nature of lien. Check all that apply.
- ❑ An agreement you made (such as mortgage or secured car loan)
- ❑ Statutory lien (such as tax lien, mechanic's lien)
- ❑ Judgment lien from a lawsuit
- ❑ Other (including a right to offset) __________

Date debt was incurred __________

Last 4 digits of account number ___ ___ ___ ___

2.2

Creditor's Name ______________________

Number Street ______________________

City State ZIP Code ______________________

Describe the property that secures the claim:

As of the date you file, the claim is: Check all that apply.
- ❑ Contingent
- ❑ Unliquidated
- ❑ Disputed

Who owes the debt? Check one.
- ❑ Debtor 1 only
- ❑ Debtor 2 only
- ❑ Debtor 1 and Debtor 2 only
- ❑ At least one of the debtors and another

❑ **Check if this claim relates to a community debt**

Nature of lien. Check all that apply.
- ❑ An agreement you made (such as mortgage or secured car loan)
- ❑ Statutory lien (such as tax lien, mechanic's lien)
- ❑ Judgment lien from a lawsuit
- ❑ Other (including a right to offset) __________

Date debt was incurred __________

Last 4 digits of account number ___ ___ ___ ___

Add the dollar value of your entries in Column A on this page. Write that number here: $__________

Fresh Start. Survivor's Guide to Bankruptcy Practice

Debtor 1 ____ Case number *(if known)* ____________________
First Name Middle Name Last Name

Part 1:	Additional Page After listing any entries on this page, number them beginning with 2.3, followed by 2.4, and so forth.	*Column A* **Amount of claim** Do not deduct the value of collateral.	*Column B* **Value of collateral that supports this claim**	*Column C* **Unsecured portion** If any

☐ ______________________________
Creditor's Name
____
Number Street
____
____
City State ZIP Code

Describe the property that secures the claim: $__________ $__________ $__________

As of the date you file, the claim is: Check all that apply.
- ☐ Contingent
- ☐ Unliquidated
- ☐ Disputed

Who owes the debt? Check one.
- ☐ Debtor 1 only
- ☐ Debtor 2 only
- ☐ Debtor 1 and Debtor 2 only
- ☐ At least one of the debtors and another

☐ **Check if this claim relates to a community debt**

Nature of lien. Check all that apply.
- ☐ An agreement you made (such as mortgage or secured car loan)
- ☐ Statutory lien (such as tax lien, mechanic's lien)
- ☐ Judgment lien from a lawsuit
- ☐ Other (including a right to offset) __________

Date debt was incurred __________

Last 4 digits of account number ___ ___ ___ ___

☐ ______________________________
Creditor's Name
____
Number Street
____
____
City State ZIP Code

Describe the property that secures the claim: $__________ $__________ $__________

As of the date you file, the claim is: Check all that apply.
- ☐ Contingent
- ☐ Unliquidated
- ☐ Disputed

Who owes the debt? Check one.
- ☐ Debtor 1 only
- ☐ Debtor 2 only
- ☐ Debtor 1 and Debtor 2 only
- ☐ At least one of the debtors and another

☐ **Check if this claim relates to a community debt**

Nature of lien. Check all that apply.
- ☐ An agreement you made (such as mortgage or secured car loan)
- ☐ Statutory lien (such as tax lien, mechanic's lien)
- ☐ Judgment lien from a lawsuit
- ☐ Other (including a right to offset) __________

Date debt was incurred __________

Last 4 digits of account number ___ ___ ___ ___

☐ ______________________________
Creditor's Name
____
Number Street
____
____
City State ZIP Code

Describe the property that secures the claim: $__________ $__________ $__________

As of the date you file, the claim is: Check all that apply.
- ☐ Contingent
- ☐ Unliquidated
- ☐ Disputed

Who owes the debt? Check one.
- ☐ Debtor 1 only
- ☐ Debtor 2 only
- ☐ Debtor 1 and Debtor 2 only
- ☐ At least one of the debtors and another

☐ **Check if this claim relates to a community debt**

Nature of lien. Check all that apply.
- ☐ An agreement you made (such as mortgage or secured car loan)
- ☐ Statutory lien (such as tax lien, mechanic's lien)
- ☐ Judgment lien from a lawsuit
- ☐ Other (including a right to offset) __________

Date debt was incurred __________

Last 4 digits of account number ___ ___ ___ ___

Add the dollar value of your entries in Column A on this page. Write that number here: $__________

If this is the last page of your form, add the dollar value totals from all pages. Write that number here: $__________

386 of 470 Arlene A. Smith-Scott, JD

Official Form 106D Additional Page of **Schedule D: Creditors Who Have Claims Secured by Property** page ___ of ___

Fresh Start. Survivor's Guide to Bankruptcy Practice

Debtor 1 ______________________________ Case number (if known)______________________________
First Name Middle Name Last Name

Part 2: List Others to Be Notified for a Debt That You Already Listed

Use this page only if you have others to be notified about your bankruptcy for a debt that you already listed in Part 1. For example, if a collection agency is trying to collect from you for a debt you owe to someone else, list the creditor in Part 1, and then list the collection agency here. Similarly, if you have more than one creditor for any of the debts that you listed in Part 1, list the additional creditors here. If you do not have additional persons to be notified for any debts in Part 1, do not fill out or submit this page.

☐ ______________________________
Name
____
Number Street
____
____
City State ZIP Code

On which line in Part 1 did you enter the creditor? _____
Last 4 digits of account number ___ ___ ___ ___

☐ ______________________________
Name
____
Number Street
____
____
City State ZIP Code

On which line in Part 1 did you enter the creditor? _____
Last 4 digits of account number ___ ___ ___ ___

☐ ______________________________
Name
____
Number Street
____
____
City State ZIP Code

On which line in Part 1 did you enter the creditor? _____
Last 4 digits of account number ___ ___ ___ ___

☐ ______________________________
Name
____
Number Street
____
____
City State ZIP Code

On which line in Part 1 did you enter the creditor? _____
Last 4 digits of account number ___ ___ ___ ___

☐ ______________________________
Name
____
Number Street
____
____
City State ZIP Code

On which line in Part 1 did you enter the creditor? _____
Last 4 digits of account number ___ ___ ___ ___

☐ ______________________________
Name
____
Number Street
____
____
City State ZIP Code

On which line in Part 1 did you enter the creditor? _____
Last 4 digits of account number ___ ___ ___ ___

Chapter Forty-Four

SCHEDULES E/F: CREDITORS WHO HAVE UNSECURED CLAIMS

SCHEDULE E/F IS A crucial bankruptcy document that provides a comprehensive inventory of all unsecured debts and other obligations not backed by collateral. This schedule is divided into two main sections:

Part 1: Schedule E - Priority Unsecured Claims

Priority unsecured claims receive special treatment in bankruptcy and must be paid before general unsecured debts. These typically include:

- Domestic support obligations (child support, alimony)
- Certain tax debts (recent income taxes, payroll taxes)
- Wages, salaries, and commissions owed to employees
- Contributions to employee benefit plans
- Deposits by individuals (such as rental security deposits)
- Government fines and penalties

Priority claims often survive bankruptcy discharge, meaning you'll still owe them after your case concludes.

Part 2: Schedule F - Nonpriority Unsecured Claims

These are general unsecured debts that typically include:

- Credit card balances
- Medical bills
- Personal loans without collateral
- Student loans (listed here but may not be dischargeable)
- Utility bills
- Rent arrears
- Business debts
- Deficiency balances (remaining debt after repossession/foreclosure)
- Civil judgments

Required Information for Each Creditor

For each unsecured debt, you must provide:

- Creditor's name and contact information
- Account number (last 4 digits)
- Date debt was incurred
- Total amount owed
- Description of the claim
- Whether the claim is disputed, contingent, or unliquidated
- Codebtor information (if someone else is also responsible)

Importance of Schedule E/F

This schedule serves several critical functions:

- Ensures all creditors receive proper notice of your bankruptcy.
- Determines which debts may be discharged.
- Establishes payment priorities if assets are distributed.
- Creates an accurate picture of your financial situation for the court.

Being thorough and accurate with Schedule E/F is essential, as unlisted debts may not be discharged. Even if you believe a debt might not be dischargeable (like student loans), you must still list it on this schedule.

Fill in this information to identify your case:

Debtor 1 ______ First Name ______ Middle Name ______ Last Name

Debtor 2 (Spouse, if filing) ______ First Name ______ Middle Name ______ Last Name

United States Bankruptcy Court for the: District of ______

Case number (If known) ______

ptcy Practice

❑ Check if this is an amended filing

Official Form 106E/F

Schedule E/F: Creditors Who Have Unsecured Claims

12/15

Be as complete and accurate as possible. Use Part 1 for creditors with PRIORITY claims and Part 2 for creditors with NONPRIORITY claims. List the other party to any executory contracts or unexpired leases that could result in a claim. Also list executory contracts on *Schedule A/B: Property* (Official Form 106A/B) and on *Schedule G: Executory Contracts and Unexpired Leases* (Official Form 106G). Do not include any creditors with partially secured claims that are listed in *Schedule D: Creditors Who Have Claims Secured by Property*. If more space is needed, copy the Part you need, fill it out, number the entries in the boxes on the left. Attach the Continuation Page to this page. On the top of any additional pages, write your name and case number (if known).

Part 1: List All of Your PRIORITY Unsecured Claims

1. **Do any creditors have priority unsecured claims against you?**
   - ❑ No. Go to Part 2.
   - ❑ Yes.
2. **List all of your priority unsecured claims.** If a creditor has more than one priority unsecured claim, list the creditor separately for each claim. For each claim listed, identify what type of claim it is. If a claim has both priority and nonpriority amounts, list that claim here and show both priority and nonpriority amounts. As much as possible, list the claims in alphabetical order according to the creditor's name. If you have more than two priority unsecured claims, fill out the Continuation Page of Part 1. If more than one creditor holds a particular claim, list the other creditors in Part 3.

   (For an explanation of each type of claim, see the instructions for this form in the instruction booklet.)

Total claim	Priority amount	Nonpriority amount

2.1

______ Priority Creditor's Name

______ Number Street

______

______ City State ZIP Code

Who incurred the debt? Check one.

- ❑ Debtor 1 only
- ❑ Debtor 2 only
- ❑ Debtor 1 and Debtor 2 only
- ❑ At least one of the debtors and another
- ❑ **Check if this claim is for a community debt**

Is the claim subject to offset?

- ❑ No
- ❑ Yes

Last 4 digits of account number ___ ___ ___ ___ $______ $______ $______

When was the debt incurred? ______

As of the date you file, the claim is: Check all that apply.

- ❑ Contingent
- ❑ Unliquidated
- ❑ Disputed

Type of PRIORITY unsecured claim:

- ❑ Domestic support obligations
- ❑ Taxes and certain other debts you owe the government
- ❑ Claims for death or personal injury while you were intoxicated
- ❑ Other. Specify ______

2.2

______ Priority Creditor's Name

______ Number Street

______

______ City State ZIP Code

Who incurred the debt? Check one.

- ❑ Debtor 1 only
- ❑ Debtor 2 only
- ❑ Debtor 1 and Debtor 2 only
- ❑ At least one of the debtors and another
- ❑ **Check if this claim is for a community debt**

Is the claim subject to offset?

- ❑ No
- ❑ Yes

Last 4 digits of account number ___ ___ ___ ___ $______ $______ $______

When was the debt incurred? ______

As of the date you file, the claim is: Check all that apply.

- ❑ Contingent
- ❑ Unliquidated
- ❑ Disputed

Type of PRIORITY unsecured claim:

- ❑ Domestic support obligations
- ❑ Taxes and certain other debts you owe the government
- ❑ Claims for death or personal injury while you were intoxicated
- ❑ Other. Specify ______

Debtor 1 ______ First Name Middle Name Last Name

Fresh Start. Survivor's Guide to Bankruptcy Practice

Case number (if known) ______

Part 1: Your PRIORITY Unsecured Claims – Continuation Page

After listing any entries on this page, number them beginning with 2.3, followed by 2.4, and so forth.

	Total claim	Priority amount	Nonpriority amount
☐ Priority Creditor's Name ______ / Number Street ______ / ______ / City State ZIP Code ______	$______	$______	$______

Last 4 digits of account number ___ ___ ___ ___

When was the debt incurred? ______

As of the date you file, the claim is: Check all that apply.

- ☐ Contingent
- ☐ Unliquidated
- ☐ Disputed

Who incurred the debt? Check one.

- ☐ Debtor 1 only
- ☐ Debtor 2 only
- ☐ Debtor 1 and Debtor 2 only
- ☐ At least one of the debtors and another

☐ **Check if this claim is for a community debt**

Type of PRIORITY unsecured claim:

- ☐ Domestic support obligations
- ☐ Taxes and certain other debts you owe the government
- ☐ Claims for death or personal injury while you were intoxicated
- ☐ Other. Specify ______

Is the claim subject to offset?

- ☐ No
- ☐ Yes

	Total claim	Priority amount	Nonpriority amount
☐ Priority Creditor's Name ______ / Number Street ______ / ______ / City State ZIP Code ______	$______	$______	$______

Last 4 digits of account number ___ ___ ___ ___

When was the debt incurred? ______

As of the date you file, the claim is: Check all that apply.

- ☐ Contingent
- ☐ Unliquidated
- ☐ Disputed

Who incurred the debt? Check one.

- ☐ Debtor 1 only
- ☐ Debtor 2 only
- ☐ Debtor 1 and Debtor 2 only
- ☐ At least one of the debtors and another

☐ **Check if this claim is for a community debt**

Type of PRIORITY unsecured claim:

- ☐ Domestic support obligations
- ☐ Taxes and certain other debts you owe the government
- ☐ Claims for death or personal injury while you were intoxicated
- ☐ Other. Specify ______

Is the claim subject to offset?

- ☐ No
- ☐ Yes

	Total claim	Priority amount	Nonpriority amount
☐ Priority Creditor's Name ______ / Number Street ______ / ______ / City State ZIP Code ______	$______	$______	$______

Last 4 digits of account number ___ ___ ___ ___

When was the debt incurred? ______

As of the date you file, the claim is: Check all that apply.

- ☐ Contingent
- ☐ Unliquidated
- ☐ Disputed

Who incurred the debt? Check one.

- ☐ Debtor 1 only
- ☐ Debtor 2 only
- ☐ Debtor 1 and Debtor 2 only
- ☐ At least one of the debtors and another

☐ **Check if this claim is for a community debt**

Type of PRIORITY unsecured claim:

- ☐ Domestic support obligations
- ☐ Taxes and certain other debts you owe the government
- ☐ Claims for death or personal injury while you were intoxicated
- ☐ Other. Specify ______

Is the claim subject to offset?

- ☐ No
- ☐ Yes

Debtor 1 ______________________________ Case number (if known) ______________________
First Name Middle Name Last Name

Fresh Start. Survivor's Guide to Bankruptcy Practice

Part 2: List All of Your NONPRIORITY Unsecured Claims

3. **Do any creditors have nonpriority unsecured claims against you?**
   - ❑ No. You have nothing to report in this part. Submit this form to the court with your other schedules.
   - ❑ Yes

4. **List all of your nonpriority unsecured claims in the alphabetical order of the creditor who holds each claim.** If a creditor has more than one nonpriority unsecured claim, list the creditor separately for each claim. For each claim listed, identify what type of claim it is. Do not list claims already included in Part 1. If more than one creditor holds a particular claim, list the other creditors in Part 3.If you have more than three nonpriority unsecured claims fill out the Continuation Page of Part 2.

Total claim

4.1 ______________________________
Nonpriority Creditor's Name
____
Number Street
____
City State ZIP Code

Last 4 digits of account number ___ ___ ___ ___ $__________

When was the debt incurred? __________

As of the date you file, the claim is: Check all that apply.
- ❑ Contingent
- ❑ Unliquidated
- ❑ Disputed

Who incurred the debt? Check one.
- ❑ Debtor 1 only
- ❑ Debtor 2 only
- ❑ Debtor 1 and Debtor 2 only
- ❑ At least one of the debtors and another

❑ **Check if this claim is for a community debt**

Is the claim subject to offset?
- ❑ No
- ❑ Yes

Type of NONPRIORITY unsecured claim:
- ❑ Student loans
- ❑ Obligations arising out of a separation agreement or divorce that you did not report as priority claims
- ❑ Debts to pension or profit-sharing plans, and other similar debts
- ❑ Other. Specify ______________________

4.2 ______________________________
Nonpriority Creditor's Name
____
Number Street
____
City State ZIP Code

Last 4 digits of account number ___ ___ ___ ___ $__________

When was the debt incurred? __________

As of the date you file, the claim is: Check all that apply.
- ❑ Contingent
- ❑ Unliquidated
- ❑ Disputed

Who incurred the debt? Check one.
- ❑ Debtor 1 only
- ❑ Debtor 2 only
- ❑ Debtor 1 and Debtor 2 only
- ❑ At least one of the debtors and another

❑ **Check if this claim is for a community debt**

Is the claim subject to offset?
- ❑ No
- ❑ Yes

Type of NONPRIORITY unsecured claim:
- ❑ Student loans
- ❑ Obligations arising out of a separation agreement or divorce that you did not report as priority claims
- ❑ Debts to pension or profit-sharing plans, and other similar debts
- ❑ Other. Specify ______________________

4.3 ______________________________
Nonpriority Creditor's Name
____
Number Street
____
City State ZIP Code

Last 4 digits of account number ___ ___ ___ ___ $__________

When was the debt incurred? __________

As of the date you file, the claim is: Check all that apply.
- ❑ Contingent
- ❑ Unliquidated
- ❑ Disputed

Who incurred the debt? Check one.
- ❑ Debtor 1 only
- ❑ Debtor 2 only
- ❑ Debtor 1 and Debtor 2 only
- ❑ At least one of the debtors and another

❑ **Check if this claim is for a community debt**

Is the claim subject to offset?
- ❑ No
- ❑ Yes

Type of NONPRIORITY unsecured claim:
- ❑ Student loans
- ❑ Obligations arising out of a separation agreement or divorce that you did not report as priority claims
- ❑ Debts to pension or profit-sharing plans, and other similar debts
- ❑ Other. Specify ______________________

Debtor 1 ______________________________ Case number *(if known)*______________________________
First Name Middle Name Last Name

Fresh Start. Survivor's Guide to Bankruptcy Practice

Part 2: Your NONPRIORITY Unsecured Claims — Continuation Page

After listing any entries on this page, number them beginning with 4.4, followed by 4.5, and so forth. **Total claim**

☐

____
Nonpriority Creditor's Name

____
Number Street

____
City State ZIP Code

Who incurred the debt? Check one.

- ❑ Debtor 1 only
- ❑ Debtor 2 only
- ❑ Debtor 1 and Debtor 2 only
- ❑ At least one of the debtors and another

❑ **Check if this claim is for a community debt**

Is the claim subject to offset?

- ❑ No
- ❑ Yes

Last 4 digits of account number ___ ___ ___ ___ $__________

When was the debt incurred? __________

As of the date you file, the claim is: Check all that apply.

- ❑ Contingent
- ❑ Unliquidated
- ❑ Disputed

Type of **NONPRIORITY** unsecured claim:

- ❑ Student loans
- ❑ Obligations arising out of a separation agreement or divorce that you did not report as priority claims
- ❑ Debts to pension or profit-sharing plans, and other similar debts
- ❑ Other. Specify______________________

☐

____
Nonpriority Creditor's Name

____
Number Street

____
City State ZIP Code

Who incurred the debt? Check one.

- ❑ Debtor 1 only
- ❑ Debtor 2 only
- ❑ Debtor 1 and Debtor 2 only
- ❑ At least one of the debtors and another

❑ **Check if this claim is for a community debt**

Is the claim subject to offset?

- ❑ No
- ❑ Yes

Last 4 digits of account number ___ ___ ___ ___ $__________

When was the debt incurred? __________

As of the date you file, the claim is: Check all that apply.

- ❑ Contingent
- ❑ Unliquidated
- ❑ Disputed

Type of **NONPRIORITY** unsecured claim:

- ❑ Student loans
- ❑ Obligations arising out of a separation agreement or divorce that you did not report as priority claims
- ❑ Debts to pension or profit-sharing plans, and other similar debts
- ❑ Other. Specify______________________

☐

____
Nonpriority Creditor's Name

____
Number Street

____
City State ZIP Code

Who incurred the debt? Check one.

- ❑ Debtor 1 only
- ❑ Debtor 2 only
- ❑ Debtor 1 and Debtor 2 only
- ❑ At least one of the debtors and another

❑ **Check if this claim is for a community debt**

Is the claim subject to offset?

- ❑ No
- ❑ Yes

$__________

Last 4 digits of account number ___ ___ ___ ___

When was the debt incurred? __________

As of the date you file, the claim is: Check all that apply.

- ❑ Contingent
- ❑ Unliquidated
- ❑ Disputed

Type of **NONPRIORITY** unsecured claim:

- ❑ Student loans
- ❑ Obligations arising out of a separation agreement or divorce that you did not report as priority claims
- ❑ Debts to pension or profit-sharing plans, and other similar debts
- ❑ Other. Specify______________________

Debtor 1 ______________________________ Case number *(if known)*______________________
First Name Middle Name Last Name

Fresh Start. Survivor's Guide to Bankruptcy Practice

Part 3: List Others to Be Notified About a Debt That You Already Listed

5. **Use this page only if you have others to be notified about your bankruptcy, for a debt that you already listed in Parts 1 or 2. For example, if a collection agency is trying to collect from you for a debt you owe to someone else, list the original creditor in Parts 1 or 2, then list the collection agency here. Similarly, if you have more than one creditor for any of the debts that you listed in Parts 1 or 2, list the additional creditors here. If you do not have additional persons to be notified for any debts in Parts 1 or 2, do not fill out or submit this page.**

____
Name

____
Number Street

____

____
City State ZIP Code

On which entry in Part 1 or Part 2 did you list the original creditor?

Line _____ of *(Check one)*: ☐ Part 1: Creditors with Priority Unsecured Claims
☐ Part 2: Creditors with Nonpriority Unsecured Claims

Last 4 digits of account number ___ ___ ___ ___

____
Name

____
Number Street

____

____
City State ZIP Code

On which entry in Part 1 or Part 2 did you list the original creditor?

Line _____ of *(Check one)*: ☐ Part 1: Creditors with Priority Unsecured Claims
☐ Part 2: Creditors with Nonpriority Unsecured
Claims

Last 4 digits of account number ___ ___ ___ ___

____
Name

____
Number Street

____

____
City State ZIP Code

On which entry in Part 1 or Part 2 did you list the original creditor?

Line _____ of *(Check one)*: ☐ Part 1: Creditors with Priority Unsecured Claims
☐ Part 2: Creditors with Nonpriority Unsecured
Claims

Last 4 digits of account number ___ ___ ___ ___

____
Name

____
Number Street

____

____
City State ZIP Code

On which entry in Part 1 or Part 2 did you list the original creditor?

Line _____ of *(Check one)*: ☐ Part 1: Creditors with Priority Unsecured Claims
☐ Part 2: Creditors with Nonpriority Unsecured
Claims

Last 4 digits of account number ___ ___ ___ ___

____
Name

____
Number Street

____

____
City State ZIP Code

On which entry in Part 1 or Part 2 did you list the original creditor?

Line _____ of *(Check one)*: ☐ Part 1: Creditors with Priority Unsecured Claims
☐ Part 2: Creditors with Nonpriority Unsecured
Claims

Last 4 digits of account number ___ ___ ___ ___

____
Name

____
Number Street

____

____
City State ZIP Code

On which entry in Part 1 or Part 2 did you list the original creditor?

Line _____ of *(Check one)*: ☐ Part 1: Creditors with Priority Unsecured Claims
☐ Part 2: Creditors with Nonpriority Unsecured
Claims

Last 4 digits of account number ___ ___ ___ ___

____
Name

____
Number Street

____

____
City State ZIP Code

On which entry in Part 1 or Part 2 did you list the original creditor?

Line _____ of *(Check one)*: ☐ Part 1: Creditors with Priority Unsecured Claims
☐ Part 2: Creditors with Nonpriority Unsecured
Claims

Last 4 digits of account number ___ ___ ___ ___

Chapter Forty-Five

SCHEDULE G: EXECUTORY CONTRACTS AND UNEXPIRED LEASES

THE PRIMARY PURPOSE OF Schedule G is to list and detail any unexpired leases or executory contracts that the debtor wishes to assume or reject during the bankruptcy process. Unexpired leases and executory contracts are where both parties have ongoing obligations, and neither party has fully performed their duties.

Schedule G lists and discloses executory contracts and unexpired leases that the debtor is a party to. Something that has not yet been fully performed or completed and is therefore considered imperfect or unassured until its full execution. Executory contract is a contract that was entered into by the Debtor, and it is still ongoing at the time of the bankruptcy filing. For example, a lease of an apartment is an executory contract.

SCHEDULE G SERVES SEVERAL PURPOSES

1. Identification of Contracts and Leases.

The primary purpose of Schedule G is to identify and list all executory contracts and unexpired leases that the debtor is involved in at the time of filing for bankruptcy.

2. Provide Detailed Information.

Debtors are required to provide detailed information about each contract or lease, including the name and address of the other party or parties involved, the nature of the contract or lease, and the terms and conditions of the agreement.

3. Assisting Creditors and the Trustee.

Schedule G is important because it helps creditors, the bankruptcy trustee, and the bankruptcy court understand the debtor's ongoing financial obligations.

4. Treatment of Executory Contracts and Leases.

Depending on the type of bankruptcy (Chapter 7, Chapter 11, Chapter 13, etc.), the treatment of executory contracts and leases can vary. In Chapter 7 bankruptcy, the trustee may have the option to assume or reject these contracts. In Chapter 11 or Chapter 13, debtors may have the opportunity to propose a plan to continue or modify these agreements.

5. Implications for Creditors and Debtors.

Creditors with whom the debtor has executory contracts or unexpired leases listed on Schedule G will receive notice of the bankruptcy filing. They will have the opportunity to assert any claims they may have related to these agreements. The bankruptcy court will determine how these claims are addressed and whether the contracts should be assumed, rejected, or modified.

QUESTIONS THAT ARE ON SCHEDULE G

1. Do you have any executory contracts or unexpired leases? If not, check the box and file the form with the court with your other schedules. Fill in all of the information below even if the contracts or leases are listed on Schedule A/B: Property.

2. List separately each person or company with whom you have the contract or lease. Then state what each contract or lease is for (for example, rent, vehicle lease, cell phone). Person or company

with whom you have the contract or lease. Please state what purpose the contract or lease is for. Make sure to provide the Name, Address, City, State and Zip Code for each person or company.

Fresh Start. Survivor's Guide to Bankruptcy Practice

Fill in this information to identify your case:

Debtor ______ First Name ______ Middle Name ______ Last Name

Debtor 2 (Spouse If filing) ______ First Name ______ Middle Name ______ Last Name

United States Bankruptcy Court for the: District of ______

Case number (If known) ______

❑ Check if this is an amended filing

Official Form 106G

Schedule G: Executory Contracts and Unexpired Leases

12/15

Be as complete and accurate as possible. If two married people are filing together, both are equally responsible for supplying correct information. If more space is needed, copy the additional page, fill it out, number the entries, and attach it to this page. On the top of any additional pages, write your name and case number (if known).

1. **Do you have any executory contracts or unexpired leases?**
   - ❑ No. Check this box and file this form with the court with your other schedules. You have nothing else to report on this form.
   - ❑ Yes. Fill in all of the information below even if the contracts or leases are listed on *Schedule A/B: Property* (Official Form 106A/B).

2. **List separately each person or company with whom you have the contract or lease. Then state what each contract or lease is for (for example, rent, vehicle lease, cell phone).** See the instructions for this form in the instruction booklet for more examples of executory contracts and unexpired leases.

	Person or company with whom you have the contract or lease	State what the contract or lease is for
2.1	Name Number Street City State ZIP Code	
2.2	Name Number Street City State ZIP Code	
2.3	Name Number Street City State ZIP Code	
2.4	Name Number Street City State ZIP Code	
2.5	Name Number Street City State ZIP Code	

Fresh Start. Survivor's Guide to Bankruptcy Practice

Debtor 1 ______________________________ Case number *(if known)* ______________________
First Name   Middle Name   Last Name

Additional Page if You Have More Contracts or Leases

Person or company with whom you have the contract or lease	What the contract or lease is for
22 ____________________ Name ____________________ Number Street ____________________ City State ZIP Code	
2._ ____________________ Name ____________________ Number Street ____________________ City State ZIP Code	
2._ ____________________ Name ____________________ Number Street ____________________ City State ZIP Code	
2._ ____________________ Name ____________________ Number Street ____________________ City State ZIP Code	
2._ ____________________ Name ____________________ Number Street ____________________ City State ZIP Code	
2._ ____________________ Name ____________________ Number Street ____________________ City State ZIP Code	
2._ ____________________ Name ____________________ Number Street ____________________ City State ZIP Code	
2._ ____________________ Name ____________________ Number Street ____________________ City State ZIP Code	

Chapter Forty-Six

SCHEDULE H - YOUR CODEBTORS

SCHEDULE H IS USED to disclose and provide information about any individuals or entities who have co-signed or guaranteed the debtor's debts. These individuals or entities are known as "codebtors" or "cosigners."

The primary purpose of Schedule H is to identify and list all codebtors associated with the debtor's debts. This includes anyone who may be legally responsible for the same debts as the debtor, such as cosigners on loans or guarantors of financial obligations.

Debtors are required to provide detailed information about each codebtor, including their name, address, relationship to the debtor, the nature of the debt, the name of the creditor, and the amount owed. This information ensures that all codebtors are properly identified and their obligations are clearly documented.

Schedule H serves an important function in safeguarding the rights and interests of codebtors. It provides notice to codebtors that the debtor has filed for bankruptcy, which can be critical information for them to understand their potential liability and the impact on their credit.

In Chapter 13 bankruptcy, where a repayment plan is established, Schedule H may also be used to indicate whether any of the debtor's plan payments are intended to cover codebtor obligations.

The information on Schedule H is made available to creditors, the bankruptcy trustee, and the court. Creditors may take actions regarding codebtors based on this information, and the trustee may consider it when administering the bankruptcy estate.

While the debtor's bankruptcy filing may provide some relief from debt collection efforts, codebtors may remain liable for the full amount of the debt. The treatment of codebtor obligations depends on the type of bankruptcy (Chapter 7, Chapter 13, etc.) and whether the debtor chooses to reaffirm or discharge the debt.

QUESTIONS THAT ARE ON SCHEDULE H

1. Do you have any codebtors? (If you are filing a joint case, do not list either spouse as a codebtor.) Please answer by checking No or Yes.

2. Within the last 8 years, have you lived in a community property state or territory? (Community property states and territories include Arizona, California, Idaho, Louisiana, Nevada, New Mexico, Puerto Rico, Texas, Washington, and Wisconsin.) If not, go to line 3. If yes, did your spouse, former spouse, or legal equivalent live with you at the time? Please answer no or yes and state which community state or territory do you live? Please provide the current address of that person. Name of your spouse, former spouse, or legal equivalent include street address, city, state, and zip code.

3. In Column 1, list all your codebtors. Do not include your spouse as a codebtor if your spouse is filing with you. List the person shown in line 2 again as a codebtor only if that person is a guarantor or cosigner. Make sure you have listed the creditor on Schedule D, Schedule E/F, or Schedule G. Remember to use information as found on your Schedule D, Schedule E/F, or Schedule G to fill out Column 2. Please state the creditor to whom you owe the debt. Include their name, street address, city, state, and zip code. Check the box as to where the creditor is listed. Schedule D, Schedule E/F, and Schedule G.

Fresh Start. Survivor's Guide to Bankruptcy Practice

Fill in this information to identify your case:

Debtor 1 ______________________________
First Name Middle Name Last Name

Debtor 2 ______________________________
(Spouse, if filing) First Name Middle Name Last Name

United States Bankruptcy Court for the: District of __________

Case number ______________________________
(If known)

☐ Check if this is an amended filing

Official Form 106H

Schedule H: Your Codebtors

12/15

Codebtors are people or entities who are also liable for any debts you may have. Be as complete and accurate as possible. If two married people are filing together, both are equally responsible for supplying correct information. If more space is needed, copy the Additional Page, fill it out, and number the entries in the boxes on the left. Attach the Additional Page to this page. On the top of any Additional Pages, write your name and case number (if known). Answer every question.

1. **Do you have any codebtors?** (If you are filing a joint case, do not list either spouse as a codebtor.)
   - ☐ No
   - ☐ Yes
2. **Within the last 8 years, have you lived in a community property state or territory?** (*Community property states and territories* include Arizona, California, Idaho, Louisiana, Nevada, New Mexico, Puerto Rico, Texas, Washington, and Wisconsin.)
   - ☐ No. Go to line 3.
   - ☐ Yes. Did your spouse, former spouse, or legal equivalent live with you at the time?
     - ☐ No
     - ☐ Yes. In which community state or territory did you live? ________________. Fill in the name and current address of that person.

   ____
   Name of your spouse, former spouse, or legal equivalent

   ____
   Number Street

   ____
   City State ZIP Code

3. **In Column 1, list all of your codebtors. Do not include your spouse as a codebtor if your spouse is filing with you. List the person shown in line 2 again as a codebtor only if that person is a guarantor or cosigner. Make sure you have listed the creditor on *Schedule D* (Official Form 106D), *Schedule E/F* (Official Form 106E/F), or *Schedule G* (Official Form 106G). Use *Schedule D, Schedule E/F, or Schedule G* to fill out Column 2.**

	Column 1: **Your codebtor**	*Column 2:* **The creditor to whom you owe the debt** Check all schedules that apply:
3.1	Name Number Street City State ZIP Code	☐ Schedule D, line ______ ☐ Schedule E/F, line ______ ☐ Schedule G, line ______
3.2	Name Number Street City State ZIP Code	☐ Schedule D, line ______ ☐ Schedule E/F, line ______ ☐ Schedule G, line ______
3.3	Name Number Street City State ZIP Code	☐ Schedule D, line ______ ☐ Schedule E/F, line ______ ☐ Schedule G, line ______

Debtor 1 Fresh Start. Survivor's Guide to Bankruptcy Practice Case number (if known)

First Name Middle Name Last Name

Additional Page to List More Codebtors

Column 1: **Your codebtor**	*Column 2:* **The creditor to whom you owe the debt**
	Check all schedules that apply:
3._ Name Number Street City State ZIP Code	❑ Schedule D, line ______ ❑ Schedule E/F, line ______ ❑ Schedule G, line ______
3._ Name Number Street City State ZIP Code	❑ Schedule D, line ______ ❑ Schedule E/F, line ______ ❑ Schedule G, line ______
3._ Name Number Street City State ZIP Code	❑ Schedule D, line ______ ❑ Schedule E/F, line ______ ❑ Schedule G, line ______
3._ Name Number Street City State ZIP Code	❑ Schedule D, line ______ ❑ Schedule E/F, line ______ ❑ Schedule G, line ______
3._ Name Number Street City State ZIP Code	❑ Schedule D, line ______ ❑ Schedule E/F, line ______ ❑ Schedule G, line ______
3._ Name Number Street City State ZIP Code	❑ Schedule D, line ______ ❑ Schedule E/F, line ______ ❑ Schedule G, line ______
3._ Name Number Street City State ZIP Code	❑ Schedule D, line ______ ❑ Schedule E/F, line ______ ❑ Schedule G, line ______
3._ Name Number Street City State ZIP Code	❑ Schedule D, line ______ ❑ Schedule E/F, line ______ ❑ Schedule G, line ______

Chapter Forty-Seven

SCHEDULE I - YOUR INCOME

SCHEDULE I ALLOWS FOR a comprehensive overview of the debtor's current financial situation, including their income, expenses, and certain other financial aspects. Its primary purpose is to disclose the debtor's income and enable the bankruptcy trustee, creditors, and the court to assess the debtor's ability to repay their outstanding debts. Accurate disclosure of expenses is vital to assess the debtor's disposable income available for debt repayment. This disclosure is essential in determining whether the debtor qualifies for Chapter 7 bankruptcy or whether they should be required to file under Chapter 13, which involves a repayment plan.

Schedule I require the debtor to list all sources of income, including but not limited to wages and salary, self-employment income, rental income, retirement benefits, social security, unemployment compensation, other sources of income, etc.

The debtor must specify the amount and frequency of each income source.

Deductions and Expenses: Along with income, Schedule I also prompts the debtor to list their monthly expenses including rent or mortgage payments, utilities, food and groceries, transportation costs, insurance premiums, child support or alimony payments, taxes, healthcare, etc.

Schedule I plays a significant role in determining the debtor's eligibility for Chapter 7 bankruptcy. If the debtor's disposable income, as calculated from Schedule I, falls below a certain threshold established by the means test (Form 122A-2), they may qualify for Chapter 7. However, if their disposable income exceeds this threshold, they may be required to file under Chapter 13, where they will propose a repayment plan based on their disposable income.

QUESTIONS IN SCHEDULE I

1. Fill in your employment information. If you have more than one job, attach a separate page with information about additional employers. Include part-time, seasonal, or self-employed work. Occupation may include students or homemakers, if it applies. For both Debtor 1 and Debtor 2, please state employment status. Check whether employed or not employed. If Debtor 1 and Debtor 2 are employed, please provide the name of the employer, street address, city, state, and state zip code.

2. List monthly gross wages, salary, and commissions (before all payroll deductions). If not paid monthly, calculate what the monthly wage would be. (Go back to the "Be Prepared" module and take the number you calculated for your gross wages, salary, and commission.

3. Estimate and list monthly overtime pay. (Go Back to the "Be Prepared" module.)

4. Calculate gross income. Add line 2 + line 3.

5. List of all payroll deductions:

- 5a. Tax, Medicare, and Social Security deductions
- 5b. Mandatory contributions for retirement plans
- 5c. Voluntary contributions for retirement plans
- 5d. Required repayments of retirement fund loans
- 5e. Insurance
- 5f. Domestic support obligations
- 5g. Union dues
- 5h. Other deductions.

6. Add the payroll deductions. Add lines 5a through 6.

7. Calculate total monthly take-home pay. Subtract line 6 from line 4.

8. List all other income regularly received:

- 8a. Net income from rental property and from operating a business, profession, or farm.

Attach a statement for each property and business showing gross receipts, ordinary and necessary business expenses, and the total monthly net income.

- 8b. Interest and dividends
- 8c. Family support payments that you, a non-filing spouse, or a dependent regularly receive Include alimony, spousal support, child support, maintenance, divorce settlement, and property settlement.8
- 8d. Unemployment compensation
- 8e. Social Security
- 8f. Other government assistance that you regularly receive Include cash assistance and the value (if known) of any non-cash assistance that you receive, such as food stamps (benefits under the Supplemental Nutrition Assistance Program) or housing subsidies.
- 8g. Pension or retirement income
- 8h. Other monthly income.

9. Add all other income. Add lines 8a through 8h.

10. Calculate monthly income. Add line 7 + line 9. Add the entries in line 10 for Debtor 1 and Debtor 2 or non-filing spouse.

11. State all other regular contributions to the expenses that you list in Schedule J. Include contributions from an unmarried partner, members of your household, your dependents, your roommates, and other friends or relatives. Do not include any amounts already included in lines 2-10 or amounts that are not available to pay expenses listed in Schedule J. Please specify.

12. Add the amount in the last column of line 10 to the amount in line 11. The result is the combined monthly income. Write that amount on the Summary of Your Assets and Liabilities and Certain Statistical Information, if it applies 12. Combined monthly income.

13. Do you expect an increase or decrease within the year after you file this form?

Please answer no or yes, if yes, please describe.

Fresh Start. Survivor's Guide to Bankruptcy Practice

Fill in this information to identify your case:

Debtor 1 ______________________________
First Name Middle Name Last Name

Debtor 2 ______________________________
(Spouse, if filing) First Name Middle Name Last Name

United States Bankruptcy Court for the: ________ District of ________

Case number ______________________________
(If known)

Check if this is:

- ❑ An amended filing
- ❑ A supplement showing postpetition chapter 13 income as of the following date:

____
MM / DD / YYYY

Official Form 106I

Schedule I: Your Income

12/15

Be as complete and accurate as possible. If two married people are filing together (Debtor 1 and Debtor 2), both are equally responsible for supplying correct information. If you are married and not filing jointly, and your spouse is living with you, include information about your spouse. If you are separated and your spouse is not filing with you, do not include information about your spouse. If more space is needed, attach a separate sheet to this form. On the top of any additional pages, write your name and case number (if known). Answer every question.

Part 1: Describe Employment

1. **Fill in your employment information.**

   If you have more than one job, attach a separate page with information about additional employers.

   Include part-time, seasonal, or self-employed work.

   Occupation may include student or homemaker, if it applies.

	Debtor 1	Debtor 2 or non-filing spouse
Employment status	❑ Employed ❑ Not employed	❑ Employed ❑ Not employed
Occupation	________	________
Employer's name	________	________
Employer's address	________ Number Street ________ ________ ________ City State ZIP Code	________ Number Street ________ ________ ________ City State ZIP Code
How long employed there?	________	________

Part 2: Give Details About Monthly Income

Estimate monthly income as of the date you file this form. If you have nothing to report for any line, write $0 in the space. Include your non-filing spouse unless you are separated.

If you or your non-filing spouse have more than one employer, combine the information for all employers for that person on the lines below. If you need more space, attach a separate sheet to this form.

		For Debtor 1	For Debtor 2 or non-filing spouse
2. **List monthly gross wages, salary, and commissions** (before all payroll deductions). If not paid monthly, calculate what the monthly wage would be.	2.	$________	$________
3. **Estimate and list monthly overtime pay.**	3.	+ $________	+ $________
4. **Calculate gross income.** Add line 2 + line 3.	4.	$________	$________

Fresh Start. Survivor's Guide to Bankruptcy Practice

Debtor 1 ________________________________ Case number *(if known)*____________________

First Name Middle Name Last Name

		For Debtor 1	For Debtor 2 or non-filing spouse
Copy line 4 here ...... ➔	4.	$____	$____
5. **List all payroll deductions:**			
5a. **Tax, Medicare, and Social Security deductions**	5a.	$____	$____
5b. **Mandatory contributions for retirement plans**	5b.	$____	$____
5c. **Voluntary contributions for retirement plans**	5c.	$____	$____
5d. **Required repayments of retirement fund loans**	5d.	$____	$____
5e. **Insurance**	5e.	$____	$____
5f. **Domestic support obligations**	5f.	$____	$____
5g. **Union dues**	5g.	$____	$____
5h. **Other deductions.** Specify: ____	5h.	+ $____	+ $____
6. **Add the payroll deductions.** Add lines 5a + 5b + 5c + 5d + 5e +5f + 5g + 5h.	6.	$____	$____
7. **Calculate total monthly take-home pay.** Subtract line 6 from line 4.	7.	$____	$____
8. **List all other income regularly received:**			
8a. **Net income from rental property and from operating a business, profession, or farm** Attach a statement for each property and business showing gross receipts, ordinary and necessary business expenses, and the total monthly net income.	8a.	$____	$____
8b. **Interest and dividends**	8b.	$____	$____
8c. **Family support payments that you, a non-filing spouse, or a dependent regularly receive** Include alimony, spousal support, child support, maintenance, divorce settlement, and property settlement.	8c.	$____	$____
8d. **Unemployment compensation**	8d.	$____	$____
8e. **Social Security**	8e.	$____	$____
8f. **Other government assistance that you regularly receive** Include cash assistance and the value (if known) of any non-cash assistance that you receive, such as food stamps (benefits under the Supplemental Nutrition Assistance Program) or housing subsidies. Specify: ____	8f.	$____	$____
8g. **Pension or retirement income**	8g.	$____	$____
8h. **Other monthly income.** Specify: ____	8h.	+ $____	+ $____
9. **Add all other income.** Add lines 8a + 8b + 8c + 8d + 8e + 8f +8g + 8h.	9.	$____	$____
10. **Calculate monthly income.** Add line 7 + line 9. Add the entries in line 10 for Debtor 1 and Debtor 2 or non-filing spouse.	10.	$____ +	$____ = $____

11. **State all other regular contributions to the expenses that you list in *Schedule J.***

Include contributions from an unmarried partner, members of your household, your dependents, your roommates, and other friends or relatives.

Do not include any amounts already included in lines 2-10 or amounts that are not available to pay expenses listed in *Schedule J.*

Specify: ____________________ 11. + $____

12. **Add the amount in the last column of line 10 to the amount in line 11.** The result is the combined monthly income. Write that amount on the *Summary of Your Assets and Liabilities and Certain Statistical Information,* if it applies 12. $____

Combined monthly income

13. **Do you expect an increase or decrease within the year after you file this form?**

❑ No.

❑ Yes. Explain: ____

Chapter Forty-Eight

SCHEDULE J - YOUR EXPENSES

IN BANKRUPTCY PROCEEDINGS, SCHEDULE J is a vital document that serves the purpose of detailing the debtor's monthly expenses. Schedule J reflects the net income or the monthly amount of disposable income after all expenses are paid by the Debtor(s). The disposable income or monthly amount remaining can be used as a tool to determine that the Debtor(s) are not eligible for Chapter 7 if there is sufficient income remaining after expenses.

The primary purpose of Schedule J is to provide a comprehensive breakdown of the debtor's monthly living expenses. By itemizing these expenses, it helps establish a clear picture of the debtor's financial obligations and standard of living.

When completing Schedule J, debtors are required to list a variety of monthly expenses, including but not limited to the following items.

- Housing expenses include mortgage or rent payments, property taxes, homeowner association fees, and home insurance.
- Utility expenses related to electricity, gas, water, and trash removal.
- Transportation costs related to vehicle ownership and operation, including car loan payments, fuel, insurance, maintenance, and public transportation costs.
- Food, groceries, meals, and other essential food-related expenses.

- Healthcare expenses include health insurance premiums, prescription medications, medical co-pays, and other healthcare-related costs.
- Childcare expenses related to the care and support of dependent children.
- Any ongoing tax obligations that are not dischargeable in bankruptcy.
- Other miscellaneous expenses are necessary for the debtor's maintenance and support, such as clothing, personal hygiene products, and education-related costs.

Impact on Bankruptcy Proceedings

Schedule J aids in the calculation of the debtor's disposable income, which is the amount left over after deducting allowable expenses from the debtor's monthly income.

By accurately and honestly disclosing monthly expenses on Schedule J, debtors can ensure that their Chapter 13 repayment plan reflects their true financial situation.

QUESTIONS ON SCHEDULE J.

1. Is this a joint case? If not, please go to line 2. If yes, does Debtor 2 live in a separate household? If the answer is yes, Debtor 2 must fill out Official Form 106J-2, Expenses for Separate Household of Debtor 2.

2. Do you have dependents? Do not include Debtor 1 or Debtor 2. If not, please go to line 3. If yes, state the defendant's relationship to Debtor 1, Debtor 2, etc., however, do not state the dependent's name. Include their age and whether they live with you.

3. Do your expenses include the expenses of people other than yourself and your dependents? If not, go to Line 4. If yes, please check.

Part II: Estimate Your Monthly Expenses.

Estimate your expenses as of your bankruptcy filing date unless you are using this form as a supplement in a Chapter 13 case to report expenses as of a date after the bankruptcy is filed.

Include expenses paid for with non-cash government assistance if you know the value of such assistance and have included it on Schedule I: Your Income (Official Form 106I.) Your expenses

4. The rental or home ownership expenses for your residence. Include first mortgage payments and any rent for the ground or lot. If not included in line 4, please include Real estate taxes, Property, homeowner's, or renter's insurance, home maintenance, repair, and upkeep expenses, and homeowners' association or condominium dues.

5. Additional mortgage payments for your residence, such as home equity loans.

6. Utilities. Lists electricity, heat, and natural gas on line 6a. List water, sewer, garbage collection on line 6b. Lists telephone, cell phone, Internet, satellite, and cable services on line 6c. Lists any other expenses and please specify on line 6d.

7. Food and housekeeping supplies on line 7.

8. Childcare and children's education costs on line 8.

9. Clothing, laundry, and dry cleaning on line 9.

10. Personal care products and services on line 10.

11. Medical and dental expenses on line 11.

12. Transportation. Include gas, maintenance, bus or train fare. Do not include car payments on line 12.

13. Entertainment, clubs, recreation, newspapers, magazines, and books on line 13.

14. Charitable contributions and religious donations on line 14.

15. Insurance. Do not include insurance deducted from your pay or included in lines 4 or 20. Life insurance on line 15a. Health insurance on line 15b. Vehicle insurance on line 15c. Other insurance, please specify on line 15d.

16. Taxes. Do not include taxes deducted from your pay or included in lines 4 or 20. Please specify on line 16.

17. Installment or lease payments. Please state car payments for vehicle 1 on line 17 a. Car payments for Vehicle 2 on line 17b. Please specify any other vehicle on line 17c. State any other vehicle on line 17d. If you have more vehicles, please state on separate paper.

18. Your payments of alimony, maintenance, and support that you did not report as deducted from your pay on line 5, Schedule I, Your Income (Official Form 106I).

19. Other payments you make to support others who do not live with you. Please specify or describe support.

20. Other real property expenses not included in lines 4 or 5 of this form or on Schedule I: Your Income. Mortgages on other property one-line 20a. Real estate taxes on line 20b. Property, homeowner's, or renter's insurance on line 20c. Maintenance, repair, and upkeep expenses on line 20d. Homeowner's association or condominium dues on line 20e.

21. Other. If there is additional expenses, not already disclosed, please specify on line 21.

22. Calculate your monthly expenses. Add lines 4 through 21 and place on line 22a.

- 22b. Copy line 22, which is separate expenses for Debtor 2 and add any additional expenses from supplemental or separate sheet, if applicable, and place on line 22b.
- 22c. Add line 22a and 22b. The result is your monthly expenses which you should place on line 22c.

23. Calculate your monthly net income. Copy line 12 (your combined monthly income) from Schedule I and place it on line 23a.

- 23b. Copy your monthly expenses from line 22c above and place on line 23b. Subtract your monthly income as found on line 23a from from your monthly expenses as found on 22c
- The result is your monthly net income which is found on line 23c.

****Important to note: If you have $250.00 or more remaining after all of your expenses, a Chapter 7 Trustee could ask that you pay towards your creditors. Each jurisdiction and Trustee is different, but make sure you check your expenses and account for everything.

24. Do you expect an increase or decrease in your expenses within the year after you file this form? For example, do you expect to finish paying for your car loan within the year or do you expect

your mortgage payment to increase or decrease because of a modification to the terms of your mortgage? Please state no or yes, if yes, explain.

Fresh Start. Survivor's Guide to Bankruptcy Practice

Fill in this information to identify your case:

Debtor 1 ______________________________
First Name Middle Name Last Name

Debtor 2 ______________________________
(Spouse, if filing) First Name Middle Name Last Name

United States Bankruptcy Court for the: District of __________

Case number ______________________________
(If known)

Check if this is:

- ❑ An amended filing
- ❑ A supplement showing postpetition chapter 13 expenses as of the following date:

____
MM / DD / YYYY

Official Form 106J

Schedule J: Your Expenses

12/15

Be as complete and accurate as possible. If two married people are filing together, both are equally responsible for supplying correct information. If more space is needed, attach another sheet to this form. On the top of any additional pages, write your name and case number (if known). Answer every question.

Part 1: Describe Your Household

1. **Is this a joint case?**
   - ❑ No. Go to line 2.
   - ❑ Yes. **Does Debtor 2 live in a separate household?**
     - ❑ No
     - ❑ Yes. Debtor 2 must file Official Form 106J-2, *Expenses for Separate Household of Debtor 2.*

2. **Do you have dependents?** Do not list Debtor 1 and Debtor 2. Do not state the dependents' names.
   - ❑ No
   - ❑ Yes. Fill out this information for each dependent..........................

Dependent's relationship to Debtor 1 or Debtor 2	Dependent's age	Does dependent live with you?
______________	______	❑ No ❑ Yes
______________	______	❑ No ❑ Yes
______________	______	❑ No ❑ Yes
______________	______	❑ No ❑ Yes
______________	______	❑ No ❑ Yes

3. **Do your expenses include expenses of people other than yourself and your dependents?**
   - ❑ No
   - ❑ Yes

Part 2: Estimate Your Ongoing Monthly Expenses

Estimate your expenses as of your bankruptcy filing date unless you are using this form as a supplement in a Chapter 13 case to report expenses as of a date after the bankruptcy is filed. If this is a supplemental *Schedule J*, check the box at the top of the form and fill in the applicable date.

Include expenses paid for with non-cash government assistance if you know the value of such assistance and have included it on *Schedule I: Your Income* (Official Form 106I.)

		Your expenses
4. **The rental or home ownership expenses for your residence.** Include first mortgage payments and any rent for the ground or lot.	4.	$__________
If not included in line 4:		
4a. Real estate taxes	4a.	$__________
4b. Property, homeowner's, or renter's insurance	4b.	$__________
4c. Home maintenance, repair, and upkeep expenses	4c.	$__________
4d. Homeowner's association or condominium dues	4d.	$__________

Fresh Start. Survivor's Guide to Bankruptcy Practice

Debtor 1 ______________________________ Case number *(if known)*______________________
First Name Middle Name Last Name

		Your expenses
5. **Additional mortgage payments for your residence**, such as home equity loans	5.	$________
6. **Utilities:**		
6a. Electricity, heat, natural gas	6a.	$________
6b. Water, sewer, garbage collection	6b.	$________
6c. Telephone, cell phone, Internet, satellite, and cable services	6c.	$________
6d. Other. Specify: ________________	6d.	$________
7. **Food and housekeeping supplies**	7.	$________
8. **Childcare and children's education costs**	8.	$________
9. **Clothing, laundry, and dry cleaning**	9.	$________
10. **Personal care products and services**	10.	$________
11. **Medical and dental expenses**	11.	$________
12. **Transportation.** Include gas, maintenance, bus or train fare. Do not include car payments.	12.	$________
13. **Entertainment, clubs, recreation, newspapers, magazines, and books**	13.	$________
14. **Charitable contributions and religious donations**	14.	$________
15. **Insurance.** Do not include insurance deducted from your pay or included in lines 4 or 20.		
15a. Life insurance	15a.	$________
15b. Health insurance	15b.	$________
15c. Vehicle insurance	15c.	$________
15d. Other insurance. Specify:________________	15d.	$________
16. **Taxes.** Do not include taxes deducted from your pay or included in lines 4 or 20. Specify: ________________	16.	$________
17. **Installment or lease payments:**		
17a. Car payments for Vehicle 1	17a.	$________
17b. Car payments for Vehicle 2	17b.	$________
17c. Other. Specify:________________	17c.	$________
17d. Other. Specify:________________	17d.	$________
18. **Your payments of alimony, maintenance, and support that you did not report as deducted from your pay on line 5, *Schedule I, Your Income* (Official Form 106I).**	18.	$________
19. **Other payments you make to support others who do not live with you.** Specify:________________	19.	$________
20. **Other real property expenses not included in lines 4 or 5 of this form or on *Schedule I*: *Your Income*.**		
20a. Mortgages on other property	20a.	$________
20b. Real estate taxes	20b.	$________
20c. Property, homeowner's, or renter's insurance	20c.	$________
20d. Maintenance, repair, and upkeep expenses	20d.	$________
20e. Homeowner's association or condominium dues	20e.	$________

Fresh Start. Survivor's Guide to Bankruptcy Practice

Debtor 1 ______________________________ Case number *(if known)*______________________

First Name Middle Name Last Name

21. **Other**. Specify: ______________________________ 21. +$__________

22. **Calculate your monthly expenses.**

22a. Add lines 4 through 21. 22a. $__________

22b. Copy line 22 (monthly expenses for Debtor 2), if any, from Official Form 106J-2 22b. $__________

22c. Add line 22a and 22b. The result is your monthly expenses. 22c. $__________

23. **Calculate your monthly net income.**

23a. Copy line 12 (*your combined monthly income*) from *Schedule I.* 23a. $__________

23b. Copy your monthly expenses from line 22c above. 23b. – $__________

23c. Subtract your monthly expenses from your monthly income.
The result is your *monthly net income.* 23c. $__________

24. **Do you expect an increase or decrease in your expenses within the year after you file this form?**

For example, do you expect to finish paying for your car loan within the year or do you expect your mortgage payment to increase or decrease because of a modification to the terms of your mortgage?

❑ No.

❑ Yes. Explain here:

Chapter Forty-Nine

STATEMENT OF FINANCIAL AFFAIRS FOR INDIVIDUALS FILING FOR BANKRUPTCY (SOFA)

THE STATEMENT OF FINANCIAL Affairs (SOFA) is a critical bankruptcy document that serves as a comprehensive financial disclosure mechanism. It verifies and expands upon information provided in your bankruptcy schedules while creating a detailed financial history. This document essentially "follows the money" by requiring you to disclose financial transactions and activities that occurred before your bankruptcy filing.

Key Functions

- Verification Tool: Confirms the accuracy of information in your bankruptcy schedules
- Financial History Record: Creates a timeline of your significant financial transactions
- Due Diligence Mechanism: Allows trustees and creditors to identify potential issues
- Fraud Prevention: Helps detect improper pre-bankruptcy financial maneuvers

Critical Nature of Accuracy

The SOFA requires meticulous attention to detail and complete honesty. Inaccuracies or omissions can:

- Lead to denial of discharge
- Result in dismissal of your bankruptcy case
- Potentially trigger criminal penalties for bankruptcy fraud
- Create grounds for adversary proceedings from the trustee or creditors
- Information Required in the SOFA

Income History

- Employment-related income
- Business income
- Interest, dividends, and royalties
- Alimony and child support
- Social Security, pension, and retirement benefits
- Other income sources

Payment History

- Payments related to debts (especially preferences to certain creditors)
- Payments to insiders (family members, business partners, etc.)
- Payments to bankruptcy consultancy services or attorneys

Legal Proceedings

- Lawsuits in which you were involved (as plaintiff or defendant)
- Foreclosures or repossessions
- Garnishments and attachments
- Seizures of property

Property Transfers

- Sales, trades, or other transfers of property
- Gifts given to others
- Charitable contributions
- Losses from theft, fire, or other disasters
- Transfers to self-settled trusts or similar devices

Financial Accounts and Instruments

- Closed financial accounts
- Safe deposit boxes and their contents
- Storage units and their contents
- Property held for another person

Business Interests

- Current and former businesses in which you had an interest

- Financial statements issued to financial institutions
- Inventory of business assets

Environmental Information

- Property that poses environmental hazards
- Notification of environmental law violations

Strategic Considerations

The SOFA not only creates a legal obligation for full disclosure but also presents strategic considerations for your bankruptcy case:

- Look-Back Periods: Different questions have different time frames to consider (90 days, 1 year, 2 years, etc.)
- Preference Actions: Payments to creditors within 90 days (or 1 year for insiders) may be recoverable by the trustee
- Fraudulent Transfers: Property transfers for less than fair market value within 2 years may be voidable
- Pre-Bankruptcy Planning: The SOFA can reveal patterns that might suggest improper pre-bankruptcy planning

Filing Tips

1. Document Everything: Gather all financial records before completing the SOFA
2. Be Exhaustive: When in doubt, disclose more rather than less.
3. Consistency Check: Ensure all information aligns with your schedules and other filings.
4. Professional Review: Have your bankruptcy attorney review your SOFA for accuracy and completeness

Amendments: If you realize you've made an error after filing, file an amendment immediately. Remember that the SOFA is signed under penalty of perjury. The bankruptcy system relies on honest disclosure, and serious consequences can result from failing to provide complete and accurate information.

Fresh Start. Survivor's Guide to Bankruptcy Practice

Fill in this information to identify your case:

Debtor 1 ______________________________
First Name Middle Name Last Name

Debtor 2 ______________________________
(Spouse, if filing) First Name Middle Name Last Name

United States Bankruptcy Court for the: District of __________

Case number ______________________________
(If known)

❑ Check if this is an amended filing

Official Form 107

Statement of Financial Affairs for Individuals Filing for Bankruptcy

04/22

Be as complete and accurate as possible. If two married people are filing together, both are equally responsible for supplying correct information. If more space is needed, attach a separate sheet to this form. On the top of any additional pages, write your name and case number (if known). Answer every question.

Part 1: Give Details About Your Marital Status and Where You Lived Before

1. **What is your current marital status?**

❑ Married
❑ Not married

2. **During the last 3 years, have you lived anywhere other than where you live now?**

❑ No
❑ Yes. List all of the places you lived in the last 3 years. Do not include where you live now.

Debtor 1:	Dates Debtor 1 lived there	Debtor 2:	Dates Debtor 2 lived there
Number Street City State ZIP Code	From ______ To ______	❑ Same as Debtor 1 Number Street City State ZIP Code	❑ Same as Debtor 1 From ______ To ______
Number Street City State ZIP Code	From ______ To ______	❑ Same as Debtor 1 Number Street City State ZIP Code	❑ Same as Debtor 1 From ______ To ______

3. **Within the last 8 years, did you ever live with a spouse or legal equivalent in a community property state or territory?** (*Community property states and territories* include Arizona, California, Idaho, Louisiana, Nevada, New Mexico, Puerto Rico, Texas, Washington, and Wisconsin.)

❑ No
❑ Yes. Make sure you fill out *Schedule H: Your Codebtors* (Official Form 106H).

Part 2: Explain the Sources of Your Income

Fresh Start. Survivor's Guide to Bankruptcy Practice

Debtor 1 ______________________________ Case number *(if known)*______________________
First Name Middle Name Last Name

4. **Did you have any income from employment or from operating a business during this year or the two previous calendar years?**
Fill in the total amount of income you received from all jobs and all businesses, including part-time activities.
If you are filing a joint case and you have income that you receive together, list it only once under Debtor 1.

❑ No
❑ Yes. Fill in the details.

	Debtor 1		**Debtor 2**	
	Sources of income Check all that apply.	**Gross income** (before deductions and exclusions)	**Sources of income** Check all that apply.	**Gross income** (before deductions and exclusions)
From January 1 of current year until the date you filed for bankruptcy:	❑ Wages, commissions, bonuses, tips ❑ Operating a business	$__________	❑ Wages, commissions, bonuses, tips ❑ Operating a business	$__________
For last calendar year: (January 1 to December 31, ______) YYYY	❑ Wages, commissions, bonuses, tips ❑ Operating a business	$__________	❑ Wages, commissions, bonuses, tips ❑ Operating a business	$__________
For the calendar year before that: (January 1 to December 31, ______) YYYY	❑ Wages, commissions, bonuses, tips ❑ Operating a business	$__________	❑ Wages, commissions, bonuses, tips ❑ Operating a business	$__________

5. **Did you receive any other income during this year or the two previous calendar years?**
Include income regardless of whether that income is taxable. Examples of *other income* are alimony; child support; Social Security, unemployment, and other public benefit payments; pensions; rental income; interest; dividends; money collected from lawsuits; royalties; and gambling and lottery winnings. If you are filing a joint case and you have income that you received together, list it only once under Debtor 1.

List each source and the gross income from each source separately. Do not include income that you listed in line 4.

❑ No
❑ Yes. Fill in the details.

	Debtor 1		**Debtor 2**	
	Sources of income Describe below.	**Gross income from each source** (before deductions and exclusions)	**Sources of income** Describe below.	**Gross income from each source** (before deductions and exclusions)
From January 1 of current year until the date you filed for bankruptcy:	__________ __________ __________	$__________ $__________ $__________	__________ __________ __________	$__________ $__________ $__________
For last calendar year: (January 1 to December 31, ______) YYYY	__________ __________ __________	$__________ $__________ $__________	__________ __________ __________	$__________ $__________ $__________
For the calendar year before that: (January 1 to December 31, ______) YYYY	__________ __________ __________	$__________ $__________ $__________	__________ __________ __________	$__________ $__________ $__________

Fresh Start. Survivor's Guide to Bankruptcy Practice

Debtor 1 ______________________________ Case number *(if known)* ______________________
First Name Middle Name Last Name

Part 3: List Certain Payments You Made Before You Filed for Bankruptcy

6. Are either Debtor 1's or Debtor 2's debts primarily consumer debts?

❑ No. **Neither Debtor 1 nor Debtor 2 has primarily consumer debts.** *Consumer debts* are defined in 11 U.S.C. § 101(8) as "incurred by an individual primarily for a personal, family, or household purpose."

During the 90 days before you filed for bankruptcy, did you pay any creditor a total of $7,575* or more?

❑ No. Go to line 7.

❑ Yes. List below each creditor to whom you paid a total of $7,575* or more in one or more payments and the total amount you paid that creditor. Do not include payments for domestic support obligations, such as child support and alimony. Also, do not include payments to an attorney for this bankruptcy case.

* Subject to adjustment on 4/01/25 and every 3 years after that for cases filed on or after the date of adjustment.

❑ Yes. **Debtor 1 or Debtor 2 or both have primarily consumer debts.**

During the 90 days before you filed for bankruptcy, did you pay any creditor a total of $600 or more?

❑ No. Go to line 7.

❑ Yes. List below each creditor to whom you paid a total of $600 or more and the total amount you paid that creditor. Do not include payments for domestic support obligations, such as child support and alimony. Also, do not include payments to an attorney for this bankruptcy case.

	Dates of payment	Total amount paid	Amount you still owe	Was this payment for...
Creditor's Name Number Street City State ZIP Code		$	$	❑ Mortgage ❑ Car ❑ Credit card ❑ Loan repayment ❑ Suppliers or vendors ❑ Other ____
Creditor's Name Number Street City State ZIP Code		$	$	❑ Mortgage ❑ Car ❑ Credit card ❑ Loan repayment ❑ Suppliers or vendors ❑ Other ____
Creditor's Name Number Street City State ZIP Code		$	$	❑ Mortgage ❑ Car ❑ Credit card ❑ Loan repayment ❑ Suppliers or vendors ❑ Other ____

Fresh Start. Survivor's Guide to Bankruptcy Practice

Debtor 1 ______________________ First Name Middle Name Last Name   Case number (if known)______________________

7. Within 1 year before you filed for bankruptcy, did you make a payment on a debt you owed anyone who was an insider?
Insiders include your relatives; any general partners; relatives of any general partners; partnerships of which you are a general partner; corporations of which you are an officer, director, person in control, or owner of 20% or more of their voting securities; and any managing agent, including one for a business you operate as a sole proprietor. 11 U.S.C. § 101. Include payments for domestic support obligations, such as child support and alimony.

- ❑ No
- ❑ Yes. List all payments to an insider.

	Dates of payment	Total amount paid	Amount you still owe	Reason for this payment
Insider's Name Number Street City State ZIP Code		$	$	
Insider's Name Number Street City State ZIP Code		$	$	

8. Within 1 year before you filed for bankruptcy, did you make any payments or transfer any property on account of a debt that benefited an insider?
Include payments on debts guaranteed or cosigned by an insider.

- ❑ No
- ❑ Yes. List all payments that benefited an insider.

	Dates of payment	Total amount paid	Amount you still owe	Reason for this payment Include creditor's name
Insider's Name Number Street City State ZIP Code		$	$	
Insider's Name Number Street City State ZIP Code		$	$	

Fresh Start. Survivor's Guide to Bankruptcy Practice

Debtor 1 ______________________________ Case number (if known) ______________________
First Name Middle Name Last Name

Part 4: Identify Legal Actions, Repossessions, and Foreclosures

9. **Within 1 year before you filed for bankruptcy, were you a party in any lawsuit, court action, or administrative proceeding?**
List all such matters, including personal injury cases, small claims actions, divorces, collection suits, paternity actions, support or custody modifications, and contract disputes.

- ☐ No
- ☐ Yes. Fill in the details.

	Nature of the case	Court or agency	Status of the case
Case title ______________ ______________ Case number ______________		______________ Court Name ______________ Number Street ______________ City State ZIP Code	☐ Pending ☐ On appeal ☐ Concluded
Case title ______________ ______________ Case number ______________		______________ Court Name ______________ Number Street ______________ City State ZIP Code	☐ Pending ☐ On appeal ☐ Concluded

10. **Within 1 year before you filed for bankruptcy, was any of your property repossessed, foreclosed, garnished, attached, seized, or levied?**
Check all that apply and fill in the details below.

- ☐ No. Go to line 11.
- ☐ Yes. Fill in the information below.

	Describe the property	Date	Value of the property
______________ Creditor's Name ______________ Number Street ______________ ______________ City State ZIP Code	 **Explain what happened** ☐ Property was repossessed. ☐ Property was foreclosed. ☐ Property was garnished. ☐ Property was attached, seized, or levied.	________	$________
______________ Creditor's Name ______________ Number Street ______________ ______________ City State ZIP Code	 **Explain what happened** ☐ Property was repossessed. ☐ Property was foreclosed. ☐ Property was garnished. ☐ Property was attached, seized, or levied.	________	$________

Fresh Start. Survivor's Guide to Bankruptcy Practice

Debtor 1 ______________________________ Case number *(if known)*______________________
First Name Middle Name Last Name

11. **Within 90 days before you filed for bankruptcy, did any creditor, including a bank or financial institution, set off any amounts from your accounts or refuse to make a payment because you owed a debt?**

- ❑ No
- ❑ Yes. Fill in the details.

	Describe the action the creditor took	Date action was taken	Amount
Creditor's Name			
Number Street		________	$________
City State ZIP Code	Last 4 digits of account number: XXXX–___ ___ ___ ___		

12. **Within 1 year before you filed for bankruptcy, was any of your property in the possession of an assignee for the benefit of creditors, a court-appointed receiver, a custodian, or another official?**

- ❑ No
- ❑ Yes

Part 5: List Certain Gifts and Contributions

13. **Within 2 years before you filed for bankruptcy, did you give any gifts with a total value of more than $600 per person?**

- ❑ No
- ❑ Yes. Fill in the details for each gift.

Gifts with a total value of more than $600 per person	Describe the gifts	Dates you gave the gifts	Value
Person to Whom You Gave the Gift		________	$________
		________	$________
Number Street			
City State ZIP Code			
Person's relationship to you ________			

Gifts with a total value of more than $600 per person	Describe the gifts	Dates you gave the gifts	Value
Person to Whom You Gave the Gift		________	$________
		________	$________
Number Street			
City State ZIP Code			
Person's relationship to you ________			

Fresh Start. Survivor's Guide to Bankruptcy Practice

Debtor 1 ______________________________ Case number *(if known)* ______________
First Name Middle Name Last Name

14. Within 2 years before you filed for bankruptcy, did you give any gifts or contributions with a total value of more than $600 to any charity?

❑ No
❑ Yes. Fill in the details for each gift or contribution.

Gifts or contributions to charities that total more than $600	**Describe what you contributed**	**Date you contributed**	**Value**
Charity's Name		________	$________
		________	$________
Number Street			
City State ZIP Code			

Part 6: List Certain Losses

15. Within 1 year before you filed for bankruptcy or since you filed for bankruptcy, did you lose anything because of theft, fire, other disaster, or gambling?

❑ No
❑ Yes. Fill in the details.

Describe the property you lost and how the loss occurred	**Describe any insurance coverage for the loss** Include the amount that insurance has paid. List pending insurance claims on line 33 of *Schedule A/B: Property.*	**Date of your loss**	**Value of property lost**
		________	$________

Part 7: List Certain Payments or Transfers

16. Within 1 year before you filed for bankruptcy, did you or anyone else acting on your behalf pay or transfer any property to anyone you consulted about seeking bankruptcy or preparing a bankruptcy petition?
Include any attorneys, bankruptcy petition preparers, or credit counseling agencies for services required in your bankruptcy.

❑ No
❑ Yes. Fill in the details.

	Description and value of any property transferred	**Date payment or transfer was made**	**Amount of payment**
Person Who Was Paid			
Number Street		________	$________
		________	$________
City State ZIP Code			
Email or website address			
Person Who Made the Payment, if Not You			

Fresh Start. Survivor's Guide to Bankruptcy Practice

Debtor 1 ______________________________ Case number (if known)______________________
First Name Middle Name Last Name

	Description and value of any property transferred	Date payment or transfer was made	Amount of payment
______________________ Person Who Was Paid ______________________ Number Street ______________________ ______________________ City State ZIP Code ______________________ Email or website address ______________________ Person Who Made the Payment, if Not You		________ ________	$__________ $__________

17. **Within 1 year before you filed for bankruptcy, did you or anyone else acting on your behalf pay or transfer any property to anyone who promised to help you deal with your creditors or to make payments to your creditors?**
Do not include any payment or transfer that you listed on line 16.

❑ No
❑ Yes. Fill in the details.

	Description and value of any property transferred	Date payment or transfer was made	Amount of payment
______________________ Person Who Was Paid ______________________ Number Street ______________________ ______________________ City State ZIP Code		________ ________	$__________ $__________

18. **Within 2 years before you filed for bankruptcy, did you sell, trade, or otherwise transfer any property to anyone, other than property transferred in the ordinary course of your business or financial affairs?**
Include both outright transfers and transfers made as security (such as the granting of a security interest or mortgage on your property).
Do not include gifts and transfers that you have already listed on this statement.

❑ No
❑ Yes. Fill in the details.

	Description and value of property transferred	Describe any property or payments received or debts paid in exchange	Date transfer was made
______________________ Person Who Received Transfer ______________________ Number Street ______________________ ______________________ City State ZIP Code Person's relationship to you __________			________
______________________ Person Who Received Transfer ______________________ Number Street ______________________ ______________________ City State ZIP Code Person's relationship to you __________			________

Fresh Start. Survivor's Guide to Bankruptcy Practice

Debtor 1 ______________________________ Case number *(if known)*______________________
First Name Middle Name Last Name

19. **Within 10 years before you filed for bankruptcy, did you transfer any property to a self-settled trust or similar device of which you are a beneficiary?** (These are often called *asset-protection devices.*)

❑ No
❑ Yes. Fill in the details.

	Description and value of the property transferred	Date transfer was made
Name of trust ______________		________

Part 8: List Certain Financial Accounts, Instruments, Safe Deposit Boxes, and Storage Units

20. **Within 1 year before you filed for bankruptcy, were any financial accounts or instruments held in your name, or for your benefit, closed, sold, moved, or transferred?**
Include checking, savings, money market, or other financial accounts; certificates of deposit; shares in banks, credit unions, brokerage houses, pension funds, cooperatives, associations, and other financial institutions.

❑ **No**
❑ **Yes. Fill in the details.**

	Last 4 digits of account number	Type of account or instrument	Date account was closed, sold, moved, or transferred	Last balance before closing or transfer
Name of Financial Institution Number Street City State ZIP Code	XXXX–__ __ __ __	❑ Checking ❑ Savings ❑ Money market ❑ Brokerage ❑ Other________	________	$________
Name of Financial Institution Number Street City State ZIP Code	XXXX–__ __ __ __	❑ Checking ❑ Savings ❑ Money market ❑ Brokerage ❑ Other________	________	$________

21. **Do you now have, or did you have within 1 year before you filed for bankruptcy, any safe deposit box or other depository for securities, cash, or other valuables?**

❑ **No**
❑ **Yes. Fill in the details.**

	Who else had access to it?	Describe the contents	Do you still have it?
Name of Financial Institution Number Street City State ZIP Code	Name Number Street City State ZIP Code		❑ No ❑ Yes

Fresh Start. Survivor's Guide to Bankruptcy Practice

Debtor 1 ______________________ First Name Middle Name Last Name Case number (if known)______________________

22. **Have you stored property in a storage unit or place other than your home within 1 year before you filed for bankruptcy?**

❑ **No**

❑ **Yes. Fill in the details.**

	Who else has or had access to it?	Describe the contents	Do you still have it?
Name of Storage Facility Number Street City State ZIP Code	Name Number Street City State ZIP Code		❑ No ❑ Yes

Part 9: Identify Property You Hold or Control for Someone Else

23. **Do you hold or control any property that someone else owns? Include any property you borrowed from, are storing for, or hold in trust for someone.**

❑ **No**

❑ **Yes. Fill in the details.**

	Where is the property?	Describe the property	Value
Owner's Name Number Street City State ZIP Code	Number Street City State ZIP Code		$________

Part 10: Give Details About Environmental Information

For the purpose of Part 10, the following definitions apply:

- ***Environmental law*** **means any federal, state, or local statute or regulation concerning pollution, contamination, releases of hazardous or toxic substances, wastes, or material into the air, land, soil, surface water, groundwater, or other medium, including statutes or regulations controlling the cleanup of these substances, wastes, or material.**
- ***Site*** **means any location, facility, or property as defined under any environmental law, whether you now own, operate, or utilize it or used to own, operate, or utilize it, including disposal sites.**
- ***Hazardous material*** **means anything an environmental law defines as a hazardous waste, hazardous substance, toxic substance, hazardous material, pollutant, contaminant, or similar term.**

Report all notices, releases, and proceedings that you know about, regardless of when they occurred.

24. **Has any governmental unit notified you that you may be liable or potentially liable under or in violation of an environmental law?**

❑ **No**

❑ **Yes. Fill in the details.**

	Governmental unit	Environmental law, if you know it	Date of notice
Name of site Number Street City State ZIP Code	Governmental unit Number Street City State ZIP Code		________

Fresh Start. Survivor's Guide to Bankruptcy Practice

Debtor 1 ______________________________ Case number (if known)______________________
First Name Middle Name Last Name

25. Have you notified any governmental unit of any release of hazardous material?

- ☐ No
- ☐ Yes. Fill in the details.

	Governmental unit	Environmental law, if you know it	Date of notice
Name of site	Governmental unit		
Number Street	Number Street		
	City State ZIP Code		
City State ZIP Code			

26. Have you been a party in any judicial or administrative proceeding under any environmental law? Include settlements and orders.

- ☐ No
- ☐ Yes. Fill in the details.

	Court or agency	Nature of the case	Status of the case
Case title______	Court Name		☐ Pending
	Number Street		☐ On appeal
Case number	City State ZIP Code		☐ Concluded

Part 11: Give Details About Your Business or Connections to Any Business

27. Within 4 years before you filed for bankruptcy, did you own a business or have any of the following connections to any business?

- ☐ A sole proprietor or self-employed in a trade, profession, or other activity, either full-time or part-time
- ☐ A member of a limited liability company (LLC) or limited liability partnership (LLP)
- ☐ A partner in a partnership
- ☐ An officer, director, or managing executive of a corporation
- ☐ An owner of at least 5% of the voting or equity securities of a corporation

- ☐ No. None of the above applies. Go to Part 12.
- ☐ Yes. Check all that apply above and fill in the details below for each business.

	Describe the nature of the business	Employer Identification number Do not include Social Security number or ITIN.
Business Name		EIN: __ __ – __ __ __ __ __ __ __
Number Street	Name of accountant or bookkeeper	Dates business existed
City State ZIP Code		From ______ To ______

	Describe the nature of the business	Employer Identification number Do not include Social Security number or ITIN.
Business Name		EIN: __ __ – __ __ __ __ __ __ __
Number Street	Name of accountant or bookkeeper	Dates business existed
City State ZIP Code		From ______ To ______

Fresh Start. Survivor's Guide to Bankruptcy Practice

Debtor 1 ________________________________ Case number *(if known)* ____________________
First Name Middle Name Last Name

____________________ **Business Name** ____________________ **Number Street** ____________________ ____________________ **City State ZIP Code**	**Describe the nature of the business** **Name of accountant or bookkeeper**	**Employer Identification number** **Do not include Social Security number or ITIN.** **EIN:** __ __ – __ __ __ __ __ __ __ **Dates business existed** **From** ______ **To** ______

28. Within 2 years before you filed for bankruptcy, did you give a financial statement to anyone about your business? Include all financial institutions, creditors, or other parties.

❑ **No**
❑ **Yes. Fill in the details below.**

	Date issued
____________________ **Name**	________ **MM / DD / YYYY**
____________________ **Number Street**	
____________________ ____________________ **City State ZIP Code**	

Part 12: Sign Below

I have read the answers on this *Statement of Financial Affairs* and any attachments, and I declare under penalty of perjury that the answers are true and correct. I understand that making a false statement, concealing property, or obtaining money or property by fraud in connection with a bankruptcy case can result in fines up to $250,000, or imprisonment for up to 20 years, or both. 18 U.S.C. §§ 152, 1341, 1519, and 3571.

✘ ____________________ ✘ ____________________
Signature of Debtor 1 **Signature of Debtor 2**

Date ________ **Date** ________

Did you attach additional pages to *Your Statement of Financial Affairs for Individuals Filing for Bankruptcy* (Official Form 107)?

❑ No
❑ Yes

Did you pay or agree to pay someone who is not an attorney to help you fill out bankruptcy forms?

❑ No
❑ Yes. Name of person ____________________. Attach the *Bankruptcy Petition Preparer's Notice, Declaration, and Signature* (Official Form 119).

Chapter Fifty

CHAPTER 7 STATEMENT OF YOUR CURRENT MONTHLY INCOME (FORM 122A-1)

THE CHAPTER 7 STATEMENT of Your Current Monthly Income (Form 122A-1) serves as the initial eligibility screening tool for Chapter 7 bankruptcy. This critical form determines whether you qualify for Chapter 7 bankruptcy through a comparison of your income to state-specific standards.

The Income Comparison Process

Step 1: Calculating Your Current Monthly Income (CMI)

The form requires calculation of your "current monthly income," which has a specific legal definition in bankruptcy:

- Average monthly income received from all sources during the 6 calendar months before filing
- Includes regular income from:

a. Wages, salary, commissions, bonuses
b. Business, profession, or farm operations
c. Rental properties
d. Interest, dividends, and royalties
e. Pension and retirement income
f. Regular contributions from others to household expenses

g. Unemployment compensation
h. State disability insurance
i. Annuity payments

Step 2: Median Income Comparison

Your calculated CMI is compared to the median income for your state and household size:

- Median income figures are updated regularly by the U.S. Trustee Program
- Household size includes you, your spouse (if filing jointly), and dependents
- Different states have different median income thresholds

Step 3: Outcome Determination

(i) Below Median: If your CMI is below the state median for your household size, you generally qualify for Chapter 7 without further testing

(ii) Above Median: If your CMI exceeds the state median, you must complete the more detailed means test (Form 122A-2)

Form 122A-1Supp: Statement of Exemption from Presumption of Abuse

In certain circumstances, even if your income is above the median, you may be exempt from the full means test through Form 122A-1Supp if:

- You are a disabled veteran whose debts were primarily incurred during active duty or homeland defense activities
- You are a reservist or National Guard member called to active duty after September 11, 2001, for at least 90 days
- You can demonstrate "special circumstances" that justify your Chapter 7 filing despite higher income

Strategic Considerations

Timing of Filing

- The 6-month lookback period for calculating CMI means timing your bankruptcy filing can be strategic
- If your income has recently decreased, waiting until higher-income months fall outside the 6-month window may help you qualify

Household Size Determination

- Accurately counting your household size is crucial as it directly affects the median income threshold
- Generally includes individuals who financially depend on or contribute to your household

Income Documentation

- Be prepared to provide pay stubs, tax returns, and other income verification
- Trustees will verify your calculations and may challenge inconsistencies

Non-Filing Spouse Income

- If married but filing individually, you must still include your non-filing spouse's income (with certain exceptions)
- May need to complete the Marital Adjustment deduction to exclude income not contributed to household expenses

CONSEQUENCES OF THE INCOME TEST

Passing the Test (Below Median)

- You may proceed with Chapter 7 bankruptcy
- No presumption of abuse arises
- Less scrutiny from the trustee regarding your ability to pay debts

Failing the Test (Above Median without Exemption)

- Required to complete the full means test (Form 122A-2)
- May still qualify for Chapter 7 if the means test shows insufficient disposable income
- If means test indicates ability to repay some debts, case may be:

- Dismissed, or
- Converted to Chapter 13 bankruptcy (repayment plan)

This form represents the gateway to Chapter 7 bankruptcy relief and must be completed with precision and honesty, as it is filed under penalty of perjury and will be scrutinized by the bankruptcy trustee.

Fill in this information to identify your case:

[redacted]

District of ________

[redacted]

uptc

Check one box only as directed in this form and in Form 122A-1Supp:

[redacted]

☐ Check if this is an amended filing

Official Form 122A–1

Chapter 7 Statement of Your Current Monthly Income

10/19

Be as complete and accurate as possible. If two married people are filing together, both are equally responsible for being accurate. If more space is needed, attach a separate sheet to this form. Include the line number to which the additional information applies. On the top of any additional pages, write your name and case number (if known). If you believe that you are exempted from a presumption of abuse because you do not have primarily consumer debts or because of qualifying military service, complete and file *Statement of Exemption from Presumption of Abuse Under § 707(b)(2)* (Official Form 122A-1Supp) with this form.

Part 1: Calculate Your Current Monthly Income

1. **What is your marital and filing status?** Check one only.
   - ☐ **Not married.** Fill out Column A, lines 2-11.
   - ☐ **Married and your spouse is filing with you.** Fill out both Columns A and B, lines 2-11.
   - ☐ **Married and your spouse is NOT filing with you. You and your spouse are:**
     - ☐ **Living in the same household and are not legally separated.** Fill out both Columns A and B, lines 2-11.
     - ☐ **Living separately or are legally separated.** Fill out Column A, lines 2-11; do not fill out Column B. By checking this box, you declare under penalty of perjury that you and your spouse are legally separated under nonbankruptcy law that applies or that you and your spouse are living apart for reasons that do not include evading the Means Test requirements. 11 U.S.C. § 707(b)(7)(B).

Fill in the average monthly income that you received from all sources, derived during the 6 full months before you file this bankruptcy case. 11 U.S.C. § 101(10A). For example, if you are filing on September 15, the 6-month period would be March 1 through August 31. If the amount of your monthly income varied during the 6 months, add the income for all 6 months and divide the total by 6. Fill in the result. Do not include any income amount more than once. For example, if both spouses own the same rental property, put the income from that property in one column only. If you have nothing to report for any line, write $0 in the space.

	Debtor 1	Debtor 2		*Column A* **Debtor 1**	*Column B* **Debtor 2 or non-filing spouse**
2. **Your gross wages, salary, tips, bonuses, overtime, and commissions** (before all payroll deductions).				$________	$________
3. **Alimony and maintenance payments.** Do not include payments from a spouse if Column B is filled in.				$________	$________
4. **All amounts from any source which are regularly paid for household expenses of you or your dependents, including child support.** Include regular contributions from an unmarried partner, members of your household, your dependents, parents, and roommates. Include regular contributions from a spouse only if Column B is not filled in. Do not include payments you listed on line 3.				$________	$________
5. **Net income from operating a business, profession, or farm**	**Debtor 1**	**Debtor 2**			
Gross receipts (before all deductions)	$______	$______			
Ordinary and necessary operating expenses	– $______	– $______			
Net monthly income from a business, profession, or farm	$______	$______	Copy here→	$________	$________
6. **Net income from rental and other real property**	**Debtor 1**	**Debtor 2**			
Gross receipts (before all deductions)	$______	$______			
Ordinary and necessary operating expenses	– $______	– $______			
Net monthly income from rental or other real property	$______	$______	Copy here→	$________	$________
7. **Interest, dividends, and royalties**				$________	$________

Fresh Start. Survivor's Guide to Bankruptcy Practice

Debtor 1 ______________________________ Case number *(if known)*______________________
First Name Middle Name Last Name

	Column A Debtor 1	Column B Debtor 2 or non-filing spouse
8. **Unemployment compensation**	$________	$________
Do not enter the amount if you contend that the amount received was a benefit under the Social Security Act. Instead, list it here: .... ↓ For you .... $________ For your spouse .... $________		
9. **Pension or retirement income.** Do not include any amount received that was a benefit under the Social Security Act. Also, except as stated in the next sentence, do not include any compensation, pension, pay, annuity, or allowance paid by the United States Government in connection with a disability, combat-related injury or disability, or death of a member of the uniformed services. If you received any retired pay paid under chapter 61 of title 10, then include that pay only to the extent that it does not exceed the amount of retired pay to which you would otherwise be entitled if retired under any provision of title 10 other than chapter 61 of that title.	$________	$________
10. **Income from all other sources not listed above.** Specify the source and amount. Do not include any benefits received under the Social Security Act; payments received as a victim of a war crime, a crime against humanity, or international or domestic terrorism; or compensation, pension, pay, annuity, or allowance paid by the United States Government in connection with a disability, combat-related injury or disability, or death of a member of the uniformed services. If necessary, list other sources on a separate page and put the total below.		
______________________	$________	$________
______________________	$________	$________
Total amounts from separate pages, if any.	+ $________	+ $________
11. **Calculate your total current monthly income.** Add lines 2 through 10 for each column. Then add the total for Column A to the total for Column B.	$________ +	$________ = $________ Total current monthly income

Part 2: Determine Whether the Means Test Applies to You

12. **Calculate your current monthly income for the year.** Follow these steps:

12a. Copy your total current monthly income from line 11. .... **Copy line 11 here➔** $________

Multiply by 12 (the number of months in a year). **x** 12

12b. The result is your annual income for this part of the form. 12b. $________

13. **Calculate the median family income that applies to you.** Follow these steps:

Fill in the state in which you live. [ ]

Fill in the number of people in your household. [ ]

Fill in the median family income for your state and size of household. .... 13. $________

To find a list of applicable median income amounts, go online using the link specified in the separate instructions for this form. This list may also be available at the bankruptcy clerk's office.

14. **How do the lines compare?**

14a. ☐ Line 12b is less than or equal to line 13. On the top of page 1, check box 1, *There is no presumption of abuse.* Go to Part 3.

14b. ☐ Line 12b is more than line 13. On the top of page 1, check box 2, *The presumption of abuse is determined by Form 122A-2.* Go to Part 3 and fill out Form 122A–2.

Fresh Start. Survivor's Guide to Bankruptcy Practice

Debtor 1 ______________________________ Case number (*if known*)______________________
First Name Middle Name Last Name

Part 3: Sign Below

By signing here, I declare under penalty of perjury that the information on this statement and in any attachments is true and correct.

✗ ______________________________ ✗ ______________________________
Signature of Debtor 1 Signature of Debtor 2

Date ______________ Date ______________
MM / DD / YYYY MM / DD / YYYY

If you checked line 14a, do NOT fill out or file Form 122A–2.

If you checked line 14b, fill out Form 122A–2 and file it with this form.

Fresh Start. Survivor's Guide to Bankruptcy Practice

AVERAGE MEDIAN INCOME -2022

Fresh Start. Survivor's Guide to Bankruptcy Practice

Census Bureau Median Family Income By Family Size

(Cases Filed Between November 1, 2022 and March 31, 2023, Inclusive)

The following table provides median family income data reproduced in a format designed for ease of use in completing Bankruptcy Forms 122A-1 and 122C-1.

Fresh Start. Survivor's Guide to Bankruptcy Practice

STATE	FAMILY SIZE			
	1 EARNER	2 PEOPLE	3 PEOPLE	4 PEOPLE *
ALABAMA	$52,404	$62,918	$71,682	$87,645
ALASKA	$70,545	$83,268	$104,659	$112,092
ARIZONA	$59,417	$74,303	$83,510	$96,426
ARKANSAS	$47,373	$59,105	$68,957	$79,664
CALIFORNIA	$69,660	$86,271	$97,021	$113,615
COLORADO	$70,100	$91,076	$105,388	$124,206
CONNECTICUT	$75,840	$93,182	$112,921	$132,030
DELAWARE	$65,997	$77,011	$95,922	$113,801
DISTRICT OF COLUMBIA	$79,970	$135,589	$135,589	$189,519
FLORIDA	$55,951	$68,638	$77,217	$93,031
GEORGIA	$56,008	$71,464	$81,241	$95,959
HAWAII	$72,950	$85,718	$96,946	$116,313
IDAHO	$58,089	$71,960	$81,442	$90,009
ILLINOIS	$62,130	$78,602	$94,397	$113,228
INDIANA	$56,225	$70,159	$83,146	$95,002
IOWA	$56,453	$75,323	$88,645	$106,775
KANSAS	$56,626	$73,843	$81,730	$104,767
KENTUCKY	$51,824	$61,945	$70,091	$87,902
LOUISIANA	$49,099	$59,963	$67,955	$84,596
MAINE	$56,887	$73,159	$88,452	$110,295
MARYLAND	$74,074	$95,445	$113,317	$140,379
MASSACHUSETTS	$74,505	$93,086	$117,749	$150,387
MICHIGAN	$58,684	$69,789	$86,917	$103,336
MINNESOTA	$66,334	$84,207	$105,800	$130,852
MISSISSIPPI	$45,002	$56,462	$65,693	$80,158
MISSOURI	$56,633	$69,699	$82,882	$101,203
MONTANA	$60,032	$72,102	$77,793	$101,329
NEBRASKA	$60,390	$77,581	$92,447	$106,728
NEVADA	$58,770	$70,353	$80,200	$88,840
NEW HAMPSHIRE	$77,662	$90,968	$126,743	$140,317
NEW JERSEY	$77,681	$91,716	$113,460	$143,987
NEW MEXICO	$50,177	$64,080	$66,001	$76,026
NEW YORK	$63,715	$78,663	$95,779	$116,818
NORTH CAROLINA	$55,621	$69,303	$80,895	$99,190
NORTH DAKOTA	$64,929	$83,377	$86,331	$115,080
OHIO	$57,364	$70,490	$84,176	$101,907
OKLAHOMA	$51,256	$64,056	$71,448	$83,371
OREGON	$64,492	$78,163	$94,432	$109,713
PENNSYLVANIA	$61,530	$74,369	$93,412	$113,037
RHODE ISLAND	$65,608	$83,513	$101,399	$120,481
SOUTH CAROLINA	$55,101	$67,050	$76,030	$93,154
SOUTH DAKOTA	$53,011	$75,960	$85,918	$96,645
TENNESSEE	$53,004	$66,506	$78,715	$88,698
TEXAS	$55,591	$71,860	$80,765	$94,213
UTAH	$67,380	$75,831	$95,313	$102,835
VERMONT	$64,754	$79,992	$96,074	$117,173
VIRGINIA	$69,791	$86,413	$102,791	$124,304
WASHINGTON	$76,962	$89,711	$107,724	$128,225
WEST VIRGINIA	$52,239	$58,308	$75,891	$83,570
WISCONSIN	$58,467	$75,789	$91,906	$109,665
WYOMING	$60,607	$76,416	$86,712	$96,745

* *Add $9,900 for each individual in excess of 4.*

Fresh Start. Survivor's Guide to Bankruptcy Practice

COMMONWEALTH OR U.S. TERRITORY	1 EARNER	FAMILY SIZE		
		2 PEOPLE	3 PEOPLE	4 PEOPLE *
GUAM	$45,332	$54,202	$61,766	$74,744
NORTHERN MARIANA ISLANDS	$30,442	$30,442	$35,417	$52,091
PUERTO RICO	$27,013	$27,013	$30,376	$37,997
VIRGIN ISLANDS	$35,968	$43,228	$46,090	$50,496

* *Add $9,900 for each individual in excess of 4.*

Chapter Fifty-One

MEANS TEST CALCULATION (FORM 122A-2)

THE MEANS TEST CALCULATION (Form 122A-2) determines whether someone with above-median income can still qualify for Chapter 7 bankruptcy or must file for Chapter 13 bankruptcy instead. This form helps ensure that Chapter 7 relief is reserved for those who truly cannot afford to repay their debts.

When Required

- Only required if your income exceeds your state's median income on Form 122A-1
- Serves as the second step in determining Chapter 7 eligibility for higher-income filers

Process Overview

- Takes your Current Monthly Income (CMI) from Form 122A-1
- Deducts allowable living expenses and certain debt payments
- Calculates remaining disposable income that could potentially repay debts
- If disposable income is substantial, it creates a "presumption of abuse"

Key Components

- Current Monthly Income: Based on 6-month average before filing (calculated in Form 122A-1)
- Allowable Expenses: Includes housing, transportation, healthcare, and other necessary costs
- Disposable Income: Amount remaining after deducting allowable expenses

- Presumption of Abuse: Legal term indicating you may have enough income to repay debts

Important Considerations

- A "presumption of abuse" doesn't imply intentional misuse of the bankruptcy system
- You can rebut this presumption by demonstrating special circumstances affecting income or expenses
- If disqualified from Chapter 7, you can still pursue debt relief through Chapter 13
- Chapter 13 requires creating a repayment plan based on your financial capacity

Completion Steps

- Gather financial documentation (pay stubs, tax returns, expense records)
- Use your previously calculated six-month income average (CMI)
- Complete all sections of Form 122A-2 with detailed income and expense information
- Calculate final disposable income after all allowable deductions
- Determine if this amount triggers the presumption of abuse

This calculation is critical for determining the appropriate bankruptcy path based on your financial situation.

Fresh Start. Survivor's Guide to Bankruptcy Practice

Fill in this information to identify your case:

Debtor 1 ______________________________
First Name Middle Name Last Name

Debtor 2 ______________________________
(Spouse, if filing) First Name Middle Name Last Name

United States Bankruptcy Court for the: District of ________

Case number ______________________
(If known)

Check the appropriate box as directed in lines 40 or 42:

According to the calculations required by this Statement:

❑ 1. There is no presumption of abuse.

❑ 2. There is a presumption of abuse.

❑ Check if this is an amended filing

Official Form 122A–2

Chapter 7 Means Test Calculation

04/22

To fill out this form, you will need your completed copy of *Chapter 7 Statement of Your Current Monthly Income* (Official Form 122A-1).

Be as complete and accurate as possible. If two married people are filing together, both are equally responsible for being accurate. If more space is needed, attach a separate sheet to this form. Include the line number to which the additional information applies. On the top of any additional pages, write your name and case number (if known).

Part 1: Determine Your Adjusted Income

1. **Copy your total current monthly income.** .... **Copy line 11 from Official Form 122A-1 here** ➔ .... $________

2. **Did you fill out Column B in Part 1 of Form 122A–1?**

   ❑ No. Fill in $0 for the total on line 3.

   ❑ Yes. Is your spouse filing with you?

   ❑ No. Go to line 3.

   ❑ Yes. Fill in $0 for the total on line 3.

3. **Adjust your current monthly income by subtracting any part of your spouse's income not used to pay for the household expenses of you or your dependents.** Follow these steps:

   On line 11, Column B of Form 122A–1, was any amount of the income you reported for your spouse NOT regularly used for the household expenses of you or your dependents?

   ❑ No. Fill in 0 for the total on line 3.

   ❑ Yes. Fill in the information below:

State each purpose for which the income was used For example, the income is used to pay your spouse's tax debt or to support people other than you or your dependents	**Fill in the amount you are subtracting from your spouse's income**
______________________	$________
______________________	$________
______________________	+ $________
Total.	$________

Copy total here .... ➔ – $________

4. **Adjust your current monthly income.** Subtract the total on line 3 from line 1. $________

Fresh Start. Survivor's Guide to Bankruptcy Practice

Debtor 1 ______ First Name Middle Name Last Name Case number (if known)______

Part 2: Calculate Your Deductions from Your Income

The Internal Revenue Service (IRS) issues National and Local Standards for certain expense amounts. Use these amounts to answer the questions in lines 6-15. To find the IRS standards, go online using the link specified in the separate instructions for this form. This information may also be available at the bankruptcy clerk's office.

Deduct the expense amounts set out in lines 6-15 regardless of your actual expense. In later parts of the form, you will use some of your actual expenses if they are higher than the standards. Do not deduct any amounts that you subtracted from your spouse's income in line 3 and do not deduct any operating expenses that you subtracted from income in lines 5 and 6 of Form 122A–1.

If your expenses differ from month to month, enter the average expense.

Whenever this part of the form refers to *you*, it means both you and your spouse if Column B of Form 122A–1 is filled in.

5. **The number of people used in determining your deductions from income**

Fill in the number of people who could be claimed as exemptions on your federal income tax return, plus the number of any additional dependents whom you support. This number may be different from the number of people in your household. [ ]

National Standards You must use the IRS National Standards to answer the questions in lines 6-7.

6. **Food, clothing, and other items:** Using the number of people you entered in line 5 and the IRS National Standards, fill in the dollar amount for food, clothing, and other items. $______

7. **Out-of-pocket health care allowance:** Using the number of people you entered in line 5 and the IRS National Standards, fill in the dollar amount for out-of-pocket health care. The number of people is split into two categories—people who are under 65 and people who are 65 or older—because older people have a higher IRS allowance for health care costs. If your actual expenses are higher than this IRS amount, you may deduct the additional amount on line 22.

People who are under 65 years of age

7a. Out-of-pocket health care allowance per person $______

7b. Number of people who are under 65 X ______

7c. **Subtotal.** Multiply line 7a by line 7b. $______ **Copy here➔** $______

People who are 65 years of age or older

7d. Out-of-pocket health care allowance per person $______

7e. Number of people who are 65 or older X ______

7f. **Subtotal.** Multiply line 7d by line 7e. $______ **Copy here➔** + $______

7g. **Total**. Add lines 7c and 7f... $______ **Copy total here➔** $______

Fresh Start. Survivor's Guide to Bankruptcy Practice

Debtor 1 ______________________ Case number (if known) ______________________
First Name Middle Name Last Name

Local Standards You must use the IRS Local Standards to answer the questions in lines 8-15.

Based on information from the IRS, the U.S. Trustee Program has divided the IRS Local Standard for housing for bankruptcy purposes into two parts:

- **Housing and utilities – Insurance and operating expenses**
- **Housing and utilities – Mortgage or rent expenses**

To answer the questions in lines 8-9, use the U.S. Trustee Program chart.

To find the chart, go online using the link specified in the separate instructions for this form.
This chart may also be available at the bankruptcy clerk's office.

8. **Housing and utilities – Insurance and operating expenses:** Using the number of people you entered in line 5, fill in the dollar amount listed for your county for insurance and operating expenses. .... $______

9. **Housing and utilities – Mortgage or rent expenses:**

9a. Using the number of people you entered in line 5, fill in the dollar amount listed for your county for mortgage or rent expenses........ $______

9b. Total average monthly payment for all mortgages and other debts secured by your home.

To calculate the total average monthly payment, add all amounts that are contractually due to each secured creditor in the 60 months after you file for bankruptcy. Then divide by 60.

Name of the creditor	Average monthly payment
______________	$______
______________	$______
______________	+ $______
Total average monthly payment	$______

Copy here → – $______ Repeat this amount on line 33a.

9c. Net mortgage or rent expense.
Subtract line 9b (*total average monthly payment*) from line 9a (*mortgage or rent expense*). If this amount is less than $0, enter $0. .... $______ Copy here → $______

10. **If you claim that the U.S. Trustee Program's division of the IRS Local Standard for housing is incorrect and affects the calculation of your monthly expenses, fill in any additional amount you claim.** $______

Explain why: ______________________

11. **Local transportation expenses:** Check the number of vehicles for which you claim an ownership or operating expense.

- ❑ 0. Go to line 14.
- ❑ 1. Go to line 12.
- ❑ 2 or more. Go to line 12.

12. **Vehicle operation expense:** Using the IRS Local Standards and the number of vehicles for which you claim the operating expenses, fill in the *Operating Costs* that apply for your Census region or metropolitan statistical area. $______

13. **Vehicle ownership or lease expense:** Using the IRS Local Standards, calculate the net ownership or lease expense for each vehicle below. You may not claim the expense if you do not make any loan or lease payments on the vehicle. In addition, you may not claim the expense for more than two vehicles.

Vehicle 1 **Describe Vehicle 1:** _______________

13a. Ownership or leasing costs using IRS Local Standard. .... $________

13b. Average monthly payment for all debts secured by Vehicle 1.
Do not include costs for leased vehicles.

To calculate the average monthly payment here and on line 13e, add all amounts that are contractually due to each secured creditor in the 60 months after you filed for bankruptcy. Then divide by 60.

Name of each creditor for Vehicle 1	Average monthly payment
________	$________
________	+ $________

Total average monthly payment $________ **Copy here➔** – $________ Repeat this amount on line 33b.

13c. Net Vehicle 1 ownership or lease expense
Subtract line 13b from line 13a. If this amount is less than $0, enter $0. .... $________ **Copy net Vehicle 1 expense here.....➔** $________

Vehicle 2 **Describe Vehicle 2:** _______________

13d. Ownership or leasing costs using IRS Local Standard. .... $________

13e. Average monthly payment for all debts secured by Vehicle 2.
Do not include costs for leased vehicles.

Name of each creditor for Vehicle 2	Average monthly payment
________	$________
________	+ $________

Total average monthly payment $________ **Copy here➔** – $________ Repeat this amount on line 33c.

13f. Net Vehicle 2 ownership or lease expense
Subtract line 13e from 13d. If this amount is less than $0, enter $0. .... $________ **Copy net Vehicle 2 expense here ...➔** $________

14. **Public transportation expense**: If you claimed 0 vehicles in line 11, using the IRS Local Standards, fill in the *Public Transportation* expense allowance regardless of whether you use public transportation. $________

15. **Additional public transportation expense:** If you claimed 1 or more vehicles in line 11 and if you claim that you may also deduct a public transportation expense, you may fill in what you believe is the appropriate expense, but you may not claim more than the IRS Local Standard for *Public Transportation*. $________

Other Necessary Expenses In addition to the expense deductions listed above, you are allowed your monthly expenses for the following IRS categories.

16. **Taxes:** The total monthly amount that you will actually owe for federal, state and local taxes, such as income taxes, self-employment taxes, Social Security taxes, and Medicare taxes. You may include the monthly amount withheld from your pay for these taxes. However, if you expect to receive a tax refund, you must divide the expected refund by 12 and subtract that number from the total monthly amount that is withheld to pay for taxes. $________

    Do not include real estate, sales, or use taxes.

17. **Involuntary deductions:** The total monthly payroll deductions that your job requires, such as retirement contributions, union dues, and uniform costs.

    Do not include amounts that are not required by your job, such as voluntary 401(k) contributions or payroll savings. $________

18. **Life insurance:** The total monthly premiums that you pay for your own term life insurance. If two married people are filing together, include payments that you make for your spouse's term life insurance. Do not include premiums for life insurance on your dependents, for a non-filing spouse's life insurance, or for any form of life insurance other than term. $________

19. **Court-ordered payments:** The total monthly amount that you pay as required by the order of a court or administrative agency, such as spousal or child support payments.

    Do not include payments on past due obligations for spousal or child support. You will list these obligations in line 35. $________

20. **Education:** The total monthly amount that you pay for education that is either required:
    - as a condition for your job, or
    - for your physically or mentally challenged dependent child if no public education is available for similar services. $________

21. **Childcare:** The total monthly amount that you pay for childcare, such as babysitting, daycare, nursery, and preschool.

    Do not include payments for any elementary or secondary school education. $________

22. **Additional health care expenses, excluding insurance costs:** The monthly amount that you pay for health care that is required for the health and welfare of you or your dependents and that is not reimbursed by insurance or paid by a health savings account. Include only the amount that is more than the total entered in line 7.
    Payments for health insurance or health savings accounts should be listed only in line 25. $________

23. **Optional telephones and telephone services:** The total monthly amount that you pay for telecommunication services for you and your dependents, such as pagers, call waiting, caller identification, special long distance, or business cell phone service, to the extent necessary for your health and welfare or that of your dependents or for the production of income, if it is not reimbursed by your employer. + $________

    Do not include payments for basic home telephone, internet and cell phone service. Do not include self-employment expenses, such as those reported on line 5 of Official Form 122A-1, or any amount you previously deducted.

24. **Add all of the expenses allowed under the IRS expense allowances.**

    Add lines 6 through 23. $________

Additional Expense Deductions These are additional deductions allowed by the Means Test.
Note: Do not include any expense allowances listed in lines 6-24.

25. **Health insurance, disability insurance, and health savings account expenses.** The monthly expenses for health insurance, disability insurance, and health savings accounts that are reasonably necessary for yourself, your spouse, or your dependents.

Health insurance	$	
Disability insurance	$	
Health savings account	+ $	
Total	$	Copy total here➔ .... $

Do you actually spend this total amount?

- ❑ No. How much do you actually spend? $
- ❑ Yes

26. **Continuing contributions to the care of household or family members.** The actual monthly expenses that you will continue to pay for the reasonable and necessary care and support of an elderly, chronically ill, or disabled member of your household or member of your immediate family who is unable to pay for such expenses. These expenses may include contributions to an account of a qualified ABLE program. 26 U.S.C. § 529A(b). $

27. **Protection against family violence.** The reasonably necessary monthly expenses that you incur to maintain the safety of you and your family under the Family Violence Prevention and Services Act or other federal laws that apply. $
By law, the court must keep the nature of these expenses confidential.

28. **Additional home energy costs.** Your home energy costs are included in your insurance and operating expenses on line 8.
If you believe that you have home energy costs that are more than the home energy costs included in expenses on line 8, then fill in the excess amount of home energy costs.
You must give your case trustee documentation of your actual expenses, and you must show that the additional amount claimed is reasonable and necessary. $

29. **Education expenses for dependent children who are younger than 18.** The monthly expenses (not more than $189.58* per child) that you pay for your dependent children who are younger than 18 years old to attend a private or public elementary or secondary school.
You must give your case trustee documentation of your actual expenses, and you must explain why the amount claimed is reasonable and necessary and not already accounted for in lines 6-23. $

* Subject to adjustment on 4/01/25, and every 3 years after that for cases begun on or after the date of adjustment.

30. **Additional food and clothing expense.** The monthly amount by which your actual food and clothing expenses are higher than the combined food and clothing allowances in the IRS National Standards. That amount cannot be more than 5% of the food and clothing allowances in the IRS National Standards. $
To find a chart showing the maximum additional allowance, go online using the link specified in the separate instructions for this form. This chart may also be available at the bankruptcy clerk's office.
You must show that the additional amount claimed is reasonable and necessary.

31. **Continuing charitable contributions.** The amount that you will continue to contribute in the form of cash or financial instruments to a religious or charitable organization. 26 U.S.C. § 170(c)(1)-(2). + $

32. **Add all of the additional expense deductions.**
Add lines 25 through 31. $

Fresh Start. Survivor's Guide to Bankruptcy Practice

Debtor 1 ______________________________ Case number (if known) ______________________
First Name Middle Name Last Name

Deductions for Debt Payment

33. **For debts that are secured by an interest in property that you own, including home mortgages, vehicle loans, and other secured debt, fill in lines 33a through 33e.**

To calculate the total average monthly payment, add all amounts that are contractually due to each secured creditor in the 60 months after you file for bankruptcy. Then divide by 60.

Average monthly payment

Mortgages on your home:

33a. Copy line 9b here .... ➔ $__________

Loans on your first two vehicles:

33b. Copy line 13b here. .... ➔ $__________

33c. Copy line 13e here. .... ➔ $__________

33d. List other secured debts:

Name of each creditor for other secured debt	Identify property that secures the debt	Does payment include taxes or insurance?	
__________	__________	❑ No ❑ Yes	$__________
__________	__________	❑ No ❑ Yes	$__________
__________	__________	❑ No ❑ Yes	+ $__________

33e. Total average monthly payment. Add lines 33a through 33d. .... $__________ **Copy total here**➔ $__________

34. **Are any debts that you listed in line 33 secured by your primary residence, a vehicle, or other property necessary for your support or the support of your dependents?**

❑ No. Go to line 35.

❑ Yes. State any amount that you must pay to a creditor, in addition to the payments listed in line 33, to keep possession of your property (called the *cure amount*). Next, divide by 60 and fill in the information below.

Name of the creditor	Identify property that secures the debt	Total cure amount		Monthly cure amount
__________	__________	$__________	÷ 60 =	$__________
__________	__________	$__________	÷ 60 =	$__________
__________	__________	$__________	÷ 60 =	+ $__________

Total $__________ **Copy total here**➔ $__________

35. **Do you owe any priority claims such as a priority tax, child support, or alimony — that are past due as of the filing date of your bankruptcy case?** 11 U.S.C. § 507.

❑ No. Go to line 36.

❑ Yes. Fill in the total amount of all of these priority claims. Do not include current or ongoing priority claims, such as those you listed in line 19.

Total amount of all past-due priority claims .... $__________ ÷ 60 = $__________

36. **Are you eligible to file a case under Chapter 13?** 11 U.S.C. § 109(e).
For more information, go online using the link for *Bankruptcy Basics* specified in the separate instructions for this form. *Bankruptcy Basics* may also be available at the bankruptcy clerk's office.

❑ No. Go to line 37.

❑ Yes. Fill in the following information.

Projected monthly plan payment if you were filing under Chapter 13 $_______

Current multiplier for your district as stated on the list issued by the Administrative Office of the United States Courts (for districts in Alabama and North Carolina) or by the Executive Office for United States Trustees (for all other districts). x _____

To find a list of district multipliers that includes your district, go online using the link specified in the separate instructions for this form. This list may also be available at the bankruptcy clerk's office.

Average monthly administrative expense if you were filing under Chapter 13 $_______ **Copy total here➔** $_______

37. **Add all of the deductions for debt payment.**
Add lines 33e through 36. .... $_______

Total Deductions from Income

38. **Add all of the allowed deductions.**

Copy line 24, *All of the expenses allowed under IRS expense allowances* .... $_______

Copy line 32, *All of the additional expense deductions*.......... $_______

Copy line 37, *All of the deductions for debt payment*.......... + $_______

Total deductions $_______ **Copy total here** .... ➔ $_______

Part 3: Determine Whether There Is a Presumption of Abuse

39. **Calculate monthly disposable income for 60 months**

39a. Copy line 4, *adjusted current monthly income* ..... $_______

39b. Copy line 38, *Total deductions*.......... − $_______

39c. Monthly disposable income. 11 U.S.C. § 707(b)(2). Subtract line 39b from line 39a. $_______ **Copy here➔** $_______

For the next 60 months (5 years).......... x 60

39d. **Total.** Multiply line 39c by 60. .... $_______ **Copy here➔** $_______

40. **Find out whether there is a presumption of abuse.** Check the box that applies:

❑ **The line 39d is less than $9,075*.** On the top of page 1 of this form, check box 1, *There is no presumption of abuse.* Go to Part 5.

❑ **The line 39d is more than $15,150*.** On the top of page 1 of this form, check box 2, *There is a presumption of abuse.* You may fill out Part 4 if you claim special circumstances. Then go to Part 5.

❑ **The line 39d is at least $9,075*, but not more than $15,150*.** Go to line 41.

* Subject to adjustment on 4/01/25, and every 3 years after that for cases filed on or after the date of adjustment.

Fresh Start. Survivor's Guide to Bankruptcy Practice

41. 41a. **Fill in the amount of your total nonpriority unsecured debt.** If you filled out *A Summary of Your Assets and Liabilities and Certain Statistical Information Schedules* (Official Form 106Sum), you may refer to line 3b on that form. .... $______

x .25

41b. **25% of your total nonpriority unsecured debt.** 11 U.S.C. § 707(b)(2)(A)(i)(I). Multiply line 41a by 0.25. .... $______ **Copy here➔** $______

42. **Determine whether the income you have left over after subtracting all allowed deductions is enough to pay 25% of your unsecured, nonpriority debt.**
Check the box that applies:

❑ **Line 39d is less than line 41b.** On the top of page 1 of this form, check box 1, *There is no presumption of abuse.* Go to Part 5.

❑ **Line 39d is equal to or more than line 41b.** On the top of page 1 of this form, check box 2, *There is a presumption of abuse.* You may fill out Part 4 if you claim special circumstances. Then go to Part 5.

Part 4: Give Details About Special Circumstances

43. **Do you have any special circumstances that justify additional expenses or adjustments of current monthly income for which there is no reasonable alternative?** 11 U.S.C. § 707(b)(2)(B).

❑ No. Go to Part 5.

❑ Yes. Fill in the following information. All figures should reflect your average monthly expense or income adjustment for each item. You may include expenses you listed in line 25.

You must give a detailed explanation of the special circumstances that make the expenses or income adjustments necessary and reasonable. You must also give your case trustee documentation of your actual expenses or income adjustments.

Give a detailed explanation of the special circumstances	Average monthly expense or income adjustment
______	$______
______	$______
______	$______
______	$______

Part 5: Sign Below

By signing here, I declare under penalty of perjury that the information on this statement and in any attachments is true and correct.

✘ ______
Signature of Debtor 1

Date ______
MM / DD / YYYY

✘ ______
Signature of Debtor 2

Date ______
MM / DD / YYYY

Chapter Fifty-Two

SUMMARY OF SCHEDULES

THE "SUMMARY OF SCHEDULES" serves as a concise summary or snapshot of the Schedules A through J and the Statement of Financial Affairs. The summary offers a quick reference point for creditors, the bankruptcy court, and other involved parties.

The Summary of Schedules is a critical component of a bankruptcy petition, designed to offer a brief but comprehensive view of your financial status. It serves as an at-a-glance summary for the court, your creditors, and other interested parties.

Section of Schedules

Debtor Information is requested. This section includes basic information about the debtor, such as name, address, and the type of bankruptcy (Chapter 7, Chapter 13, etc.) filed.

Schedule A/B outlines the debtor's real and personal property and assets, including their estimated value. This can include homes, vehicles, bank accounts, and other possessions.

Schedule D and E/F summarize the types of claims against the debtor, such as secured debts (like mortgages or car loans) and unsecured debts (like credit card balances). It also lists the names and addresses of the creditors.

Schedule C identifies the property that the debtor has claimed as exempt, which they can retain even in bankruptcy.

Schedule I/J outlines the debtor's monthly income and expenses, which is crucial for determining the feasibility of a Chapter 13 repayment plan.

Statement of Financial Affairs provides a concise overview of the debtor's recent financial history, including any recent financial transactions or significant events that may have led to the bankruptcy filing.

The summary of the schedules is a valuable tool for parties involved in the bankruptcy process, as it allows them to quickly grasp the debtor's financial situation.

The Summary of Schedules provides a concise overview of the debtor's financial situation and is an essential part of the bankruptcy petition. It is intended to give a snapshot of the debtor's assets, liabilities, income, and expenses.

Part 2 of the Summary of Schedules seeks the following information.

Summary of Expenditures highlights your monthly expenses, including essential living costs like housing, food, transportation, and healthcare. It helps evaluate your financial ability to make payments.

Summary of Financial Affairs provides information about your financial history, recent financial transactions, and any significant financial events, such as property sales or loans, that occurred before your bankruptcy filing.

Summary of Executory Contracts and Unexpired Leases gives detailed information as to any ongoing contracts or leases, like rental agreements or business contracts, you'll summarize them here.

The "Summary of Schedules" in a bankruptcy case serves as a concise summary or snapshot of Schedule A through J and the Statement of Financial Affairs. The summary offers a quick reference point for creditors, the bankruptcy court, and other involved parties

B 6 Summary (Official Form 6 - Summary) (12/14) Fresh Start. Survivor's Guide to Bankruptcy Practice

UNITED STATES BANKRUPTCY COURT

In re ______________________________________,
Debtor

Case No. ____________________

Chapter ____________

SUMMARY OF SCHEDULES

Indicate as to each schedule whether that schedule is attached and state the number of pages in each. Report the totals from Schedules A, B, D, E, F, I, and J in the boxes provided. Add the amounts from Schedules A and B to determine the total amount of the debtor's assets. Add the amounts of all claims from Schedules D, E, and F to determine the total amount of the debtor's liabilities. Individual debtors also must complete the "Statistical Summary of Certain Liabilities and Related Data" if they file a case under chapter 7, 11, or 13.

NAME OF SCHEDULE	ATTACHED (YES/NO)	NO. OF SHEETS	ASSETS	LIABILITIES	OTHER
A - Real Property			$		
B - Personal Property			$		
C - Property Claimed as Exempt					
D - Creditors Holding Secured Claims				$	
E - Creditors Holding Unsecured Priority Claims (Total of Claims on Schedule E)				$	
F - Creditors Holding Unsecured Nonpriority Claims				$	
G - Executory Contracts and Unexpired Leases					
H - Codebtors					
I - Current Income of Individual Debtor(s)					$
J - Current Expenditures of Individual Debtors(s)					$
TOTAL			$	$	

 Fresh Start. Survivor's Guide to Bankruptcy Practice

UNITED STATES BANKRUPTCY COURT

In re ________________________________,
Debtor

Case No. ________________

Chapter ___________

STATISTICAL SUMMARY OF CERTAIN LIABILITIES AND RELATED DATA (28 U.S.C. § 159)

If you are an individual debtor whose debts are primarily consumer debts, as defined in § 101(8) of the Bankruptcy Code (11 U.S.C. § 101(8)), filing a case under chapter 7, 11 or 13, you must report all information requested below.

☐Check this box if you are an individual debtor whose debts are NOT primarily consumer debts. You are not required to report any information here.

This information is for statistical purposes only under 28 U.S.C. § 159.

Summarize the following types of liabilities, as reported in the Schedules, and total them.

Type of Liability	Amount
Domestic Support Obligations (from Schedule E)	$
Taxes and Certain Other Debts Owed to Governmental Units (from Schedule E)	$
Claims for Death or Personal Injury While Debtor Was Intoxicated (from Schedule E) (whether disputed or undisputed)	$
Student Loan Obligations (from Schedule F)	$
Domestic Support, Separation Agreement, and Divorce Decree Obligations Not Reported on Schedule E	$
Obligations to Pension or Profit-Sharing, and Other Similar Obligations (from Schedule F)	$
TOTAL	$

State the following:

Average Income (from Schedule I, Line 12)	$
Average Expenses (from Schedule J, Line 22)	$
Current Monthly Income (from Form 22A-1 Line 11; **OR**, Form 22B Line 14; **OR**, Form 22C-1 Line 14)	$

State the following:

1. Total from Schedule D, "UNSECURED PORTION, IF ANY" column		$
2. Total from Schedule E, "AMOUNT ENTITLED TO PRIORITY" column.	$	
3. Total from Schedule E, "AMOUNT NOT ENTITLED TO PRIORITY, IF ANY" column		$
4. Total from Schedule F		$
5. Total of non-priority unsecured debt (sum of 1, 3, and 4)		$

Chapter Fifty-Three

STATEMENT ABOUT YOUR SOCIAL SECURITY DISCLOSURE

Statement About Your Social Security Numbers known as Official Form 121. It is the only form with your full Social Security Number, so make sure it is right. The court will make only the last four digits of your numbers known to the public. However, the full numbers will be available to your creditors, the U.S. Trustee or bankruptcy administrator, and the trustee assigned to your case.

THIS IS THE ONLY DOCUMENT THAT WILL CONTAIN YOUR FULL SOCIAL SECURITY NUMBER. MAKE SURE IT IS CORRECT. CHECK TWICE FOR ERRORS.

Use this form to tell the court about any Social Security or federal Individual Taxpayer Identification numbers you have used. Do not file this form as part of the public case file.

This form must be submitted separately and must not be included in the court's public electronic records.

Please consult local court procedures for submission requirements. To protect your privacy, the court will not make this form available to the public.

You should not include a full Social Security Number or Individual Taxpayer Number on any other document filed with the court.

The court will make only the last four digits of your numbers known to the public. However, the full numbers will be available to your creditors, the U.S. Trustee or bankruptcy administrator, and the trustee assigned to your case.

Making a false statement, concealing property, or obtaining money or property by fraud in connection with a bankruptcy case can result in fines up to $250,000, or imprisonment for up to 20 years, or both. 18 U.S.C. §§ 152, 1341, 1519, and 3571.

The form asks the following:

1. Your name.
2. All Social Security Numbers you have used.
3. All federal Individual Taxpayer Identification Numbers (ITIN) you have used.
4. Must execute document by signing name.

DOUBLE CHECK FOR ACCURACY! IT IS A MESS TO FIX AN ERRONEOUS SOCIAL SECURITY NUMBER.

Fresh Start. Survivor's Guide to Bankruptcy Practice

Fill in this information to identify your case:

United States Bankruptcy Court for the:

District of __________

Case number *(If known)*: ____________________

Official Form 121

Statement About Your Social Security Numbers

12/15

Use this form to tell the court about any Social Security or federal Individual Taxpayer Identification numbers you have used. Do not file this form as part of the public case file. This form must be submitted separately and must not be included in the court's public electronic records. Please consult local court procedures for submission requirements.

To protect your privacy, the court will not make this form available to the public. You should not include a full Social Security Number or Individual Taxpayer Number on any other document filed with the court. The court will make only the last four digits of your numbers known to the public. However, the full numbers will be available to your creditors, the U.S. Trustee or bankruptcy administrator, and the trustee assigned to your case.

Making a false statement, concealing property, or obtaining money or property by fraud in connection with a bankruptcy case can result in fines up to $250,000, or imprisonment for up to 20 years, or both. 18 U.S.C. §§ 152, 1341, 1519, and 3571.

Part 1: Tell the Court About Yourself and Your spouse if Your Spouse is Filing With You

	For Debtor 1:	For Debtor 2 (Only If Spouse Is Filing):
1. Your name	____________ First name	____________ First name
	____________ Middle name	____________ Middle name
	____________ Last name	____________ Last name

Part 2: Tell the Court About all of Your Social Security or Federal Individual Taxpayer Identification Numbers

	For Debtor 1	For Debtor 2
2. All Social Security Numbers you have used	___ ___ ___ – ___ ___ – ___ ___ ___ ___	___ ___ ___ – ___ ___ – ___ ___ ___ ___
	___ ___ ___ – ___ ___ – ___ ___ ___ ___	___ ___ ___ – ___ ___ – ___ ___ ___ ___
	☐ You do not have a Social Security number.	☐ You do not have a Social Security number.
3. All federal Individual Taxpayer Identification Numbers (ITIN) you have used	9 ___ ___ – ___ ___ – ___ ___ ___ ___	9 ___ ___ – ___ ___ – ___ ___ ___ ___
	9 ___ ___ – ___ ___ – ___ ___ ___ ___	9 ___ ___ – ___ ___ – ___ ___ ___ ___
	☐ You do not have an ITIN.	☐ You do not have an ITIN.

Part 3: Sign Below

	Debtor 1	Debtor 2
	Under penalty of perjury, I declare that the information I have provided in this form is true and correct.	Under penalty of perjury, I declare that the information I have provided in this form is true and correct.
	✘ ____________ Signature of Debtor 1	✘ ____________ Signature of Debtor 2
	Date ________ MM / DD / YYYY	Date ________ MM / DD / YYYY

Chapter Fifty-Four

MEETING OF THE CREDITORS OR 341 MEETING

THE PRIMARY PURPOSE OF the Meeting of Creditors is to provide a forum where creditors can inquire about the debtor's financial affairs and the details of the bankruptcy case. It allows creditors to ask questions and seek information regarding the debtor's assets, liabilities, income, and other financial matters.

The Meeting of the Creditors or 341 Meeting gives the bankruptcy trustee and creditors an opportunity to review the debtor's bankruptcy petition, schedules, and statements, which detail their financial situation, assets, liabilities, income, and expenses. This meeting is mandatory and should not be missed. Keep in mind, most creditors do not show up and more often than not, you will spend more time waiting for your name to be called than the time you are in front of the Trustee.

Meeting of the Creditors or 341 Meeting

After filing a Chapter 7 Bankruptcy, the court will issue a case number and a date for the "meeting of the creditors" also called the "341 Meeting." The bankruptcy filer must attend. This meeting is mandatory and should not be missed. Make sure you come to the meeting of the creditors with your social security card and government issued identification.

Most people get anxious about this meeting. They picture all their creditors inside the courtroom and that creditors are beating on them with a long stick. But that is contrary to the truth. In fact, most creditors don't show up at all. If they do, they may ask one or two questions, if allowed. And the questions that are likely asked requires simple answers. For example, let's say you have a debt outstanding on a vehicle. A creditor, likely a credit union, will ask if you are planning on keeping the vehicle?

More time will be spent waiting for your turn in front of the Trustee. The questioning may take ten minutes, if all the documents were provided to the Trustee prior to the meeting of the creditors.

The meeting of the creditors serves several purposes.

It allows the bankruptcy trustee and creditors to review the debtor's bankruptcy petition, schedules, and statements, which detail their financial situation, assets, liabilities, income, and expenses. This review ensures that the information provided is accurate and complete.

The debtor is required to answer questions under oath about their financial affairs and the details provided in their bankruptcy documents. This examination helps verify the accuracy of the information and ensures transparency in the bankruptcy process.

Creditors are invited to attend the meeting, ask questions, and seek information about the bankruptcy case. They can also inquire about their prospects for repayment from the debtor's estate. Creditors may use this meeting to inquire about the debtor's assets, especially non-exempt property that might be sold to repay creditors.

Sometimes, the meeting of creditors can help resolve disputes or issues that may arise during the bankruptcy process. Creditors may voice concerns or objections, and the trustee may seek clarification or propose solutions.

The meeting serves to confirm the debtor's identity to prevent fraudulent filings.

For some debtors, the meeting serves as an educational opportunity, where they can learn more about the bankruptcy process and their obligations.

COMMONLY ASKED QUESTIONS

1. Did you sign the petition, schedules, statements, and related documents?

2. Did you read the petition, schedules, statements, and related documents before you signed them?

3. Are you personally familiar with the information contained in the petition, schedules, statements, and related documents?

4. Is the information contained in the petition and all accompanying documents true and correct? Are there any errors or omissions that you are aware of at this time?

5. Have you identified all of your assets on the schedules? (assets include anything of value including accounts of all kinds, real property no matter if it is located out of the country, or personal property including even clothes and wedding rings).

6. Have you listed all of your creditors on the schedules? (creditors include relatives and anyone to whom you owe money)

7. Have you previously filed bankruptcy? (generally bankruptcies older than 8 years for Chapter 7 and less for Chapter 13 are fine, but they still need to be disclosed to the Bankruptcy Court and rustee)

8. Is the copy of the tax return your attorney provided to my office before this meeting a true copy of the most recent tax return you filed? (if you have filed a more recent tax return, be sure to give a copy to your attorney a week prior to the meeting, or bring a copy to the meeting if it is even more recent than that).

9. Do you have a domestic support obligation such as child support or alimony that you owe another? To whom? You will be asked to fill out a form to provide the claimant's address and telephone number, but do not state it on the record for privacy reasons.

10. You will be asked if you are current on your post-petition domestic support obligations?

11. Have you filed all the required tax returns for the past four years? If you have not, you likely are not going to be eligible for bankruptcy relief unless you can get these done and quickly filed before a motion to dismiss is filed.

12. If you are expecting a tax refund for the year prior to filing your bankruptcy, you will need to send the refund check to the Trustee (do not direct deposit) and the Trustee will do a calculation after the meeting to pro-rate the amounts over the 365 days of the preceding year. The Trustee will return a portion to you representing any exemptions claimed and for the time period after you file bankruptcy.

13. Did you review the bankruptcy information sheet (this was provided to you when you hired us and explains the various types of bankruptcies)?

14. Have you repaid any debts to family or friends in the last year?

15. What is the reason for your bankruptcy filing?

16. How did you arrive at the values you listed for your personal property on your schedules?

17. Are you paid by the hour or salary? What is your hourly rate/salary?

18. Identify any ownership interest and mortgages for real estate, even out of the country (all of this should be listed on your petition also)?

19. Any transfers (giving or selling) anything to relatives or insiders in the past two years?

20. Anyone holding any property for you?

21. Have a claim against anyone else such as a slip and fall, car accident, someone owing you money etc.?

22. Entitled to life insurance proceeds or an inheritance upon someone's death?

23. Are you a beneficiary or trustee of a trust?

24. Do you own a business?

THE END

ABOUT THE AUTHOR

Arlene A. Smith-Scott brings a wealth of knowledge and experience to the table, making her an authority in bankruptcy practice, business development, and legal consulting. With over 14 years of ownership and leadership in the mortgage industry, Arlene purchased, renovated, and managed real property, developing a keen understanding of the real estate and financial sectors from the inside out. As a licensed attorney, her career flourished until she was unfairly targeted due to her personal and business assets, an experience that deepened her resolve and sharpened her insight into systemic legal and financial challenges.

Her impressive tenure includes packaging compelling grant proposals and business plans, developing transformative course content, and authoring several influential books, notably "Grant Writing: The Unofficial Rulebook." Known for her meticulous research and analytical skills, Arlene excels at translating complex issues into clear, comprehensive strategies and reports that empower both professionals and entrepreneurs.

As Managing Attorney at Strategic Law Group, LLC, Arlene oversaw more than 200 legal cases, specializing in client relationship management and legal retention. Her work involved drafting contracts, researching intricate legal matters, writing appellate briefs, and litigating civil and criminal cases. In her capacity as a certified Civil Mediator, she promoted effective communication, empathy, and balanced problem-solving to help parties reach lasting resolutions.

Previously, as CEO of Strategic Alliance Funding, Inc., Arlene brokered both residential and commercial mortgage loans, originating, processing, and closing them with precision. She performed in-depth credit assessments, created dynamic cash flow models, launched impactful marketing campaigns, and built a high-performing team of loan officers and processors.

Arlene's extensive experience in grant writing, legal consulting, and business development, combined with her ability to leverage CRM platforms, video production tools, and emerging technologies like AI, makes her an invaluable asset to clients, students, and readers alike. Her books and teachings continue to educate and inspire those by navigating the intricate landscapes of funding, law, and entrepreneurship.

STAY CONNECTED

Unlock a wealth of knowledge and exclusive deals! Sign up now to receive free updates and special discounts on services and products related to grant writing, commercial lending, and much more. Don't miss out, join our community today!

Website: www.DocWriteReview.com

Email: Info@DocWriteReview.com

Made in the USA
Monee, IL
05 November 2026

67979976R00260